Contents

TOP 10 OF EVERYTHING 2018

PAUL TERRY

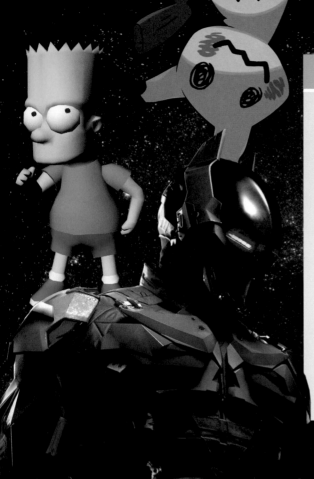

AUTHOR'S **INTRO**

A long time ago, in a galaxy far, far away... someone was, no doubt, compiling Top 10 lists. These days, some fact-packed books only cover strange "number ones," but we remain obsessed with bringing you Top 10 charts on subjects that we hope you'll find informative, entertaining and inspiring. For example, with new *Star Wars* movies such as *The Force Awakens*, *Rogue One*, and *The Last Jedi* taking the box office by storm, a special section of this book's Movies & TV zone is dedicated to facts about the past 40+ years of the sci-fi franchise.

Galactic adventures aside, *Top 10 of Everything 2018* proudly presents a smorgasbord of other information, including the likes of: the longest crocodiles, deepest canyons, most popular metal albums, first Nobel Prize winners, biggest TV tie-in video games, fastest people in the world, most popular theme parks, fastest Maglev trains, the biggest zombie movies, and more than 10,000 other facts to go wide-eyed about.

So sit back, lean away from that "jump-to-light-speed" button, put down your Darth Vader figure, and let your mind take a slow trip through our 10 eclectic zones...

ABOUT THE **AUTHOR**

PAUL TERRY is a best-selling author, music artist, and producer. He has written/edited official publications for the Bad Robot TV shows *Alias*, *Lost* and *Fringe*, as well as for *Stars Wars*, LEGO, DreamWorks, *The Simpsons*, and *Futurama*.

He coauthored (with Tara Bennett) *The Official Making of Big Trouble in Little China*, the official *Lost Encyclopedia*, *The Blacklist: Elizabeth Keen's Dossier*, *Sleepy Hollow: Creating Heroes, Demons & Monsters*, and *Fringe: September's Notebook* (an Amazon Book of the Year 2013).

When he's not writing books, Paul writes music. His film scores include *Emily* (starring Oscar-nominee Felicity Jones and Emmy-winner Christopher Eccleston), feature documentary *Sidney & Friends*, and the chiller *Care*. Under the moniker of Cellarscape, Paul's albums include *Exo Echo* and the IMA-nominated *The Act of Letting Go*.

www.paulterryprojects.com

Animal KINGDOM

ZONE 1

TOP 10 FASTEST **ANIMAL SPECIES**

Combining all of the different organisms on our planet from the land, sea, and sky, these 10 are the fastest of their kinds...

	TYPE	ANIMAL	RECORDED SPEED (MPH)	(KPH)
1	RAPTOR	PEREGRINE FALCON	242	389
2	BAT	MEXICAN FREE-TAILED BAT	99.4	160
3	BONY FISH	BLACK MARLIN	80	128.7
4	BIG CAT	CHEETAH	75	120.7
5	ARTIODACTYL MAMMAL	PRONGHORN	61	98.2
6	SHARK	SHORTFIN MAKO SHARK	60	96.6
=	FLIGHTLESS BIRD	OSTRICH	60	96.6
8	HORSE	AMERICAN QUARTER HORSE	55	88.5
9	DOLPHIN	ORCA WHALE	40.1	65
10	REPTILE	CENTRAL BEARDED DRAGON	24.9	40

6 SHORTFIN MAKO SHARK

The Maori word *mako* literally means "shark." It often travels more than 1,300 miles (2,092 km) and its diet consists mainly of squid and other fast-swimming fish like tuna. This results in their accidental netting (and death) during large commercial tuna catches. The IUCN (International Union for Conservation of Nature) lists this shark as vulnerable, meaning it is an endangered species.

SEA LAMPREY

1

This prehistoric fish latches onto its prey as a parasite. Its circular, multihooked maw clamps onto its victim so its probing tongue can burrow into their flesh. Classified as an invasive species in many regions, sea lampreys can decimate local fish populations. Weighing more than 5 lb (2.3 kg), lampreys have cartilage like sharks instead of a skeleton of bones. Although their bite isn't fatal to humans, they will happily latch onto our skin and feed when given the opportunity.

BLOODSUCKERS' RANKS

Here's how these blood-drinkers rank by air, water, and land creatures...

AIR	WATER	LAND
4	3	3

TOP 10 LARGEST **BLOODSUCKERS**

Vampires may be mythological creatures, but the animal kingdom is full of entities that feed exclusively on blood...

	NAME	LENGTH (IN)	(CM)
1	SEA LAMPREY	35.5	90
2	GIANT AMAZON LEECH	18	45.7
3	CANDIRU	16	40
4	VAMPIRE BAT	7	18
5	VAMPIRE FINCH	4.7	12
6	MADRILENIAL BUTTERFLY	2.76	7
7	ASSASSIN BUG	1.6	4
8	FEMALE MOSQUITO	0.6	1.6
9	BEDBUG	0.2	0.5
10	FLEA	0.09	0.25

7 ▷ POLAR BEAR

Due to spending the majority of its life on the Arctic Ocean's sea ice, the polar bear is actually categorized as a marine mammal. However, climate change is melting their habitat and making them an endangered species. They are incredible swimmers and can do so for days. On land, they can sprint at 25 mph (40.3 kph). Although they mainly hunt seals, whale carcasses and walruses also feature in their diet. Standing on its hind legs, the polar bear can exceed 11 ft (3.4 m).

TOP 10 BIGGEST **CARNIVORES**

This top 10 chart is made up of some of the largest creatures on Earth that eat other creatures...

	TYPE	ANIMAL	WEIGHT (LB)	(KG)
1	WHALE	BLUE WHALE	418,877	189,999.4
2	SHARK	WHALE SHARK	47,000	21,318
3	DOLPHIN	ORCA WHALE	22,000	9,979
4	SEAL	SOUTHERN ELEPHANT SEAL	11,000	4,989.5
5	CROCODILE	SALTWATER CROCODILE	4,409.2	2,000
6	WALRUS	PACIFIC WALRUS	4,151.3	1,883
7	BEAR	POLAR BEAR	2,209	1,002
8	STINGRAY	GIANT FRESHWATER STINGRAY	1,320	600
9	SQUID	COLOSSAL SQUID	1,091.3	495
10	BIG CAT	SIBERIAN TIGER	1,025.2	465

TOP **10**

HEAVIEST **HERBIVORES**

Although these animals' diets consist purely of vegetation, this doesn't stop them reaching immense weights...

	TYPE	ANIMAL	WEIGHT (LB)	(KG)
1	ELEPHANT	AFRICAN BUSH ELEPHANT	26,455	12,000
2	HIPPOPOTAMUS	COMMON HIPPOPOTAMUS	9,920.8	4,500
3	RHINO	SOUTHERN WHITE RHINO	8,818.5	4,000
4	GIRAFFE	ROTHSCHILD GIRAFFE	4,254.9	1,930
5	BOVINE	CHIANINA	3,924.2	1,780
6	HORSE	SHIRE HORSE	3,306.9	1,500
7	DEER	CHUKOTKA MOOSE	1,598.4	725
8	TORTOISE	GALÁPAGOS TORTOISE	919.3	417
9	GORILLA	EASTERN LOWLAND GORILLA	595.2	270
10	KANGAROO	RED KANGAROO	200.6	91

8 GALÁPAGOS TORTOISE

This huge tortoise can live for more than 150 years. Its name comes from the 19 Galápagos Islands which they inhabit. When a Spanish bishop accidentally sailed toward the archipelago in 1535, the islands were named as such because *galápago* is Spanish for "tortoise." They rest (but not fully asleep) for around 16 hours a day and have the ability not to require food or water for a year. Males make a kind of "mooing" noise when mating, but females do not communicate with any kind of sound.

TOP 10 LONGEST **SLEEPERS**

Adult humans sleep an average of seven hours a day, which makes us seem extremely active compared to these restful creatures...

	ANIMAL	APPROX. HOURS ASLEEP PER DAY
1	LARGE HAIRY ARMADILLO	20.4
2	LITTLE POCKET MOUSE	20
3	LITTLE BROWN BAT	19
4	PYTHON	18
5	NIGHT MONKEY	17
6	TREE SHREW	15.5
7	SQUIRREL	14.9
8	KOALA	14.5
9	AMERICAN BADGER	14
=	CHILEAN MOUSE OPOSSUM	14

SLOTH

Contrary to its reputation as the laziest animal, the sloth only sleeps for an average of 10 hours a day, so it doesn't make it into this top 10. They do rest for between 15 and 20 hours, but not in a deep sleep. Their 12 in (30.5 cm) tongue helps them reach leaves, and their 4 in (10.2 cm) curved claws provide excellent grip on branches, especially while hanging upside down. Sloths' long arms also make them very good swimmers.

1 LARGE HAIRY ARMADILLO

Gestation can last up to 75 days, and large hairy armadillos often give birth to twins. It is the most abundant species of armadillo in South America. A master burrower, it can breathe in oxygen underground due to special nasal membranes preventing soil from being inhaled. It favors foraging for insects and worms.

TOP 10 LARGEST BURROWERS

Making subterranean dens, nests, and shelters isn't just an activity carried out by the likes of small animals...

	ANIMAL	LENGTH (IN)	(CM)
1	POLAR BEAR	133.5	339
2	AARDVARK	86.6	220
3	NORTH AMERICAN RIVER OTTER	61.8	157
4	GIANT ARMADILLO	59.1	150
5	EUROPEAN OTTER	55.1	140
=	RED FOX	55.1	140
7	COMMON WOMBAT	51.2	130
8	MONGOOSE	47.2	120
9	NORTHERN HAIRY-NOSED WOMBAT	39.4	100
10	COYPU	37.4	95

2 AARDVARK

Like the sloth, the aardvark also has a 12 in (30.5 cm) tongue, but this nocturnal African mammal uses it to reach inside termite and ant hills for a meal. As many as 50,000 can be consumed in one feeding period. The aardvark can weigh more than 160 lb (72.6 kg), and also burrows to make a home.

TOP 10 BIGGEST **CRUSTACEANS**

Crabs, lobsters, prawns and shrimps are the most well-known types of crustacean, and you may not have heard of these giants...

	NAME	SIZE (IN)	(CM)
1	JAPANESE SPIDER CRAB	149.6	380
2	ALASKAN KING CRAB	60	152.4
3	AMERICAN LOBSTER	43.3	110
4	COCONUT CRAB	39.4	100
5	COLOSSENDEIS COLOSSEA SEA SPIDER	35.8	91
=	TASMANIAN GIANT CRAB	35.8	91
7	GIANT ISOPOD	29.9	76
8	ATLANTIC HORSESHOE CRAB	23.6	60
9	PENNELLA BALAENOPTERAE (PARASITIC BARNACLE)	12.6	32
10	SUPERGIANT AMPHIPOD	11	28

2 BLACK CAIMAN

The Alligatoridae family of reptiles includes alligators and caimans. The black caiman, the biggest member of this family, has much larger eyes than its caiman relatives. Its skull is also visibly bigger. It resides in the waterways of South America, especially the Amazon basin, where it is the region's biggest predator. Females stay close to their nest, which can contain 65 eggs.

2 ALASKAN KING CRAB

There are three types of this Alaskan creature: red king crab, blue king crab, and golden king crab. They can weigh more than 20 lb (9.1 kg) and live up to 20 years. Spawning season lasts from January through June. Unusually for a crab, this species only has six (instead of eight) legs.

TOP 10 HEAVIEST REPTILE FAMILIES

Examining all of the different families there are in the reptile kingdom, these are the 10 that tip the scales in each of them...

	REPTILE FAMILY	ANIMAL	WEIGHT (LB)	(KG)
1	CROCODYLIDAE	SALTWATER CROCODILE	4,409.2	2,000
2	ALLIGATORIDAE	BLACK CAIMAN	2,900	1,310
3	GAVIALIDAE	GHARIAL	2,150	977
4	DERMOCHELYIDAE	LEATHERBACK SEA TURTLE	2,120	961.1
5	TESTUDINIDAE	GALÁPAGOS TORTOISE	919.3	417
6	BOIDAE	GREEN ANACONDA	550	249.5
7	VARANIDAE	KOMODO DRAGON	366	166
8	PYTHONIDAE	RETICULATED PYTHON	350.1	158.8
9	VIPERIDAE	GABOON VIPER	44.1	20
10	ELAPIDAE	KING COBRA	28	12.7

8 ▶ EURASIAN LYNX

This is the largest of the four lynx species. It consumes around 5 lb (2.3 kg) of food every day, and is a pure carnivore, hunting prey as large as reindeer and roe deer. Eurasian lynxes that reside in Siberia are on record as the largest of the species, reaching 4.3 ft (1.3 m) in length.

TOP 10 BIGGEST **BIG CATS**

Compare this top 10 to the one opposite to get a better sense of just how big the "big cats" of the wild get...

	CAT	WEIGHT (LB)	(KG)
1	SIBERIAN TIGER	1,025.2	465
2	LION	595.2	270
3	JAGUAR	308.6	140
4	COUGAR	264.5	120
5	SNOW LEOPARD	160.9	73
6	LEOPARD	141.1	64
7	CHEETAH	121.2	55
8	EURASIAN LYNX	77.2	35
9	CLOUDED LEOPARD	55.1	25
10	CARACAL	44.1	20

TOP 10 BIGGEST DOMESTICATED CATS

Even though pet cats are generally dwarfed by their wild relatives, the largest cat on this chart isn't that much smaller than a caracal...

	CAT	WEIGHT (LB)	(KG)
1	SAVANNAH	30	13.6
2	SIBERIAN	25	11.3
3	MAINE COON	24.5	11.1
4	CHAUSIE	20	9.1
5	RAGDOLL	19	8.6
6	NORWEGIAN FOREST CAT	17.5	7.9
7	BRITISH SHORTHAIR	17	7.7
=	CHEETOH	17	7.7
9	RAGAMUFFIN	16	7.3
10	AMERICAN BOBTAIL	15	6.8

1 SAVANNAH

This is a hybrid, bred between an African wild cat called a serval and a common domestic cat. It is a relatively new breed, and was only accepted by The International Cat Association as a legitimate breed for cat shows in 2012. Savannah owners are known to walk their cats on a leash because their personalities are described as more like a dog than a cat. They even wag their tails as a sign of happiness.

TOP 10 BIGGEST **WILD CANINES**

Other large species of wild dogs include black-backed jackal, dhole, and the deer wolf, but these 10 are the ones that dominate the canine weight chart…

GREAT DANE
WOLF

	WILD DOG	WEIGHT	
		(LB)	(KG)
1	EURASIAN WOLF	190	86.2
2	NORTHWESTERN WOLF	175	79.4
3	ARCTIC WOLF	155	70.3
4	GREAT PLAINS WOLF	150	68
5	TUNDRA WOLF	115	52.2
6	INDIAN WOLF	90	40.8
=	RED WOLF	90	40.8
8	STEPPE WOLF	88	39.9
9	MEXICAN WOLF	80	36.3
10	DINGO	77	34.9

2 NORTHWESTERN WOLF

This well-known canine also goes by the names Canadian timber wolf and Mackenzie Valley wolf. Often exceeding 6 ft (1.8 m) in length, these wolves live and hunt in packs. A unit is made up of an alpha male and female, their young, and other younger wolves. The pack hunt and travel together for hours at a time, often through the night. They are widespread across Northwestern America and Canada.

▶ GREAT DANE

Originally a working dog, this breed's 19th-century name was the German boarhound, referencing the wild boars it would catch under the command of a human-led hunt. During this period, its famously floppy ears were cropped to prevent injury during a boar encounter. The largest Great Dane to date was named Zeus, whose height is registered on the below top 10. He died in September 2014. One of the most famous examples of a Great Dane is the cartoon character Scooby-Doo, whose animated TV series first aired in 1969.

TOP 10 — TALLEST DOMESTICATED DOGS

How big is the tallest dog in your neighbourhood? See how it measures up against this top 10 chart of huge hounds...

	DOG	HEIGHT (IN)	(CM)
1	GREAT DANE	44	112
2	IRISH WOLFHOUND	34	86.4
3	GREAT PYRENEES	32	81.3
4	LEONBERGER	31.5	80
5	NEAPOLITAN MASTIFF	31	78.7
6	NEWFOUNDLAND	28	71.1
7	SAINT BERNARD	27.5	69.9
=	BERNESE MOUNTAIN DOG	27.5	69.9
9	BULLMASTIFF	27	68.6
=	DOGUE DE BORDEAUX	27	68.6

1 SPINOSAURUS

Until experts dig up an even bigger prehistoric hunter, *Spinosaurus* remains the king of the carnivorous land lizards. Experts speculate its sail could have helped thermoregulate the animal, much like the ears of an elephant. Others have posited it helped *Spinosaurus* move faster through water, and that its crocodile-esque jaws made hunting fish a priority over land animals.

TOP 10 LARGEST PREHISTORIC **BIPEDAL CARNIVORES**

Meat-eating dinosaurs are some of the biggest animals ever to walk the Earth, with these 10 holding the current length records...

	DINOSAUR	LENGTH (FT)	(M)
1	SPINOSAURUS	59	18
2	CARCHARODONTOSAURUS	43.3	13.2
=	GIGANOTOSAURUS	43.3	13.2
4	CHILANTAISAURUS	42.7	13
5	TYRANNOSAURUS REX	40.4	12.3
6	TYRANNOTITAN	40	12.2
7	TORVOSAURUS	39.4	12
=	ALLOSAURUS	39.4	12
9	ACROCANTHOSAURUS	37.7	11.5
10	DELTADROMEUS	36.1	11

TOP 10 BIGGEST PREHISTORIC CARNIVOROUS MAMMALS

It's not just the dinosaurs that grew to monstrous sizes. Some mammals from millions of years ago weighed thousands of pounds too...

	CREATURE	WEIGHT (LB)	(KG)
1	ARCTOTHERIUM	3,855.9	1,749
2	ANDREWSARCHUS	2,204.6	1,000
3	SHORT-FACED BEAR	2,109.8	957
4	PSEUDOCYON	1,704.2	773
5	AMPHICYON	1,322.8	600
6	SMILODON	1,036.2	470
7	THYLACOSMILUS	264.6	120
8	PACHYCROCUTA	242.5	110
9	DIRE WOLF	174.2	79
10	EPICYON	150	68

1 ARCTOTHERIUM

Standing 14 ft (4.3 m) on its hind legs, the extinct *Arctotherium* is currently the largest bear on record. It lived two million years ago. Its hard-to-pronounce name translates aptly as "bear beast," which is a perfect description for an animal that was more than 1,000 lb (453.6 kg) heavier than the largest modern-day bear.

2 ARGENTINOSAURUS

Its name means "Argentine lizard," due to the first fossilized bone being unearthed by rancher Guillermo Heredia in Argentina in 1987. He initially thought it was an ancient piece of wood. Scientists have calculated that this sauropod likely traveled at 3 mph (4.8 kph). A plant-eater of this size would have needed to consume 100,000 calories per day.

TOP 10 LARGEST PREHISTORIC **HERBIVORES**

Until experts unearth new, record-breaking fossils, these 10 are the largest land-based animals of all time...

	DINOSAUR	LENGTH (FT)	(M)
1	AMPHICOELIAS	196.8	60
2	ARGENTINOSAURUS	118.1	36
3	MAMENCHISAURUS	114.8	35
4	FUTALOGNKOSAURUS	111.5	34
=	SAUROPOSEIDON	111.5	34
6	DIPLODOCUS	108.3	33
7	XINJIANGTITAN	105	32
8	PUERTASAURUS	98.4	30
=	TURIASAURUS	98.4	30
10	DREADNOUGHTUS	85.3	26

TOP 10 SMALLEST PREHISTORIC **ANIMALS**

Our planet's ancient history was not just populated by skyscraping creatures, as this top 10 chart proves...

	CREATURE	WEIGHT (LB)	(KG)
1	PARVICURSOR REMOTUS	0.31	0.14
2	EPIDEXIPTERYX HUI	0.35	0.16
3	COMPSOGNATHUS LONGIPES	0.57	0.26
4	CERATONYKUS OCULATUS	0.66	0.3
5	JURAVENATOR STARKI	0.75	0.34
6	LIGABUEINO ANDESI	0.77	0.35
7	MICRORAPTOR ZHAOIANUS	0.88	0.4
8	SINOSAUROPTERYX PRIMA	1.2	0.55
9	RAHONAVIS OSTROMI	1.3	0.58
10	MAHAKALA OMNOGOVAE	1.7	0.76

2 EPIDEXIPTERYX HUI

This dinosaur is the earliest example of the prehistoric reptiles that had feathers purely for ornamental display. No bigger than a modern-day pigeon, it lived in the region we now call China. It was formally announced as a discovery in 2008.

6 ▶ LION

Males rarely live longer than 14 years due to injuries they receive from hunting and battling other male lions. Lionesses are more successful at hunting as they are built for speed. The stockier, mane-covered males overheat faster, slowing them down. A dark and full mane is an indication of good health.

TOP 10 FASTEST ON LAND

Most of these speed record-holders are quadrupeds, but there are two animals that make it into this top 10 by sprinting on two legs...

	ANIMAL	SPEED (MPH)	(KPH)
1	CHEETAH	75	120.7
2	PRONGHORN	60.9	98
3	SPRINGBOK	60.3	97
4	OSTRICH	60	96.6
5	AMERICAN QUARTER HORSE	53.4	86
6	LION	49.7	80
7	AFRICAN WILD DOG	44.7	72
=	ELK	44.7	72
9	EASTERN GREY KANGAROO	43.5	70
10	COYOTE	42.9	69

6 ▶ PACIFIC WALRUS

Found mostly in the Arctic Circle region, these 11.5 ft (3.5 m) mammals live in huge herds that number in the hundreds. Their striking tusks serve multiple purposes. They can break breathing holes in the ice, help them to climb out of the water, and can be used to assert dominance.

TOP 10 HEAVIEST ON LAND

The weights in this top 10 are the heaviest known examples of these animals. Most are mammals, but one reptile made it into the chart...

	ANIMAL	WEIGHT (LB)	(KG)
1	AFRICAN BUSH ELEPHANT	26,455	12,000
2	ASIAN ELEPHANT	11,464	5,200
3	SOUTHERN ELEPHANT SEAL	11,000	5,000
4	COMMON HIPPOPOTAMUS	9,920.8	4,500
5	SOUTHERN WHITE RHINOCEROS	8,818.5	4,000
▶ 6	PACIFIC WALRUS	5,000	2,268
7	SALTWATER CROCODILE	4,409	2,000
8	ROTHSCHILD GIRAFFE	4,254.9	1,930
9	CHIANINA	3,924.2	1,780
10	SHIRE HORSE	3,306.9	1,500

LONGEST **CROCODILES & ALLIGATORS**

These cunning predators are known for their long snouts and tails, but these 10 beat all their relatives when it comes to being the longest of them all...

	ANIMAL	LENGTH (FT)	(M)
1	GHARIAL	23	7
2	NILE CROCODILE	21.2	6.45
3	SALTWATER CROCODILE	20.7	6.32
4	AMERICAN ALLIGATOR	17.4	5.31
5	AMERICAN CROCODILE	17.1	5.2
6	ORINOCO CROCODILE	16.8	5.1
7	BLACK CAIMAN	16	4.9
8	MORELET'S CROCODILE	14.8	4.5
9	SLENDER-SNOUTED CROCODILE	13.8	4.2
10	FRESHWATER CROCODILE	13.1	4

OFF THE CHART

ANIMAL	LENGTH (FT)	(M)
PHILIPPINE CROCODILE	10.2	3.1
CHINESE ALLIGATOR	6.9	2.1

1 GHARIAL

Also known as the gavial and the fish-eating crocodile, this unusually jawed reptile comes from India. They spend more time in water than any other crocodile, preferring rivers and deep pools. Young gharial will eat frogs and insects. Unlike other species such as the saltwater crocodile, gharial have not been recorded attacking humans.

3 L I V Y A T A N

This ancient oceanic mammal closely resembled the modern sperm whale. Its name comes from the original Hebrew spelling of the word "leviathan," a creature described in the *Tanakh*. Its teeth measured 14 in (35.6 cm) in length. Scientists currently believe this apex predator lived between 12 and 13 million years ago.

TOP 10 BIGGEST PREHISTORIC **OCEAN BEASTS**

Of all the different kinds of prehistoric fish, reptiles, and mammals that we currently know existed, these were the largest...

	ANIMAL	TYPE	LENGTH (FT)	(M)
1	SHONISAURUS	REPTILE	66	21
2	BASILOSAURUS	MAMMAL	65.6	20
3	LIVYATAN	MAMMAL	57.4	17.5
4	MEGALODON	FISH	52.5	16
5	MOSASAURUS	REPTILE	49.9	15.2
=	HAINOSAURUS	REPTILE	49.9	15.2
7	ELASMOSAURUS	REPTILE	46	14
8	PLIOSAURUS	REPTILE	42	12.8
9	DUNKLEOSTEUS	FISH	32.8	10
=	LEEDSICHTHYS	FISH	32.8	10

3 GREAT WHITE SHARK

The maximum size of the most famous shark of them all has been debated for nearly 150 years. Unverified claims of a 37 ft (11.3 m) great white shark occurred in the 1930s in Canada, and a supposed 36 ft (11 m) specimen was caught in Australian waters in the 1870s. However, bite measurements on whale carcasses have given scientists the data required to determine 24.6 ft (7.5 m) giants exist. Females can exceed 4,000 lb (1,814.4 kg). Great whites are commonly found off the coast of Australia, Hawaii, Mexico, and California, USA, and gravitate toward warm, coastal waters.

5 PYGMY SHARK

Unlike the classic shark-shaped dorsal fin, the pygmy shark only has a small one that is more flag-shaped, located further down its back. They give birth to eight pups in one litter, each measuring just 2.4 in (6.1 cm) in length. Living at depths of up to 32,600 ft (9,936.5 m), the pygmy shark has visibly luminous organs on its underside.

TOP 10 SMALLEST SHARKS

Reports about shark sightings often highlight their frightening size, but there are several species that could fit inside your pocket...

	SHARK	LENGTH (IN)	(CM)
1	DWARF LANTERNSHARK	8.3	21.2
2	PANAMA GHOST CATSHARK	9.1	23
3	PYGMY RIBBONTAIL CATSHARK	9.4	24
4	GREEN LANTERNSHARK	10.2	26
5	PYGMY SHARK	10.6	27
6	GRANULAR DOGFISH	11	28
=	LOLLIPOP CATSHARK	11	28
=	SPINED PYGMY SHARK	11	28
9	BRISTLY CATSHARK	11.4	29
=	FRINGEFIN LANTERNSHARK	11.4	29

TOP 10 BIGGEST SHARKS

Recording the lengths of sharks is notoriously problematic, but these 10 species are currently considered the largest...

	SHARK	LENGTH (FT)	(M)
1	WHALE SHARK	41.7	12.7
2	BASKING SHARK	40.4	12.3
3	GREAT WHITE SHARK	24.6	7.5
4	PACIFIC SLEEPER SHARK	24.3	7.4
5	GREENLAND SHARK	21	6.4
6	GOBLIN SHARK	20.24	6.17
7	GREAT HAMMERHEAD SHARK	20	6.1
8	TIGER SHARK	19.7	6
=	THRESHER SHARK	19.7	6
10	MEGAMOUTH SHARK	18.4	5.6

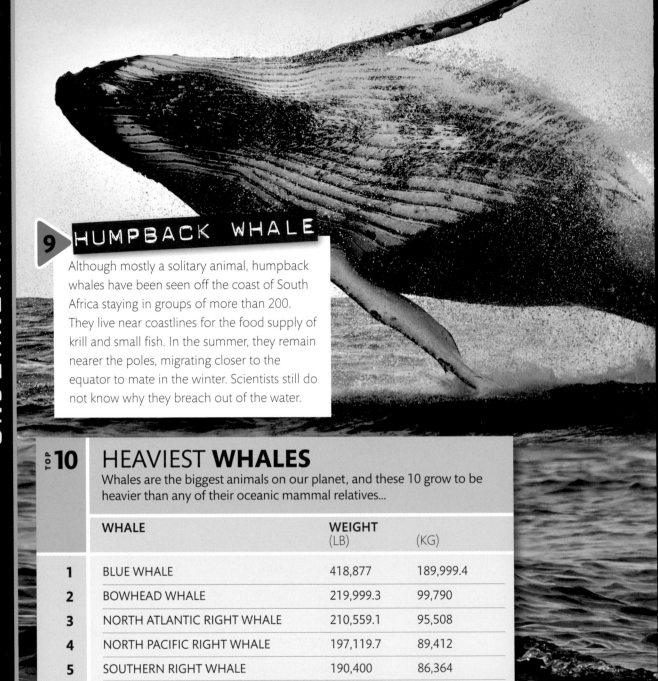

9 HUMPBACK WHALE

Although mostly a solitary animal, humpback whales have been seen off the coast of South Africa staying in groups of more than 200. They live near coastlines for the food supply of krill and small fish. In the summer, they remain nearer the poles, migrating closer to the equator to mate in the winter. Scientists still do not know why they breach out of the water.

TOP 10 HEAVIEST WHALES

Whales are the biggest animals on our planet, and these 10 grow to be heavier than any of their oceanic mammal relatives...

	WHALE	WEIGHT (LB)	(KG)
1	BLUE WHALE	418,877	189,999.4
2	BOWHEAD WHALE	219,999.3	99,790
3	NORTH ATLANTIC RIGHT WHALE	210,559.1	95,508
4	NORTH PACIFIC RIGHT WHALE	197,119.7	89,412
5	SOUTHERN RIGHT WHALE	190,400	86,364
6	FINBACK WHALE	165,760	75,187.5
7	SPERM WHALE	125,440	56,898.6
8	GRAY WHALE	88,184	39,999.6
9	HUMPBACK WHALE	88,050	39,938.8
10	SEI WHALE	62,720	28,449.3

TOP 10 BIGGEST **DOLPHINS & PORPOISES**

The difference between first and second highlights just how big the orca (also known as blackfish and the killer whale) is...

	ANIMAL	WEIGHT (LB)	(KG)
1	ORCA WHALE	22,000	9,979
2	SHORT-FINNED PILOT WHALE	6,613.9	3,000
3	LONG-FINNED PILOT WHALE	5,070.6	2,300
4	FALSE KILLER WHALE	4,850.2	2,200
5	COMMON BOTTLENOSE DOLPHIN	1,433	650
6	MONK DOLPHIN	1,102	500
7	BURRUNAN DOLPHIN	992.1	450
8	MELON-HEADED WHALE	606.3	275
9	LONG-BEAKED COMMON DOLPHIN	518.1	235
10	CHINESE WHITE DOLPHIN	507.1	230

5 COMMON BOTTLENOSE DOLPHIN

They can create more than 1,000 clicking sounds per second to communicate and for echolocation purposes. This allows them to use sound to understand their surroundings and to hunt fish. They have very flexible necks because fewer of their vertebrae are fused (unlike other dolphins). Highly social, they live in pods of a dozen up to 1,000 individuals.

3 WELS CATFISH

The wels is one of 3,000 different species of catfish. Although mainly a bottom feeder of fish, grubs and crustaceans, the wels catfish is also cannibalistic. What's more, it has a fearsome reputation for attacking large birds and even humans. Its jaws are lined with tiny teeth that create a rasping, sandpaper-like effect. The largest specimen of this freshwater giant was caught in Italy's Po river in 2015.

TOP 10 BIGGEST **CATFISH**

Some species of catfish grow so large that they have been known to attack humans, as documented on TV series like *River Monsters*...

	CATFISH	WEIGHT (LB)	(KG)
1	MEKONG GIANT CATFISH	646	293
2	PIRAIBA	341.7	155
3	WELS CATFISH	317	144
4	GIANT LAKE BIWA CATFISH	308.6	140
5	GOONCH	230	104
6	REDTAIL CATFISH	176.4	80
7	BLUE CATFISH	143	64.86
8	AFRICAN SHARPTOOTH CATFISH	132.3	60
9	FLATHEAD CATFISH	123	55.79
10	LEOPARD CATFISH	118	53.5

TOP **10** LARGEST **RAYS**

To give an idea of the immense size of these fishes' wingspans, a surfboard's length ranges between just 6 and 8 ft (1.82 and 2.43 m)...

	RAY	WIDTH (FT)	(M)
1	GIANT OCEANIC MANTA RAY	29.9	9.1
2	REEF MANTA RAY	18	5.5
3	GIANT DEVIL RAY	17.1	5.2
4	SPINETAIL DEVIL RAY	10.2	3.1
5	SPOTTED EAGLE RAY	9.8	3
6	GIANT FRESHWATER STINGRAY	7.9	2.4
7	CHUPARE STINGRAY	6.6	2
8	BENTFIN DEVIL RAY	5.9	1.8
9	DEEPWATER STINGRAY	4.9	1.5
=	PORCUPINE RAY	4.9	1.5

29.9 FT (9.1 M)

1 GIANT OCEANIC MANTA RAY

Due to its size, this ancient fish has very few predators, but it is common for it to have scars from nonfatal shark bites. Its weight can top 3,000 lb (1,360.8 kg), with young rays weighing a mere 20 lb (9.1 kg). Biologists still have a lot to uncover about this mysterious fish, but it is thought to live up to 100 years. Although an intimidating sight, divers often comment on their gentle and inquisitive nature.

TOP 10 HEAVIEST **BONY FISH**

Sharks have cartilage, so they do not qualify for this top 10 chart.
The fish here have a skeleton of bones, like humans...

	FISH	WEIGHT (LB)	(KG)
1	BELUGA STURGEON	7,054.8	3,200
2	OCEAN SUNFISH	5,070.6	2,300
3	SHARPTAIL MOLA	4,409	2,000
4	SOUTHERN SUNFISH	4,400	1,995.8
5	KALUGA STURGEON	2,205	1,000.2
6	ATLANTIC BLUEFIN TUNA	2,010	911.7
7	ATLANTIC BLUE MARLIN	1,803	817.8
8	WHITE STURGEON	1,799	816
9	BLACK MARLIN	1,653.5	750
10	SWORDFISH	1,433	650

6 ATLANTIC BLUEFIN TUNA

This amazing 12 ft (3.7 m) long fish can retract its pectoral and dorsal fins into special grooves on its body. It's a technique that makes the body even more streamlined, reducing friction against the water and increasing speed. They hunt and eat continuously, chasing down squid and small fish at depths of 1,500 ft (457.2 m).

7 ATLANTIC BLUE MARLIN

This 14 ft (4.3 m) long predator uses its spear-like snout to stun or injure its prey, rapidly swiping through schools of fish. They can live for 27 years and weigh more than 1,950 lb (884.5 kg). Mako sharks and great white sharks are known to attack and eat Atlantic blue marlin. Their terrific speed means they can cover more than 4,500 mi (7,242 km) in four months.

TOP 10 LONGEST **BONY FISH**

Some of these fish resemble what boat captains of yesteryear would describe as sea serpents, and other entries have been accused of being lake monsters...

	FISH	LENGTH (FT)	(M)
1	GIANT OARFISH	49.9	15.2
2	BELUGA STURGEON	26.2	8
=	OARFISH	26.2	8
4	WHITE STURGEON	20	6.1
5	EUROPEAN SEA STURGEON	19.7	6
6	KALUGA STURGEON	18.4	5.6
7	ATLANTIC BLUE MARLIN	16.4	5
=	CHINESE STURGEON	16.4	5
9	BLACK MARLIN	15.3	4.65
10	OCEAN SUNFISH	15.1	4.6

1 LEATHERBACK SEA TURTLE

These deep-diving turtles can exceed 7 ft (2 m) in length. Their shell is uniquely flexible, similar to hard rubber, and not rigid and bony like other turtles. This endangered species is another victim of humankind's pollution. They accidentally eat floating plastic waste because it looks like their favored food source, jellyfish.

TOP 10 BIGGEST TURTLES

Tortoises are not true turtles, because they remain on land, and so this top 10 deals exclusively with turtles of the aquatic variety...

TURTLE	WEIGHT (LB)	(KG)
1 LEATHERBACK SEA TURTLE	2,120	961.1
2 LOGGERHEAD TURTLE	1,202	545.2
3 GREEN SEA TURTLE	871	395.1
4 YANGTZE GIANT SOFTSHELL TURTLE	550	249.5
5 HAWKSBILL TURTLE	280	127
6 INDIAN NARROW-HEADED SOFTSHELL TURTLE	260	117.9
7 ALLIGATOR SNAPPING TURTLE	236	107
8 CANTOR'S GIANT SOFTSHELL TURTLE	220	99.8
9 FLATBACK SEA TURTLE	198	89.8
10 KEMP'S RIDLEY SEA TURTLE	110	49.9

TOP 10 FASTEST **IN THE SEA**

These 10 fish have the natural ability to accelerate to speeds we are used to experiencing behind the wheel of a car...

	ANIMAL	SPEED (MPH)	(KPH)
1	BLACK MARLIN	80	128.7
2	SAILFISH	68.3	110
3	MAKO SHARK	59	95
4	WAHOO	48.5	78
5	BLUEFIN TUNA	43.5	70
6	GREAT BLUE SHARK	42.9	69
7	ORCA WHALE	40.1	65
8	BONEFISH	39.8	64
=	SWORDFISH	39.8	64
10	GREAT WHITE SHARK	35	56.3

SPEED CHART

Ranked by the number of bony fish, sharks, and mammals, this speed chart looks like this...

6	BONY FISH
3	SHARKS
1	MAMMAL

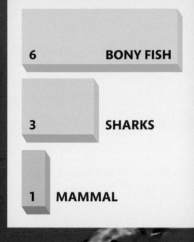

4 WAHOO

Also known as the peto and the ono, the wahoo is a muscular, mostly solitary fish. It can grow to more than 8 ft (2.4 m) in length and weigh 180 lb (81.6 kg). It is often found near reefs and shipwrecks because its diet of small fish tends to stay close by for protection. The wahoo resembles the barracuda, and it's often mistaken for this ferocious, but less fast fish (26 mph / 41.8 kph).

BIGGEST BEES, WASPS & HORNETS

Common bees and wasps are famous for invoking fear in humans, but these massive species will for some people truly be the stuff of nightmares...

	NAME	TYPE	LENGTH (IN)	(CM)
1	TARANTULA HAWK SPIDER WASP	WASP	2.5	6.4
2	EASTERN CICADA KILLER	WASP	2	5
=	WESTERN CICADA KILLER	WASP	2	5
4	GIANT SCOLIID	WASP	1.9	4.8
5	JAPANESE GIANT HORNET	HORNET	1.8	4.5
6	ASIAN GIANT HORNET	HORNET	1.6	4
=	BOMBUS DAHLBOMII	BEE	1.6	4
8	MEGACHILE PLUTO	BEE	1.5	3.9
9	EUROPEAN HORNET	HORNET	1.4	3.5
10	GREATER BANDED HORNET	HORNET	0.9	2.5

5 JAPANESE GIANT HORNET

This species targets bees for food. A few dozen Japanese giant hornets can devour tens of thousands of bees in a matter of hours. They are also attracted to human sweat as well as sweet aromas. The venom in this giant-sized hornet can be fatal to humans, especially if the victim is stung multiple times. Thousands of people are injured, and dozens die, each year from attacks by this deadly hornet.

TOP **10** FASTEST **INSECT WINGS**

The buzzing sound made by winged insects comes from their wings beating at an incredibly high rate, and these are the fastest...

	INSECT	BEATS PER SECOND (MAX)
1	MIDGE	1,046
2	GNAT	950
3	MOSQUITO	600
=	BUMBLEBEE	600
5	FRUIT FLY	300
6	WASP	247
7	HOUSEFLY	190
8	BLOWFLY	150
9	HOVERFLY	120
10	HORNET	100

1 MIDGE

The midge group of insects actually encompasses many species, of which some 4,000 different kinds of biting midges spread diseases. Sandflies, muffleheads, no-see-ums, punkies, and five-os are other names given to midge species. Many types that live near water are mistakenly identified, and feared, as mosquitoes. Predatory fish, such as carp, eat large quantities of midge larvae.

TOP 10 LARGEST **BUTTERFLIES**

The frequent use of the term "birdwing" with some of these butterflies is accurate, as all of these have wingspans as large as birds...

	BUTTERFLY	SIZE (WIDTH)	
		(IN)	(CM)
1	QUEEN ALEXANDRA'S BIRDWING	11.8	30
2	GOLIATH BIRDWING	11	28
3	GIANT AFRICAN SWALLOWTAIL	9.8	25
4	RIPPON'S BIRDWING	7.9	20
=	WALLACE'S GOLDEN BIRDWING	7.9	20
6	PALAWAN BIRDWING	7.5	19
=	PRIAM'S BIRDWING	7.5	19
8	MAGELLAN BIRDWING	7.1	18
9	RAJAH BROOKE'S BIRDWING	6.7	17
10	CHIMAERA BIRDWING	6.3	16

3 MADAGASCAN MOON MOTH

This Madagascan native can lay up to 170 eggs. Baby caterpillars hatch after two weeks, and grow to full size after two months. Once they cocoon themselves, metamorphosis into an adult Madagascan moon moth (also known as the comet moth) can take up to six months. After hatching, the adult moth lives for only five days.

4 RIPPON'S BIRDWING

Dutch entomologist Pieter Cramer first described this butterfly in 1775. Their chrysalises (the protective case the caterpillar turns into prior to metamorphosis) resemble dead leaves to avoid being eaten. Unlike the Madagascan moon moth, the Rippon's birdwing can live for three months. A female is pictured here. The male has a lighter brown coloration.

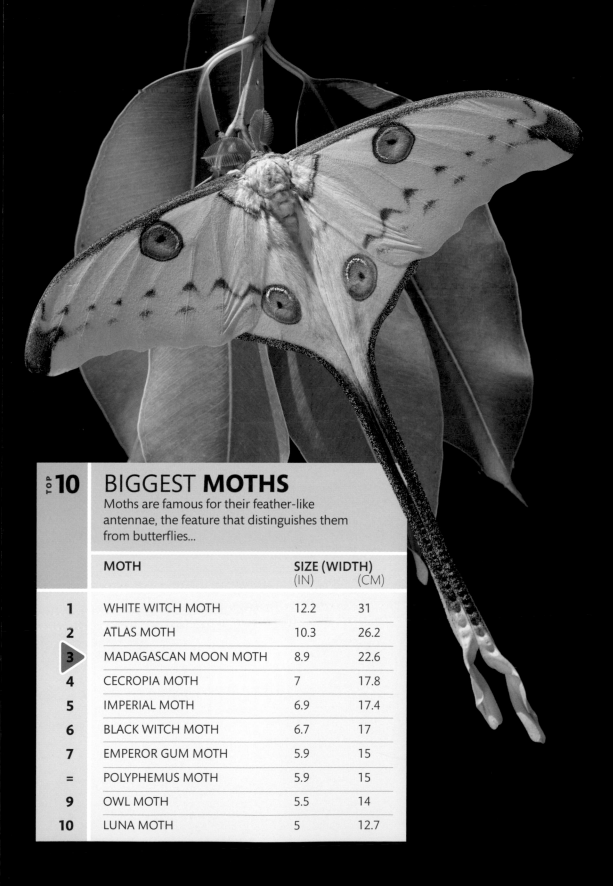

TOP **10** BIGGEST **MOTHS**

Moths are famous for their feather-like antennae, the feature that distinguishes them from butterflies...

	MOTH	SIZE (WIDTH) (IN)	(CM)
1	WHITE WITCH MOTH	12.2	31
2	ATLAS MOTH	10.3	26.2
3	MADAGASCAN MOON MOTH	8.9	22.6
4	CECROPIA MOTH	7	17.8
5	IMPERIAL MOTH	6.9	17.4
6	BLACK WITCH MOTH	6.7	17
7	EMPEROR GUM MOTH	5.9	15
=	POLYPHEMUS MOTH	5.9	15
9	OWL MOTH	5.5	14
10	LUNA MOTH	5	12.7

WINGED CREATURES

FASTEST **IN THE AIR**

Some of the birds in this top 10 achieve their incredible speed during a dive toward their prey...

BIRD	MAXIMUM KNOWN SPEED (MPH)	(KPH)
1 PEREGRINE FALCON	241.7	389
2 GOLDEN EAGLE	198.8	320
3 GYRFALCON	129.9	209
4 SWIFT	106.3	171
5 WHITE-THROATED NEEDLETAIL	105	169
6 EURASIAN HOBBY	100	161
7 FRIGATEBIRD	95.1	153
8 SPUR-WINGED GOOSE	88.2	142
9 RED-BREASTED MERGANSER	80.8	130
10 GREY-HEADED ALBATROSS	78.9	127

1 PEREGRINE FALCON

The fastest animal on Earth is also one of the farthest travelers. Its name comes from the Medieval Latin *peregrinus*, meaning "pilgrim" or "wanderer." The incredible record speed was captured by a skydiver for a *National Geographic* television program. This raptor (bird of prey) hunts other birds, as well as small reptiles and mammals.

1 WEDGE-TAILED EAGLE

Found throughout Australia, Tasmania, Indonesia, and parts of New Guinea, this eagle can live for up to 45 years. Also known as the eaglehawk, its wedge-tailed name comes from the distinctive shape of its tail feathers. This eagle features as an emblem on several crests of Australia, including the New South Wales Police Force and the Royal Australian Air Force.

TOP **10** WIDEST **EAGLE WINGSPANS**

Eagles are some of the biggest birds of prey, also known as raptors, and these 10 are the largest species...

	EAGLE	WINGSPAN (FT)	(M)
1	WEDGE-TAILED EAGLE	9.32	2.84
2	HIMALAYAN GOLDEN EAGLE	9.22	2.81
3	MARTIAL EAGLE	8.53	2.6
4	WHITE-TAILED SEA EAGLE	8.3	2.53
5	STELLAR'S SEA EAGLE	8.2	2.5
6	BALD EAGLE	7.55	2.3
=	VERREAUX'S EAGLE	7.55	2.3
8	HARPY EAGLE	7.35	2.24
9	PHILIPPINE EAGLE	7.22	2.2
10	CROWNED EAGLE	6.23	1.9

The tiniest bird in the world is found in Cuba. It favors between nine and 10 species of plant for nectar, which is its primary food source. Its eggs are the size of garden peas and are laid inside nests barely 1 in (2.6 cm) wide, constructed from lichen and spiderwebs. They can begin breeding at one year of age. Mating aside, the bee hummingbird is a solitary animal.

TOP 10 SMALLEST **BIRDS**

Some of the birds in this top 10 are so tiny that when they're feeding on plant nectar, they are often mistaken for insects...

	BIRD	LENGTH (IN)	(CM)
1	BEE HUMMINGBIRD	1.97	5
2	BANANAQUIT	2.96	7.5
3	WEEBILL	3.15	8
=	STRIATED PARDOLATE	3.15	8
5	GOLDCREST	3.35	8.5
6	BROWN GERYGONE	3.54	9
=	LESSER GOLDFINCH	3.54	9
8	CRIMSON CHAT	3.94	10
=	GOLDEN-HEADED CISTICOLA	3.94	10
10	TROPICAL PARULA	4.33	11

TOP 10 BIGGEST **BATS**

Some species of bats are very small, like the common pipistrelle, but its 8 in (20.3 cm) wingspan comes nowhere near the qualifying size to get into this top 10...

	BAT	WIDTH (FT)	(M)
1	LARGE FLYING FOX	7	2.1
2	BLACK FLYING FOX	6	1.8
3	GIANT GOLDEN-CROWNED FLYING FOX	5.6	1.7
4	PEMBA FLYING FOX	5.2	1.6
5	GREY-HEADED FLYING FOX	5	1.53
6	INDIAN FLYING FOX	4.9	1.5
=	GREAT FLYING FOX	4.9	1.5
8	LIVINGSTONE'S FRUIT BAT	4.6	1.4
9	MADAGASCAN FLYING FOX	4.1	1.25
10	LITTLE RED FLYING FOX	3.9	1.2

1 LARGE FLYING FOX

This, the biggest of the megabats (fruit bats), is known by many other names including kalang, the Malaysian flying fox, and the large fruit bat. Unlike its smaller bat relatives (which feed on moths and small insects), the large flying fox eats solely fruits, flowers, and their nectar. It seeks out its diet with its exceptional senses of smell and sight.

TOP **10** LARGEST PREHISTORIC **FLYERS**

Although the largest flying animals on the planet today are birds, in the prehistoric era they were winged reptiles...

	PTEROSAUR	WINGSPAN (FT)	(M)
1	HATZEGOPTERYX	34.4	10.5
=	QUETZALCOATHUS	34.4	10.5
3	ARAMBOURGIANIA	32.8	10
4	ORNITHOCHEIRUS	23	7
5	PTERANODON	21.3	6.5
6	COLOBORHYNCHUS	19.7	6
7	MOGANOPTERUS	15.4	4.7
8	ISTIODACTYLUS	14.1	4.3
9	TUPUXUARA	13.1	4
10	ZHENYUANOPTERUS	11.5	3.5

10 ZHENYUANOPTERUS

This giant pterosaur's 172 needle-like, interlocking teeth made it an expert at catching fish. Its longest teeth were at the front of its jaws, slowly getting smaller in length toward the back of the mouth. It also had disproportionately tiny feet, meaning it would have spent the majority of its life in the air.

2 ▶ BLAKISTON'S FISH OWL

Fish owls hunt areas between land and water. Due to its endangered status, the Blakiston's Fish Owl Project (an international scientific collaboration between the Wildlife Conservation Society's Russia Program, the Institute of Biology and Soils, and the Amur-Ussuri Centre for Avian Biodiversity) has been set up to help the declining numbers in Russia.

TOP **10** LARGEST **OWLS**

These majestic birds of prey are popular throughout different cultures and are the biggest of the 216 owl species...

	OWL	LENGTH (IN)	(CM)
1	GREAT GREY OWL	33.1	84
▶ 2	BLAKISTON'S FISH OWL	28.3	72
3	SNOWY OWL	28	71
4	EURASIAN EAGLE-OWL	27.6	70
5	MILKY EAGLE-OWL	26	66
6	SPOT-BELLIED EAGLE-OWL	25.6	65
7	GREAT HORNED OWL	25.2	64
8	PEL'S FISHING OWL	24.8	63
9	CAPE EAGLE-OWL	24	61
=	TAWNY FISH OWL	24	61

Forces of NATURE

TOP 10 BIGGEST COUNTRIES

There are nearly 200 areas of land that are recognized / classified as a country, and these are the 10 largest...

	COUNTRY	SIZE (SQUARE MI)	(SQUARE KM)
1	RUSSIA	6,601,668	17,098,242
2	CANADA	3,855,100	9,984,670
3	CHINA	3,747,879	9,706,961
4	USA	3,705,407	9,629,091
5	BRAZIL	3,287,612	8,514,877
6	AUSTRALIA	2,969,907	7,692,024
7	INDIA	1,222,559	3,166,414
8	ARGENTINA	1,073,500	2,780,400
9	KAZAKHSTAN	1,052,100	2,724,900
10	ALGERIA	919,595	2,381,741

8 ARGENTINA

This South American country has an eclectic landscape that includes a coastline thousands of miles long, a portion of Antarctica's tundra, mountains, and deserts. It is home to 43.5 million people and the peso is its national currency, depicted by a dollar sign (like the US).

4 **INDONESIA**

More than 263 million people live on 8,000 of Indonesia's 17,000 islands. Indonesian is the official language of the country, but along with Javanese and Sundanese, more than 700 different languages are spoken across the islands. It is home to plants native to Australia and more than 500 different mammals, including tigers and leopards, and more than 1,500 species of bird.

TOP 10 LONGEST **COASTLINES**

This chart helps convey just how vast the coasts are of the countries most connected to the sea...

	COUNTRY	LENGTH (MI)	(KM)
1	CANADA	164,988.34	265,523
2	UNITED STATES	82,836.24	133,312
3	RUSSIA	68,543.46	110,310
4	INDONESIA	59,142.73	95,181
5	CHILE	48,816.78	78,563
6	AUSTRALIA	41,339.83	66,530
7	NORWAY	33,056.33	53,199
8	PHILIPPINES	21,064.48	33,900
9	BRAZIL	20,740.75	33,379
10	FINLAND	19,336.45	31,119

LAKE ASSAL

This saltwater lake in Djibouti is located in the Horn of Africa. This is the most easterly point of the continent, which is also home to Ethiopia, Eritrea, and Somalia. Lake Assal's water is 10 times saltier than the sea. It is protected under Djibouti's National Environmental Action Plan.

TOP 10

COUNTRIES WITH
THE LOWEST POINTS OF ELEVATION

Living lower than sea level can be a strange concept to visualize, and these places are up to a quarter of a mile below it...

	PLACE	COUNTRY/COUNTRIES	LOWEST POINT BELOW SEA LEVEL (FT)	(M)
1	DEAD SEA	ISRAEL, JORDAN, PALESTINE	-1,402	-428
2	SEA OF GALILEE	SYRIA	-702	-214
3	LAKE ASSAL	DJIBOUTI	-509	-155
4	AYDINGKOL	CHINA	-505	-154
5	QATTARA DEPRESSION	EGYPT	-436	-133
6	KARAGIYE DEPRESSION	KAZAKHSTAN	-433	-132
7	DANAKIL DEPRESSION	ETHIOPIA	-410	-125
8	LAGUNA DEL CARBÓN	ARGENTINA	-344	-105
9	BADWATER BASIN	USA	-279	-85
10	VPADINA AKCHANAYA	TURKMENISTAN	-266	-81

1 LA PAZ

The full name of Bolivia's capital city is Nuestra Señora de La Paz, which translates as "Our Lady of Peace." La Paz was founded in 1548 by Spanish conquistador Alonso de Mendoza (1471 – 1476). The highest and longest cable car system in the world (called Mi Teleférico, "my cable car") connects its residents to the various towns. Bolivian composer Alberto Villalpando was born in La Paz on November 21, 1940.

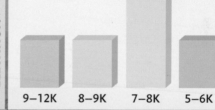

RANKS OF ELEVATION

9–12K   8–9K   7–8K   5–6K

TOP 10 HIGHEST **CAPITAL CITIES**

The number one entry is more than four times higher up than the tallest building in the world (Dubai's Burj Khalifa at 2,717 ft / 828 m)...

	CITY	COUNTRY	ELEVATION ABOVE SEA LEVEL (FT)	(M)
1	LA PAZ	BOLIVIA	11,942	3,640
2	QUITO	ECUADOR	9,350	2,850
3	THIMPHU	BHUTAN	8,688	2,648
4	BOGOTÁ	COLOMBIA	8,612	2,625
5	ADDIS ABABA	ETHIOPIA	7,726	2,355
6	ASMARA	ERITREA	7,628	2,325
7	SANA'A	YEMEN	7,382	2,250
8	MEXICO CITY	MEXICO	7,350	2,240
9	NAIROBI	KENYA	5,889	1,795
10	KABUL	AFGHANISTAN	5,873	1,790

COUNTRIES WITH
THE LARGEST FOREST AREAS

Our planet enjoys a wide range of different climates, creating millions of square miles of luscious, dense vegetation as well as vast, arid plains...

	COUNTRY	FORESTED AREA (SQUARE MI)	(SQUARE KM)
1	RUSSIA	3,146,466.2	8,149,310
2	BRAZIL	1,905,560.9	4,935,380
3	CANADA	1,340,040.9	3,470,690
4	USA	1,197,283.5	3,100,950
5	CHINA	804,331.9	2,083,210
6	DEMOCRATIC REPUBLIC OF THE CONGO	589,107	1,525,780
7	AUSTRALIA	481,666.3	1,247,510
8	INDONESIA	351,391.6	910,100
9	PERU	285,611.4	739,730
10	INDIA	272,904.8	706,820

3 CANADA

The indigenous people of Canada—the Inuit, Métis, and the First Nations—inhabited the country thousands of years before European settlers came to the shores. The name of the country comes from an indigenous language known as Iroquoian. Their word *kanata* means "land" or "settlement." As well as its sprawling forests and mountains, its two million lakes hold most of the planet's fresh water. Canada is also home to more than 200 mammals, including the silver-haired bat, Canadian lynx, and the North American beaver, which is one of the country's official animal symbols.

TOP 10 COUNTRIES / TERRITORIES WITH
THE SMALLEST FOREST AREAS

Smaller land masses and extreme temperatures contribute to these countries having very little forestry...

	COUNTRY	FORESTED AREA (SQUARE MI)	(SQUARE KM)
1	QATAR	0	0
2	FAROE ISLANDS	0.4	1
=	SAN MARINO	0.4	1
4	GREENLAND	0.8	2
5	MALTA	1.2	3
6	ARUBA	1.5	4
7	BAHRAIN	1.9	5
8	CHANNEL ISLANDS	3.1	8
9	BERMUDA	3.9	10
=	MALDIVES	3.9	10

2 FAROE ISLANDS

At only 540 square mi (1,398.6 square km), the population of the 18 Faroe Islands is little more than 49,000. The Faroes are situated 250 mi (402.3 km) north of Scotland, and between Iceland and Norway. Although trees are extremely sparse, the islands are home to 400 species of plants. More than 100 species of birds frequent the Faroe Islands, with the Eurasian oystercatcher celebrated for signifying the beginning of spring.

LARGEST **OCEANS & SEAS**

The data here should not be a surprise because 71 percent of the Earth's surface is covered in water...

	NAME	TYPE	AREA (SQUARE MI)	(SQUARE KM)
1	PACIFIC	OCEAN	64,196,000	166,266,876
2	ATLANTIC	OCEAN	33,400,000	86,505,602
3	INDIAN	OCEAN	28,400,000	73,555,662
4	SOUTHERN	OCEAN	20,327,000	52,646,688
5	ARCTIC	OCEAN	5,100,000	13,208,939
6	PHILIPPINE	SEA	2,000,000	5,179,976
7	CORAL	SEA	1,850,000	4,791,478
8	ARABIAN	SEA	1,491,000	3,861,672
9	SOUTH CHINA	SEA	1,148,000	2,973,306
10	CARIBBEAN	SEA	971,000	2,514,878

1 ▶ PACIFIC

This ocean makes up approximately a third of the Earth's surface. It has twice the amount of water as the Altantic Ocean. Its name, Latin for "peace," came from Portuguese explorer Ferdinand Magellan in 1521. He described it as *mar pacífico*—"peaceful sea." There are more than 25,000 islands in the Pacific Ocean, and it is also the ocean where the majority of commercial fishing occurs.

TOP **10** LARGEST **LAKES**

Many of the huge lakes on this chart have reports of unidentified monsters that date back hundreds of years...

	LAKE	LOCATION	AREA (SQUARE MI)	(SQUARE KM)
1	CASPIAN SEA	IRAN, RUSSIA, TURKMENISTAN, KAZAKHSTAN, AZERBAIJAN	143,000	371,000
2	SUPERIOR	CANADA, USA	31,820	82,414
3	VICTORIA	UGANDA, KENYA, TANZANIA	26,828	69,485
4	HURON	CANADA, USA	23,000	59,600
5	MICHIGAN	USA	22,000	58,000
6	TANGANYIKA	TANZANIA, DEMOCRATIC REPUBLIC OF THE CONGO, BURUNDI, ZAMBIA	12,700	32,893
7	BAIKAL	RUSSIA	12,200	31,500
8	GREAT BEAR	CANADA	12,000	31,080
9	MALAWI	MOZAMBIQUE, TANZANIA, MALAWI	11,600	30,044
10	GREAT SLAVE	CANADA	11,170	28,930

7 BAIKAL

Lake Baikal may not be high up on this chart by area, but it holds a few other records where it does come out number one. Scientists date it as 25 million years old, which makes it the oldest lake on Earth. With a depth of 5,387 ft (1,642 m), it is also the deepest lake in the world. On top of that, when measured by volume, Lake Baikal is the largest freshwater lake on the planet. Over the decades, there have been numerous reports of an unidentified lake monster and even alien-esque humanoid creatures.

TOP 10 LONGEST RIVERS

Some experts estimate than the Amazon river is home to 8,000 different species of fish...

	RIVER	OUTFLOW	LENGTH (MI)	(KM)
1	AMAZON – UCAYALI – APURÍMAC	ATLANTIC OCEAN	4,345	6,992
2	NILE – KAGERA	MEDITERRANEAN	4,258	6,853
3	YANGTZE	EAST CHINA SEA	3,917	6,300
4	MISSISSIPPI – MISSOURI – JEFFERSON	GULF OF MEXICO	3,902	6,275
5	YENISEI – ANGARA – SELENGE	KARA SEA	3,445	5,539
6	HUANG HE	BOHAI SEA	3,395	5,464
7	OB – IRTYSH	GULF OF OB	3,364	5,410
8	PARANÁ – RÍO DE LA PLATA	RÍO DE LA PLATA	3,030	4,880
9	CONGO – CHAMBESHI	ATLANTIC OCEAN	2,922	4,700
10	AMUR – ARGUN	SEA OF OKHOTSK	2,763	4,444

2 NILE

This river flows through 11 countries. Egypt and Sudan rely on the Nile as their main source of water. It is home to a vast array of wildlife, including the toothy African tigerfish, the colossal 440 lb (200 kg) Nile perch, and the African softshell turtle.

5 CATARATA YUMBILLA

This waterfall has four drops. It is one of four in the region, along with Catarata Gocta, Catarata Chinata, and Catarata Pabelló. Catarata Yumbilla is the tallest, but does not have a high volume of water. Its water comes from a cave stream from Caverna San Francisco.

TOP 10 HIGHEST WATERFALLS

To help express just how huge these waterfalls are, New York's Statue of Liberty is a mere 305 ft (93 m) high...

	WATERFALL	LOCATION	HEIGHT (FT)	(M)
1	ANGEL FALLS	BOLÍVAR STATE (VENEZUELA)	3,212	979
2	TUGELA FALLS	KWAZULU-NATAL (SOUTH AFRICA)	3,110	948
3	CATARATAS LAS TRES HERMANAS	AYACUCHO (PERU)	3,000	914
4	OLO'UPENA FALLS	MOLOKAI, HAWAII (USA)	2,953	900
5	CATARATA YUMBILLA	AMAZONAS (PERU)	2,940	896
6	VINNUFOSSEN	MØRE OG ROMSDAL (NORWAY)	2,822	860
7	BALÅIFOSSEN	HORDALAND (NORWAY)	2,788	850
8	PU'UKA'OKU FALLS	HAWAII (USA)	2,756	840
=	JAMES BRUCE FALLS	BRITISH COLUMBIA (CANADA)	2,756	840
10	BROWNE FALLS	SOUTH ISLAND (NEW ZEALAND)	2,743	836

2 KEBILI, TUNISIA

Kebili is 8,669.5 square mi (22,454 square km), with a population of around 157,000. It is one of the oldest places in Africa. Kebili is the capital of Kebili Governorate, Tunisia's second largest province behind Tataouine (famous for inspiring the name of the planet Tatooine in the *Star Wars* universe). Tunisia has 24 governorates (provinces). Tourism is highest in spring and autumn, as summer has its record-breaking extreme heat, and winter nights have freezing temperatures.

1910s
1930s
1940s
1960s
2010s

RANKS BY DECADE

TOP 10 HOTTEST PLACES

What is the highest recorded temperature of the town that you live in? Find out and compare it to these extraordinarily hot locations...

	LOCATION	DATE	TEMPERATURE (°F)	(°C)
1	DEATH VALLEY, CALIFORNIA (USA)	JUL 10, 1913	134	56.7
2	KEBILI (TUNISIA)	JUL 7, 1931	131	55
3	TIRAT ZVI (ISRAEL)	JUN 21, 1942	129	54
4	SULAIBYA (KUWAIT)	JUL 31, 2012	128.5	53.6
5	KUWAIT INTERNATIONAL AIRPORT (KUWAIT)	AUG 3, 2011	128.3	53.5
=	MOHENJO-DARO, SINDH (PAKISTAN)	MAY 26, 2010	128.3	53.5
7	NASIRIYAH, ALI AIR BASE (IRAQ)	AUG 3, 2011	127.4	53
8	BASRA (IRAQ)	JUN 14, 2010	125.6	52
=	SAN LUIS RÍO COLORADO (MEXICO)	JUL 6, 1966	125.6	52
=	JEDDAH (SAUDI ARABIA)	JUN 22, 2010	125.6	52

TOP 10 COLDEST PLACES

Frostbite can occur in humans in just 30 minutes at 0°F (-17.8°C) if the wind-chill is at -19°F (-28.3°C), so this chart's temperatures are extremely dangerous...

	LOCATION	DATE	TEMPERATURE (°C)	(°F)
1	VOSTOK STATION (ANTARCTICA)	JUL 21, 1983	-128.6	-89.2
2	AMUNDSEN-SCOTT SOUTH POLE STATION (SOUTH POLE)	JUN 23, 1982	-117	-82.8
3	DOME A (EAST ANTARCTICA)	JULY 2007	-116.5	-82.5
4	VERKHOYANSK & OYMYAKON SAKHA REPUBLIC (RUSSIA)	FEB 6, 1933	-90	-68
5	NORTH ICE (GREENLAND)	JAN 9, 1954	-87	-66.1
6	SNAG, YUKON (CANADA)	FEB 3, 1947	-81	-63
7	PROSPECT CREEK, ALASKA (USA)	JAN 23, 1971	-80	-62
8	UST-SHCHUGER (RUSSIA)	DEC 31, 1978	-72.6	-58.1
9	MALGOVIK, VÄSTERBOTTEN (SWEDEN)	DEC 13, 1941	-63.4	-53
10	MOHE COUNTY (CHINA)	FEB 13, 1969	-62.1	-52.3

1 VOSTOK STATION, ANTARCTICA

Russia's Vostok Station began its research on December 16, 1957. Its studies include magnetic fields and ice-core samples. The station is also the location of the coldest wind-chill ever recorded, -191°F (-124°C), on August 24, 2005. The word *vostok* is Russian for "east" and was the name of Captain Fabian von Bellingshausen's ship, which led Russia's first Antarctic expedition in 1820.

2 KALI GANDAKI GORGE

Also known as the Andha Gorge, this is located in Nepal's Himalaya mountains. The Kali Gandaki river runs through the gorge, separating two massifs, Annapurna (26,545 ft / 8,090.9 m) and Dhaulagiri (26,795 ft / 8,167.1 m).

TOP 10 DEEPEST CANYONS

The combined depth of all these canyons totals 21.5 mi (34.6 km), which is a third of the distance between the Earth's surface and space...

	CANYON	LOCATION	DEEPEST POINT (FT)	(M)
1	YARLUNG TSANGPO GRAND CANYON	TIBET	19,714.6	6,009
2	KALI GANDAKI GORGE	NEPAL	18,277.6	5,571
3	INDUS GORGE	PAKISTAN	17,060.4	5,200
4	COLCA CANYON	PERU	13,648.3	4,160
5	TIGER LEAPING GORGE	CHINA	12,434.4	3,790
6	COTAHUASI CANYON	PERU	11,597.8	3,535
7	URIQUE CANNON (ONE OF THE 6 COPPER CANYONS)	MEXICO	6,164.7	1,879
8	GRAND CANYON	USA	5,997.4	1,828
9	BLYDE RIVER CANYON	SOUTH AFRICA	4,537.4	1,383
10	TARA RIVER CANYON	MONTENEGRO	4,265.1	1,300

TOP 10

DEEPEST **REALMS**

The total distance here is three times that of the canyons' total, and equals the 62 mile (100 km) span between our planet and space...

	NAME	LOCATION	DEEPEST POINT BELOW SEA LEVEL (FT)	(M)
1	MARIANA TRENCH	PACIFIC OCEAN	36,197.5	11,033
2	TONGA TRENCH	PACIFIC OCEAN	35,702.1	10,882
3	JAPAN TRENCH	PACIFIC OCEAN	34,593.2	10,544
4	PHILIPPINE TRENCH	PACIFIC OCEAN	34,580	10,540
5	KURIL-KAMCHATKA TRENCH	PACIFIC OCEAN	34,448.8	10,500
6	KERMADEC TRENCH	PACIFIC OCEAN	32,962.6	10,047
7	IZU-OGASAWARA TRENCH	PACIFIC OCEAN	32,086.6	9,780
8	PUERTO RICO TRENCH	ATLANTIC OCEAN	28,372.7	8,648
9	SOUTH SANDWICH TRENCH	ATLANTIC OCEAN	27,650.9	8,428
10	ATACAMA TRENCH	PACIFIC OCEAN	26,460	8,065

3 JAPAN TRENCH

This is a feature of a U-shaped area called the Ring of Fire. Its ominous name comes from the fact that 85 percent of the world's earthquakes occur along it. The Japan Trench is home to different species of snailfish, which are currently the deepest living fish captured on film.

4 ROCKIES

The mountain range that dates back 80 million years became home to several Native Americans, including the Apache, Crow Nation, and Sioux. The range extends from Canada's British Columbia all the way down to New Mexico in the USA. Colorado's Mount Elbert is its tallest peak at 14,440 ft (4,401 m).

TOP 10 LONGEST **MOUNTAIN RANGES**

The mountain ranges on land are impressive, but two located underneath the waves dwarf them in comparison...

	RANGE	MOUNTAIN TYPE	LOCATION	LENGTH (MI)	(KM)
1	MID-OCEANIC RIDGE	OCEANIC	GLOBAL	40,389	65,000
2	MID-ATLANTIC RIDGE	OCEANIC	ATLANTIC OCEAN	6,214	10,000
3	ANDES	LAND	SOUTH AMERICA	4,350	7,000
4	ROCKIES	LAND	NORTH AMERICA	2,983	4,800
5	TRANSANTARCTIC	LAND	ANTARCTICA	2,201	3,542
6	GREAT DIVING RANGE	LAND	AUSTRALIA	1,901	3,059
7	HIMALAYAS	LAND	ASIA	1,601	2,576
8	SOUTHEAST INDIAN RIDGE	OCEANIC	INDIAN OCEAN	1,429	2,300
9	SOUTHWEST INDIAN RIDGE	OCEANIC	RODRIGUEZ ISLAND TO PRINCE EDWARD ISLANDS	1,200	1,931
10	PACIFIC-ANTARCTIC RIDGE	OCEANIC	SOUTH PACIFIC OCEAN	639	1,029

TOP 10 LARGEST DESERTS

The word "desert" conjures up an image of barren, sandy plains, but it is the snowy poles of Earth that are home to the biggest...

	DESERT	LOCATION	AREA (SQUARE MI)	(SQUARE KM)
1	ANTARCTIC POLAR DESERT	ANTARCTICA	5,500,000	14,244,935
2	ARCTIC POLAR DESERT	ARCTIC	5,400,000	13,985,936
3	SAHARA DESERT	NORTHERN AFRICA	3,500,000	9,064,959
4	ARABIAN DESERT	WESTERN ASIA	900,000	2,330,000
5	GOBI DESERT	ASIA	500,000	1,294,994
6	KALAHARI DESERT	SOUTHERN AFRICA	360,000	932,396
7	PATAGONIAN DESERT	ARGENTINA, CHILE	259,847	673,000
8	SYRIAN DESERT	SYRIA	200,773	520,000
9	GREAT BASIN DESERT	USA	190,000	492,098
10	GREAT VICTORIA DESERT	AUSTRALIA	163,862	424,400

1 ANTARCTIC POLAR DESERT

This snow-, glacier-, and tundra-covered region is larger than the Arabian, Gobi, Kalahari, and Sahara deserts combined. Temperatures range from -90°F (-67.8°C) to 30°F (-1.1°C). Its polar desert makes up the majority of Antarctica, which has less than 1.6 in (4 cm) of rain every year. Each region of this polar desert experiences a period of nine to 10 months of total darkness.

HIGHEST **RECORDED RAINFALL**

Instead of comparing the rainfall of countries, this chart looks at specific places to showcase the wettest locations on Earth...

	LOCATION	HIGHEST RAINFALL RECORDED (IN)	(MM)
1	CHERRAPUNJI, MEGHALAYA (INDIA)	1,041.8	26,461
2	MAWSYNRAM, MEGHALAYA (INDIA)	1,023.6	26,000
3	MT. WAIALEALE, KAUAI, HAWAII (USA)	681.1	17,300
4	LÓPEZ DE MICAY, CAUCA DEPARTMENT (COLOMBIA)	507.6	12,892
5	LLORÓ, CHOCÓ DEPARTMENT (COLOMBIA)	500.7	12,717
6	TUTENDO (COLOMBIA)	463.4	11,770
7	CROPP RIVER (NEW ZEALAND)	453.4	11,516
8	SAN ANTONIO DE URECA, BIOKO ISLAND (EQUATORIAL GUINEA)	411.4	10,450
9	DEBUNDSCHA (CAMEROON)	405.5	10,299
10	BIG BOG, MAUI, HAWAII (USA)	404.4	10,272

1 CHERRAPUNJI, MEGHALAYA

This town is 4,869 ft (1,484 m) above sea level. It is accessible by a winding, mist-covered road, 36 mi (58 km) from Shillong, the capital of Meghalaya. It rains every month of the year, but May to September feature the most intense rainfall. The nearby Mawsmai Falls, the fourth highest waterfall in India, is 1,035 ft (315.5 m) high.

TOP 10

LEAST ANNUAL RAINFALL

The place that takes the number one spot in this chart may surprise you, especially as we tend to associate lack of rain with deserts...

	LOCATION	COUNTRY	AVERAGE ANNUAL RAINFALL (IN)	(MM)
1	MCMURDO DRY VALLEYS	ANTARCTICA	0	0
2	ARICA	CHILE	0.029	0.76
3	KUFRA	LIBYA	0.034	0.86
=	ASWAN	EGYPT	0.034	0.86
=	LUXOR	EGYPT	0.034	0.86
6	ICA	PERU	0.09	2.3
7	WADI HALFA	SUDAN	0.1	2.45
8	IQUIQUE	CHILE	0.2	5.1
9	PELICAN POINT	NAMIBIA	0.3	8.1
10	AOULEF	ALGERIA	0.48	12.2

2 ARICA

The northern Chile seaside town is home to the Catedral de San Marcos, designed by Gustave Eiffel, most famous for the Eiffel Tower in Paris, France. Chungará lake, inside Arica's Lauca National Park, is surrounded by volcanoes. Arica's climate has led to its nickname of "the city of the eternal spring."

4 ALYESKA, ALASKA

Alyeska is a ski resort located in the resort town of Girdwood, Alaska. This town is in the valley of the 250 mi (400 km) long Chugach Mountains, the highest point of which is 13,094 ft (3,991.1 m) tall. Alyeska has hosted the US Alpine Championships five times, in 1963, 1981, 2004, 2007, and 2009.

TOP 10 MOST SNOWFALL

Do you know what the average annual snowfall is for the town that you live in? See if it comes anywhere near that of these 10 places...

	LOCATION	AVERAGE SNOWFALL (IN)	(MM)
1	PARADISE RANGER STATION, MT. RAINIER, WASHINGTON (USA)	642	16,307
2	NISEKO (JAPAN)	594	15,088
3	MT. FIDELITY, GLACIER NATIONAL PARK, BC (CANADA)	576	14,630
4	ALYESKA, ALASKA (USA)	516	13,106
5	ALTA, UTAH (USA)	510	12,954
6	KIRKWOOD MOUNTAIN, CALIFORNIA (USA)	472	11,988
7	NAGANO (JAPAN)	432	10,973
8	CHAMONIX (FRANCE)	376	9,550
9	AOMORI CITY, TOHOKU (JAPAN)	312	7,925
10	MT. WASHINGTON, NEW HAMPSHIRE (USA)	261	6,629

TOP 10 SUNNIEST LOCATIONS

Some places, like Barrow, Alaska, USA, go for weeks without any sunlight, but these 10 places require virtually all-year-round sunscreen...

	LOCATION	COUNTRY	HOURS OF SUNLIGHT PER YEAR
1	YUMA, ARIZONA	USA	4,015
2	PHOENIX, ARIZONA	USA	3,872
3	ASWAN	EGYPT	3,869
4	LAS VEGAS, NEVADA	USA	3,826
5	DONGOLA	SUDAN	3,814
6	TUCSON, ARIZONA	USA	3,808
7	FAYA-LARGEAU	CHAD	3,800
8	KHARGA	EGYPT	3,796
9	EL PASO, TEXAS	USA	3,763
10	TENNANT CREEK	AUSTRALIA	3,614

1 YUMA, ARIZONA

European explorers first set foot in Yuma in 1540. Now, around 93,000 people live in this sunny city, located in the southwestern corner of Arizona. A city which strongly supports the arts, the Yuma Art Center receives more than 100,000 annual visitors. Its top-of-the-chart sunshine hours equate to clear skies 90 percent of the daytime. Yuma gets barely more than 3 in (7.6 cm) of rain each year.

RANKS BY COUNTRY

EGYPT
SUDAN
AUSTRALIA
CHAD
USA

1 AFGHANISTAN

The main languages of Afghanistan are Dari and Pashto, but Arabic and more than 30 others are also spoken. The land-locked country is made up of 34 provinces. Kabul Province is the most populous, with nearly 4.5 million residents, and includes the country's capital city, Kabul. The country's total population exceeds 33 million.

TOP 10 MOST POLLUTED COUNTRIES

The industrial age resulted in a huge increase in air-polluting emissions, and these nations suffer with the poorest air quality...

	COUNTRY	AQI (Annual Quality Index)
1	AFGHANISTAN	187
2	GHANA	177
3	LEBANON	171
4	MONGOLIA	170
5	BANGLADESH	169
6	EGYPT	167
7	MYANMAR	166
8	CHINA	161
9	VIETNAM	158
10	PERU	157

TOP 10 COUNTRIES WITH
THE CLEANEST AIR

Conversely, these 10 countries are having the most success with cutting down emissions and making the air less polluted...

	COUNTRY	ANNUAL MEAN PM10 (UG / M3)
1	ESTONIA	11
2	MAURITIUS	12
3	AUSTRALIA	13
=	CANADA	13
5	IRELAND	15
6	BHUTAN	18
=	MONACO	18
=	USA	18
=	LUXEMBOURG	18
10	SAN MARINO	20

1 ESTONIA

With little more than 1.3 million people, Estonia covers an area of just 17,500 square mi (45,324.8 square km). Although a small developed country, Estonia has a universal healthcare system and led the way with being the first nation to conduct elections via the internet. It is situated on the opposite side of the Gulf of Finland, next to the Baltic Sea, and has 2,357 mi (3,794 km) of coastline.

TOP 10 CLOUDIEST **US CITIES**

Affected by SAD (seasonal affective disorder)? Living in any of these cities may not be a good choice for you as they hardly get any sunshine...

	CITY	NUMBER OF DAYS WITH CLOUD COVER PER YEAR
1	BUFFALO, NEW YORK	311
2	SEATTLE, WASHINGTON	308
3	PITTSBURGH, PENNSYLVANIA	306
4	ROCHESTER, NEW YORK	304
5	CLEVELAND, OHIO	299
6	PORTLAND, OREGON	296
7	COLUMBUS, OHIO	293
8	DETROIT, MICHIGAN	290
=	MIAMI, FLORIDA	290
10	CINCINNATI, OHIO	284

1 BUFFALO, NEW YORK

This city sits on the banks of Lake Erie, the 13th largest lake in the world. It is home to 26 museums and galleries, including Buffalo & Erie County Naval and Military Park, the Museum of Disability History, and Whitworth Ferguson Planetarium. As well as being a cloudy city, its temperature averages a freezing 24.9°F (-3.9°C).

8 ▶ GEORGES, FLORIDA

This hurricane's name is not pronounced "George" as you might expect. Being a French name, it's "zhorzh." It killed nearly 500 people in the USA and Caribbean, and caused destruction in multiple regions including Cuba, Puerto Rico, Haiti, the Dominican Republic, and mainland Florida, Alabama, Mississippi, and Louisiana. Florida suffered damage worth $472 million during its week-long storm.

TOP 10 US TROPICAL STORMS

From cloudiest to wettest, these tropical storms dropped a total of 35 ft (10.7 m) of rain onto these American locations...

	STORM	YEAR	LOCATION	TOTAL RAINFALL (IN)	(MM)
1	HIKI	1950	KANALOHULUHULU RANGER STATION, KAUAI, HAWAII	52	1,321
2	AMELIA	1978	MEDINA, TEXAS	48	1,219
3	EASY	1950	YANKEETOWN, FLORIDA	45.2	1,148
4	CLAUDETTE	1979	ALVIN, TEXAS	45	1,143
5	T. D. #19	1970	JAYUYA, PUERTO RICO	41.7	1,058.7
6	ALLISON	2001	NORTHWEST JEFFERSON COUNTY, TEXAS	40.7	1,033
7	PAUL	2000	KAPAPALA RANCH 36, HAWAII	38.8	985
8	GEORGES	1998	MUNSON, FLORIDA	38.5	977
9	DANNY	1997	DAUPHIN ISLAND SEA LAB, ALABAMA	36.7	932
10	PAMELA	1976	GUAM WSMO	33.7	856

HUMANKIND

ZONE 3

MOST RECENT NOBEL PEACE PRIZE
WINNERS (INDIVIDUALS)

Activists, journalists, professors, and politicians from all over the world have been honored for their work to promote peace...

	NAME	COUNTRY	YEAR
1	JUAN MANUEL SANTOS	COLOMBIA	2016
2	MALALA YOUSAFZAI	PAKISTAN	2014
=	KAILASH SATYARTHI	INDIA	2014
4	LEYMAH GBOWEE	LIBERIA	2011
=	ELLEN JOHNSON SIRLEAF	LIBERIA	2011
=	TAWAKKOL KARMAN	YEMEN	2011
7	LIU XIAOBO	CHINA	2010
8	BARACK OBAMA	USA	2009
9	MARTTI AHTISAARI	FINLAND	2008
10	AL GORE	USA	2007

1 JUAN MANUEL SANTOS

It was announced on October 7, 2016, that the current President of Colombia was to be the recipient of the Nobel Peace Prize. Santos' work helped end the country's civil war. He is Colombia's 32nd president, sworn in on August 7, 2010. Santos previously held positions as the Minister of Foreign Trade, Minister of Finance and Public Credit, and Minister of National Defense.

MEN VS. WOMEN WINNERS

WOMEN
16

MEN
87

TUNISIAN NATIONAL DIALOGUE QUARTET

This collective was awarded the Nobel Peace Prize for being key in establishing a peaceful political discourse during a period when Tunisia was close to civil war. The group is comprised of the Tunisian General Labor Union, the Tunisian Confederation of Industry, Trade and Handicrafts, the Tunisian Human Rights League, and the Tunisian Order of Lawyers.

TOP 10
MOST RECENT NOBEL PEACE PRIZE
WINNERS (ORGANIZATIONS)

This highly regarded international award is also given to groups who are working hard to increase peace around the world...

	ORGANIZATION	LOCATION	YEAR
1	TUNISIAN NATIONAL DIALOGUE QUARTET	TUNISIA	2015
2	ORGANISATION FOR THE PROHIBITION OF CHEMICAL WEAPONS	WORLDWIDE	2013
3	EUROPEAN UNION	EUROPE	2012
4	INTERGOVERNMENTAL PANEL ON CLIMATE CHANGE	UNITED NATIONS	2007
5	GRAMEEN BANK	BANGLADESH	2006
6	INTERNATIONAL ATOMIC ENERGY AGENCY	UNITED NATIONS	2005
7	UNITED NATIONS	UNITED NATIONS	2001
8	MÉDECINS SANS FRONTIÈRES	SWITZERLAND	1999
9	INTERNATIONAL CAMPAIGN TO BAN LANDMINES	SWITZERLAND	1997
10	PUGWASH CONFERENCES ON SCIENCE AND WORLD AFFAIRS	CANADA	1995

1 BOB DYLAN

The Nobel Prize organization announced Bob Dylan's award on October 13, 2016, "for having created new poetic expressions within the great American song tradition." Dylan also won a 2001 Academy Award for Best Original Song for "Things Have Changed," which he wrote for filmmaker Curtis Hanson's film *Wonderboys*. Since 1962, Dylan has released 39 solo studio albums. His latest, *Triplicate*, was released on March 31, 2017.

TOP 10 MOST RECENT NOBEL PRIZE IN LITERATURE WINNERS

Exceptional writers from the worlds of fiction, nonfiction, poetry, and even songwriting have been given this award...

	NAME	COUNTRY	YEAR
1	BOB DYLAN	USA	2016
2	SVETLANA ALEXIEVICH	BELARUS	2015
3	PATRICK MODIANO	FRANCE	2014
4	ALICE MUNRO	CANADA	2013
5	MO YAN	CHINA	2012
6	TOMAS TRANSTRÖMER	SWEDEN	2011
7	MARIO VARGAS LLOSA	PERU / SPAIN	2010
8	HERTA MÜLLER	ROMANIA / GERMANY	2009
9	J. M. G. LE CLÉZIO	FRANCE / MAURITIUS	2008
10	DORIS LESSING	IRAN / UK	2007

YOSHINORI OHSUMI

Japanese cell biologist Yoshinori Ohsumi won the Nobel Prize for his groundbreaking discoveries on autophagy. This process, which means "self-devouring," is when cells break down and recycle their components. Ohsumi's work is crucial for the study of life-threatening diseases such as dementia and cancer.

TOP 10

MOST RECENT NOBEL PRIZE IN
PHYSIOLOGY / MEDICINE WINNERS

From 1901 to 2016, a total of 211 Nobel Laureates have been awarded this prize for their outstanding scientific discoveries...

	NAME	COUNTRY	YEAR
1	YOSHINORI OHSUMI	JAPAN	2016
2	WILLIAM C. CAMPBELL	IRELAND / USA	2015
=	SATOSHI OMURA	JAPAN	2015
=	TU YOUYOU	CHINA	2015
5	JOHN O'KEEFE	USA/UK	2014
=	MAY-BRITT MOSER	NORWAY	2014
=	EDVARD I. MOSER	NORWAY	2014
8	JAMES E. ROTHMAN	USA	2013
=	RANDY W. SCHEKMAN	USA	2013
=	THOMAS C. SÜDHOF	USA / GERMANY	2013

WILHELM CONRAD RÖNTGEN

1

The discovery of X-rays, a kind of electromagnetic radiation, is what led to Wilhelm Conrad Röntgen's Nobel Prize win. Pictured below left is the world's first ever X-ray, of his wife Anna Bertha Ludwig's hand. Röntgen studied physics and mechanical engineering. He earned his PhD at the University of Zurich in Switzerland.

TOP 10

FIRST NOBEL PRIZE IN PHYSICS WINNERS

The charts on these pages show the first two years of the Nobel Prizes for Physics and Chemistry were winners for Germany and the Netherlands...

	NAME	COUNTRY	YEAR
1	WILHELM CONRAD RÖNTGEN	GERMANY	1901
2	HENDRIK LORENTZ	NETHERLANDS	1902
=	PIETER ZEEMAN	NETHERLANDS	1902
4	ANTOINE HENRI BECQUEREL	FRANCE	1903
=	PIERRE CURIE	FRANCE	1903
=	MARIA SKŁODOWSKA-CURIE	POLAND / FRANCE	1903
7	LORD RAYLEIGH	UK	1904
8	PHILIPP EDUARD ANTON VON LENARD	AUSTRIA-HUNGARY / GERMANY	1905
9	JOSEPH JOHN THOMSON	UK	1906
10	ALBERT ABRAHAM MICHELSON	USA / POLAND	1907

4 ▶ SIR WILLIAM RAMSAY

William Ramsay was born in Glasgow on October 2, 1852. His earned his Nobel Prize by collaborating with Lord Rayleigh (who won his prize in physics—see the chart on the opposite page) to discover the gaseous elements in air, such as the noble gas argon. Ramsay also appeared on a Swedish stamp printed in 1964 with Russian physiologist Ivan Petrovich Pavlov.

NOBELPRIS 1904
RAMSAY
PAVLOV
STIG ÅSBERG del   1964   ARNE WALLHORN sc
SVERIGE 40

TOP 10 FIRST NOBEL PRIZE IN CHEMISTRY WINNERS

In the 21st century, nonchemist-based experts have been given this prize as well as those responsible for breakthroughs in the field of chemistry...

	NAME	COUNTRY	YEAR
1	JACOBUS HENRICUS VAN 'T HOFF	NETHERLANDS	1901
2	HERMANN EMIL FISCHER	GERMANY	1902
3	SVANTE AUGUST ARRHENIUS	SWEDEN	1903
4 ▶	SIR WILLIAM RAMSAY	UK	1904
5	JOHANN FRIEDRICH WILHELM ADOLF VON BAEYER	GERMANY	1905
6	HENRI MOISSAN	FRANCE	1906
7	EDUARD BUCHNER	GERMANY	1907
8	ERNEST RUTHERFORD	NEW ZEALAND/UK	1908
9	WILHELM OSTWALD	GERMANY	1909
10	OTTO WALLACH	GERMANY	1910

TOP 10 WRITERS WITH THE MOST
TV / MOVIE ADAPTATIONS

Do you have a favorite writer? This chart celebrates those who have had their works turned into TV shows and films...

	WRITER	NUMBER OF ADAPTATIONS
1	WILLIAM SHAKESPEARE	1,195
2	ANTON CHEKHOV	442
3	CHARLES DICKENS	365
4	EDGAR ALLAN POE	338
5	HANS CHRISTIAN ANDERSEN	281
6	JACOB & WILHELM GRIMM	273
7	ALEXANDRE DUMAS	267
8	ROBERT LOUIS STEVENSON	263
9	ARTHUR CONAN DOYLE	260
=	MOLIÈRE (JEAN-BAPTISTE POQUELIN)	260

STAN LEE

Although Stan Lee is responsible for creating and writing some of the world's most successful comic books, he doesn't make it into this top 10. Lee is credited with 125 adaptations. Other famous writers who don't make this chart include Oscar Wilde (257 adaptations), Stephen King (225 adaptations), and Agatha Christie (147 adaptations).

J.K. ROWLING

The official eighth *Harry Potter* story, set many years after the 2007 novel *Harry Potter and the Deathly Hallows*, is *Harry Potter and the Cursed Child Parts I & II*. This stage play was based on a story conceived by *Harry Potter* creator J. K. Rowling, John Tiffany, and the play's writer, Jack Thorne. It premiered at the Palace Theatre in London, England, on July 30, 2016.

HARRY POTTER

TOP 10 FIRST PUBLICATIONS IN J. K. ROWLING'S
HARRY POTTER UNIVERSE

For more than 20 years, the wizarding world of Mr Potter has featured novels, movies, games, and beyond. These were the first books released...

	BOOK	PUBLICATION DATE
1	HARRY POTTER AND THE PHILOSOPHER'S STONE	JUN 26, 1997
2	HARRY POTTER AND THE CHAMBER OF SECRETS	JUL 2, 1998
3	HARRY POTTER AND THE PRISONER OF AZKABAN	JUL 8, 1999
4	HARRY POTTER AND THE GOBLET OF FIRE	JUL 8, 2000
5	FANTASTIC BEASTS AND WHERE TO FIND THEM	MAR 1, 2001
=	QUIDDITCH THROUGH THE AGES	MAR 1, 2001
7	HARRY POTTER AND THE ORDER OF THE PHOENIX	JUN 21, 2003
8	HARRY POTTER AND THE HALF-BLOOD PRINCE	JUL 16, 2005
9	HARRY POTTER AND THE DEATHLY HALLOWS	JUL 21, 2007
10	THE TALES OF BEEDLE THE BARD	DEC 4, 2008

TOP 10 LONGEST-RUNNING INDEPENDENT COMIC BOOKS (NO BREAK IN ORIGINAL NUMBERING)

Hundreds of millions of comic books have been sold, but these are the independent titles that have been published the longest...

	NAME TO DATE	CREATOR	PUBLISHER	LAUNCHED	ISSUES
1	2000 AD	VARIOUS	IPC / FLEETWAY / REBELLION	1977	2,016+
2	ARCHIE	BOB MONTANA	ARCHIE COMICS	1942	666+
3	SONIC THE HEDGEHOG	YUJI NAKA, NAOTO OHSHIMA, HIROKAZU YASUHARA	ARCHIE COMICS	1992	282+
4	SPAWN	TODD MCFARLANE	IMAGE COMICS	1992	267+
5	GOLD DIGGER	FRED PERRY	ANTARCTIC	1992	237+
6	SIMPSONS COMICS	MATT GROENING	BONGO COMICS	1993	234+
7	SAVAGE DRAGON	ERIK LARSEN	IMAGE COMICS	1992	217+
8	WITCHBLADE	BRIAN HABERLIN, MARC SILVESTRI, MICHAEL TURNER, DAVID WOHL	TOP COW	1995	187+
9	FEMFORCE	BILL BLACK	AC COMICS	1985	176+
10	THE WALKING DEAD	ROBERT KIRKMAN	IMAGE COMICS	2003	161+

9  FEMFORCE

AC Comics evolved from creator Bill Black's Paragon Publications in 1982. The publisher has released more than 400 comic books since then, including Black's creation *Femforce*. The "Federal Emergency Missions Force" remains the world's only all-female superhero comic book success story. The team's original line-up was Rio Rita, the Blue Bulleteer, She Cat, and Miss Victory.

TOP 10 COUNTRIES WITH THE FIRST FULL-COLOR TV CHANNELS

Decades before the plasma, curved, and LCD screens, the cathode ray tube television revolutionized how we watched at-home entertainment...

	COUNTRY	CHANNEL	YEAR LAUNCHED
1	USA	CBS	1950
2	CUBA	TELE-COLOR	1958
3	JAPAN	VARIOUS	1960
4	SOVIET BYELORUSSIA	BELTELERADIO	1961
5	MEXICO	CANAL 5	1963
6	PHILIPPINES	ABS-CBN	1966
=	CANADA	CBC / CTV	1966
8	UK	BBC 2	1967
=	GERMANY (WEST GERMANY ERA)	ARD / ZDF	1967
=	NETHERLANDS	NPO	1967

8 BILLIE JEAN KING - BBC2

On July 1, 1967, the BBC (British Broadcasting Corporation) became Europe's first broadcaster to air a full-color service. This began with a live feed on BBC 2 of that year's Wimbledon Championships, the world-renowned tennis tournament that began in 1877. American Billie Jean King defeated British finalist Ann Haydon-Jones. King won this championship the previous year, and went on to win Wimbledon a further four times.

1 USA

With almost 2,700 mi (4,345.229 km) of land between its east and west coasts, the US is famous for its scenic road trips. Route 66 involves 2,451 mi (3,944.5 km) of eclectic driving from Illinois to California, including winding rural roads and dead-straight desert sections. The latter state is famous for the PCH (Pacific Coast Highway), a 600 mi (965.6 km) long coastal road from San Francisco to San Diego.

TOP 10 COUNTRIES WITH THE MOST ROADS

The automobile revolutionized road travel in the 20th century. These countries total in excess of 15 million miles of roadways...

	COUNTRY	TOTAL LENGTH OF ALL ROADWAYS (MI)	(KM)
1	USA	4,092,729.7	6,586,610
2	INDIA	3,400,232.6	5,472,144
3	CHINA	2,796,170.4	4,500,000
4	BRAZIL	1,088,560.3	1,751,868
5	RUSSIA	867,434.2	1,396,000
6	JAPAN	754,966	1,215,000
7	CANADA	647,655.2	1,042,300
8	FRANCE	639,046.7	1,028,446
9	AUSTRALIA	511,523.3	823,217
10	SOUTH AFRICA	464,173	747,014

TOP 10

COUNTRIES WITH THE MOST AIRPORTS

With more than 5,000 airlines in operation all over the world, the number of airports in these 10 countries is not a surprise...

	COUNTRY	TOTAL AIRPORTS
1	USA	19,299
2	BRAZIL	4,093
3	MEXICO	1,714
4	CANADA	1,467
5	RUSSIA	1,218
6	ARGENTINA	1,138
7	COLOMBIA	992
8	BOLIVIA	952
9	PARAGUAY	799
10	INDONESIA	683

RANKS BY AMOUNT

Here's how the airports and countries compare visually...

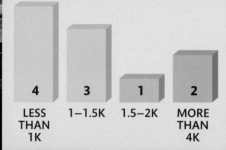

4	3	1	2
LESS THAN 1K	1–1.5K	1.5–2K	MORE THAN 4K

2 BRAZIL

GRU Airport (formerly known as São Paulo–Guarulhos International Airport) is based in the city of Guarulhos in the state of São Paulo. It serves more than 39 million people each year. Argentina's capital, Buenos Aires, and the US East Coast cities of Miami and New York remain the busiest routes for the airport, which first opened in 1985.

USA

The port of Los Angeles was founded in 1907. It covers 11.72 square mi (30.4 square km) and has 86 container cranes. It has an annual total operating revenue of more than $450 million. 976,000 Southern Californians are employed by the port, with a total of 2.8 million jobs across the country.

TOP **10**

COUNTRIES WITH THE
MOST PORTS

Ports and harbors are essential for countries' economies as they play a crucial role in the import and export of cargo...

	COUNTRY	TOTAL NUMBER OF PORTS
1	USA	554
2	UK	391
3	ITALY	311
4	JAPAN	292
5	FRANCE	268
6	CANADA	239
7	CHINA	172
8	DENMARK	159
9	INDONESIA	154
10	AUSTRALIA	106

COUNTRIES WITH THE
MOST RAILWAY PASSENGERS

TOP 10

Train travel is not only a preferred mode of transport for some people, a lot of countries rely on it so their citizens can get to work...

	COUNTRY	TOTAL ANNUAL RAILWAY PASSENGERS
1	CHINA	17,116,000,000
2	JAPAN	9,147,000,000
3	INDIA	8,397,000,000
4	GERMANY	2,023,000,000
5	UK	1,689,000,000
6	FRANCE	1,122,000,000
7	RUSSIA	1,070,000,000
8	ITALY	622,000,000
9	SPAIN	578,000,000
10	UKRAINE	485,000,000

1 CHINA

Beijing South Railway Station is Beijing's biggest train station. However, the largest train station in China is the Shanghai Hongqiao Railway Station, which has 16 platforms over an area of 1.3 million square mi (3.7 million square km). More than 200,000 people use it every day.

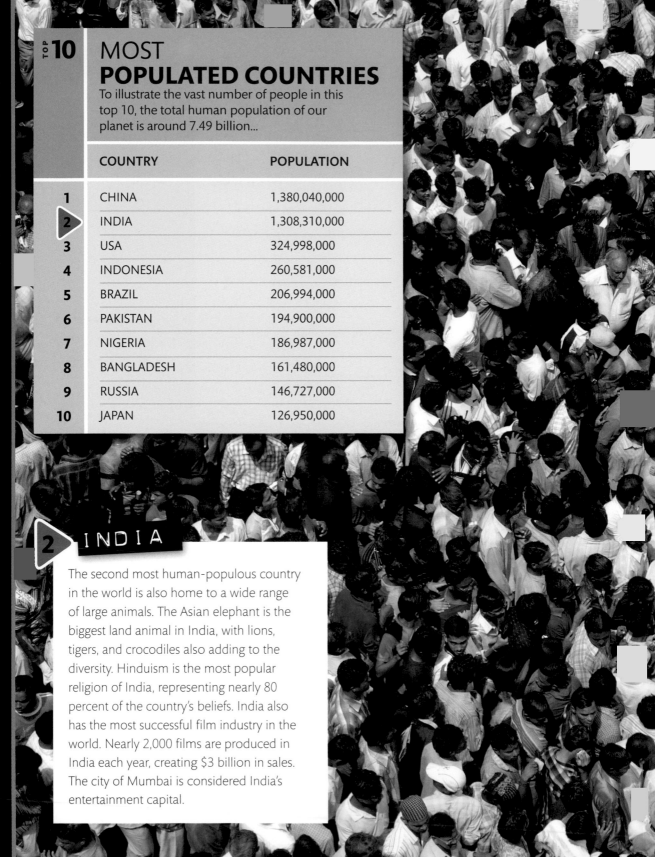

TOP 10

MOST POPULATED COUNTRIES

To illustrate the vast number of people in this top 10, the total human population of our planet is around 7.49 billion...

	COUNTRY	POPULATION
1	CHINA	1,380,040,000
2	INDIA	1,308,310,000
3	USA	324,998,000
4	INDONESIA	260,581,000
5	BRAZIL	206,994,000
6	PAKISTAN	194,900,000
7	NIGERIA	186,987,000
8	BANGLADESH	161,480,000
9	RUSSIA	146,727,000
10	JAPAN	126,950,000

2 INDIA

The second most human-populous country in the world is also home to a wide range of large animals. The Asian elephant is the biggest land animal in India, with lions, tigers, and crocodiles also adding to the diversity. Hinduism is the most popular religion of India, representing nearly 80 percent of the country's beliefs. India also has the most successful film industry in the world. Nearly 2,000 films are produced in India each year, creating $3 billion in sales. The city of Mumbai is considered India's entertainment capital.

4 TUVALU

Previously known as the Ellice Islands, this country has a total land area of just 10 square mi (25.9 square km). Tuvalu's traditional music includes a dance song called the *fatele*. All Tuvaluan songs consist of striking rhythms that build while the story is sung. Lyrically, they feature minimal lines, like a concise poem, which are repeated over and over. Percussive instruments are key in the performance of these songs.

TOP 10 LEAST POPULATED COUNTRIES

There are 196 areas of land on Earth that we have classified as countries, and these are the 10 with the smallest populations...

	COUNTRY	POPULATION
1	VATICAN CITY	842
2	NIUE	1,612
3	NAURU	10,084
4	TUVALU	10,640
5	PALAU	17,948
6	COOK ISLANDS	18,100
7	SAN MARINO	33,020
8	LIECHTENSTEIN	37,623
9	MONACO	38,400
10	SOUTH OSSETIA	53,532

TOP **10** | MOST POPULATED STATES /
TERRITORIES OF AMERICA

325 million live in the USA, which means the people living in these 10 states, a total of 174.2 million, represent 54 percent of the entire population...

	STATE	POPULATION
1	CALIFORNIA	39,144,818
2	TEXAS	27,469,114
3	FLORIDA	20,271,272
4	NEW YORK	19,859,995
5	ILLINOIS	12,860,000
6	PENNSYLVANIA	12,802,503
7	OHIO	11,613,423
8	GEORGIA	10,214,860
9	NORTH CAROLINA	10,042,802
10	MICHIGAN	9,922,576

1 CALIFORNIA

If California was a country, it would be the sixth largest economy on Earth. California's biggest city of Los Angeles (meaning "the angels") is the second biggest city in the US, following New York City. Nearly a third of Californians speak Spanish. It is home to several major film studios including 20th Century Fox, The Walt Disney Company, and James Cameron's Lightstorm Entertainment. Before European settlers, scientists calculate more than 100 different Native American tribes populated California.

1 NORTHERN MARIANA ISLANDS

These culturally diverse islands are home to several ethnicities including the indigenous Chamorro. Their traditional beliefs feature spirits of their ancestors, called *taotaomo'na*, and elemental beings called *birak*. Popular sports on the islands include mixed martial arts, outrigger sailing, and baseball.

TOP **10** LEAST POPULATED STATES / **TERRITORIES OF AMERICA**

As well as its 50 states, the US also has 16 territories. Five of these territories are populated, and four of them feature on this chart...

	STATE	POPULATION
1	NORTHERN MARIANA ISLANDS	52,344
2	AMERICAN SAMOA	54,343
3	US VIRGIN ISLANDS	103,574
4	GUAM	161,785
5	WYOMING	586,107
6	VERMONT	626,042
7	DISTRICT OF COLUMBIA	672,228
8	ALASKA	738,432
9	NORTH DAKOTA	756,927
10	SOUTH DAKOTA	858,469

TOP 10 MOST POPULATED COUNTRIES IN THE EUROPEAN UNION

As of 2017, the European Union includes 28 countries. Of all these members, the below 10 have the highest numbers of citizens...

	COUNTRY	POPULATION
1	GERMANY	81,459,000
2	FRANCE	66,484,000
3	UK	65,081,276
4	ITALY	60,963,000
5	SPAIN	46,423,064
6	POLAND	38,494,000
7	ROMANIA	19,822,000
8	NETHERLANDS	17,003,777
9	BELGIUM	11,259,000
10	GREECE	10,769,000

1

MUNICH, GERMANY

Munich is the capital city of Bavaria, one of 16 states that make up Germany. Munich is also Germany's third largest city. With a population of around 5.2 million, more than 40 percent of Bavaria's population lives in Munich and its metropolitan region. Academy Award-nominated filmmaker Werner Herzog was born in Munich on September 5, 1942. It is also the home city of seven Nobel Prize winners, including physicist Arno Allan Penzias.

1 LAGOS, NIGERIA

Lagos is a major city in Nigeria's Lagos State, a region that has approximately 18 million residents. Lagos is known for its numerous festivals, including Eko International Film Festival, Lagos Black Heritage Carnival, and the Lagos Jazz Series. Former basketball player for the Toronto Raptors and the Houston Rockets, Hakeem Olajuwon, was born in Lagos.

RANKS BY AMOUNT

This is how Africa's countries and their populations compare...

LESS THAN 40M	1
40–50M	3
50–60M	2
60–70M	0
70–80M	1
80–100M	2
MORE THAN 100M	1

TOP 10

MOST POPULATED COUNTRIES IN AFRICA

By area, Africa is the world's second largest continent. Of its 54 countries, these are the 10 with the biggest populations...

	COUNTRY	POPULATION
1	NIGERIA	182,202,000
2	ETHIOPIA	99,391,000
3	EGYPT	88,523,000
4	DEMOCRATIC REPUBLIC OF THE CONGO	77,267,000
5	SOUTH AFRICA	54,957,000
6	TANZANIA	51,046,000
7	KENYA	45,533,000
8	SUDAN	40,235,000
9	ALGERIA	40,100,000
10	UGANDA	37,102,000

SPORTS

TOP 10 FASTEST MALE & FEMALE
MARATHON RUNNERS

These long-distance endurance races are held all over the world, and the 10 women and men below hold the speed records...

	ATHLETE	SEX	COUNTRY	YEAR	TIME	AVERAGE SPEED (MPH)	(KPH)
1	DENNIS KIPRUTO KIMETTO	MALE	KENYA	2014	2:02:57	12.795	20.591
2	KENENISA BEKELE	MALE	ETHIOPIA	2016	2:03:03	12.784	20.575
3	ELIUD KIPCHOGE	MALE	KENYA	2016	2:03:05	12.781	20.569
4	EMMANUEL MUTAI	MALE	KENYA	2014	2:03:13	12.767	20.547
=	WILSON KIPSANG	MALE	KENYA	2016	2:03:13	12.767	20.547
6	PAULA RADCLIFFE	FEMALE	UK	2003	2:15:25	11.617	18.696
7	MARY KEITANY	FEMALE	KENYA	2012	2:18:37	11.349	18.264
8	CATHERINE NDEREBA	FEMALE	KENYA	2001	2:18:47	11.335	18.242
9	TIKI GELANA	FEMALE	ETHIOPIA	2012	2:18:58	11.320	18.218
10	MIZUKI NOGUCHI	FEMALE	JAPAN	2005	2:19:12	11.301	18.188

7 MARY KEITANY

The Kenyan athlete has achieved first place in marathons all over the world. These include the 2011 and 2012 London Marathons (UK), and 2011 Ras Al Khaimah Half Marathon (United Arab Emirates), for which Keitany holds the world record.

2 KENENISA BEKELE

Born on June 13, 1982, near Bekoji, in Ethiopia's Arsi Province, Bekele won his first cross-country race in 1997. His marathon time on this chart was achieved in Berlin on September 26, 2016.

FASTEST MACHINES **IN SPORT**

New data is in, which means we have a new number one champion machine in this chart of sport-focused, mechanical creations...

	SPORT	TOP SPEED (MPH)	(KPH)
1	AIR SHOW STUNT PLANE	550	885.14
2	TOP FUEL DRAGSTER	337.58	543.28
3	INDY CAR	256.95	413.52
4	FORMULA ONE CAR	231.523	372.6
5	MOTOR RALLY (NASCAR, ETC)	212.8	342.4
6	SNOWMOBILE	211.5	338
7	POWERBOAT	210	337.95
8	MOTORCYCLE (RACING)	193.24	310.99
9	JET SKI	112	180.24
10	MONSTER TRUCK	99.1	159.48

2 TOP FUEL DRAGSTER

This vehicle's fuel can be up to 90 percent nitromethane, hence the term "nitro." A Top Fuel dragster can achieve zero to 100 mph (160.9 kph) in 0.8 seconds. American Tony Schumacher has won the National Hot Rod Association championship a record 82 times.

QUICKEST **FEMALE PARALYMPIANS**

This chart is not a definitive top 10, because comparing classes is unfair.
Therefore, this is simply to show the fastest speeds achieved...

	SPORT	DISTANCE	FASTEST ATHLETE	CLASS	COUNTRY	YEAR	TIME	SPEED (MPH)	(KPH)
1	RUNNING	100 M	OMARA DURAND	T12	CUBA	2016	0:11.40	19.62	31.58
2	RUNNING	200 M	OMARA DURAND	T12	CUBA	2015	0:23.03	19.43	31.26
3	WHEELCHAIR RACING	800 M	TATYANA MCFADDEN	T54	USA	2015	1:42.72	17.42	28.03
4	WHEELCHAIR RACING	1500 M	TATYANA MCFADDEN	T53 / 54	USA	2015	3:13.27	17.36	27.94
5	RUNNING	400 M	OMARA DURAND	T12	CUBA	2016	0:51.77	17.28	27.82
6	SWIMMING: Freestyle	50 M	OXANA SAVCHENKO	S12	RUSSIA	2009	0:26.54	4.21	6.78
7	SWIMMING: Freestyle	100 M	ANNA STETSENKO	S13	UKRAINE	2016	0:58.05	3.853	6.2
8	SWIMMING: Butterfly	50 M	SOPHIE PASCOE	S10	NEW ZEALAND	2013	0:29.08	3.846	6.19
9	SWIMMING: Backstroke	50 M	SOPHIE PASCOE	S10	NEW ZEALAND	2013	0:30.49	3.67	5.9
10	SWIMMING: Freestyle	200 M	VALERIE GRAND-MAISON	S13	CANADA	2008	2:08.53	3.48	5.6

1 OMARA DURAND

The visually impaired Cuban runner achieved a new 100 m T12 world record at the 2016 Summer Olympics in Rio de Janeiro, Brazil. Durand is pictured here tethered to her guide who runs next to her. This helps Durand stay in her running lane.

6 RANOMI KROMOWIDJOJO

This three-time Olympic champion started swimming in July 1992, just before her third birthday. Her Olympic gold medals are from the 2012 London Summer Games (100 m freestyle and 50 m freestyle) and the 2008 Beijing Summer Olympics (4 x 100 m freestyle relay).

TOP 10

QUICKEST **SPORTSWOMEN**

The sports listed here utilize the sprint muscles. American Florence Griffith Joyner's records have not been bested in 30 years...

	SPORT	DISTANCE	FASTEST ATHLETE	COUNTRY	YEAR	TIME	AVERAGE SPEED (MPH)	(KPH)
1	RUNNING	100 M	FLORENCE GRIFFITH JOYNER	USA	1988	0:10.49	21.32	34.32
2	RUNNING	200 M	FLORENCE GRIFFITH JOYNER	USA	1988	0:21.34	20.96	33.74
3	RUNNING	400 M	MARITA KOCH	GERMANY	1985	0:47.60	18.8	30.25
4	RUNNING	800 M	JARMILA KRATOCHVÍLOVÁ	CZECH REPUBLIC	1983	1:53.28	15.8	25.42
5	RUNNING	1000 M	SVETLANA MASTERKOVA	RUSSIA	1996	2:28.98	15.02	24.16
6	SWIMMING: Freestyle	50 M	RANOMI KROMOWIDJOJO	NETHERLANDS	2013	0:23.24	4.81	7.74
7	SWIMMING: Butterfly	50 M	THERESE ALSHAMMAR	SWEDEN	2009	0:24.38	4.59	7.39
8	SWIMMING: Freestyle	100 M	CATE CAMPBELL	AUSTRALIA	2015	0:50.91	4.39	7.07
9	SWIMMING: Backstroke	50 M	ETIENE MEDEIROS	BRAZIL	2014	0:25.67	4.36	7.02
10	SWIMMING: Butterfly	100 M	SARAH SJÖSTRÖM	SWEDEN	2014	0:54.61	4.1	6.59

8 **TIMOTHY ANTALFY**

The visually impaired Australian swimmer, surfer, wakeboarder, and water-skier was born on April 1, 1987. Antalfy began swimming competitively in 1995. He has held top 10 world rankings in the S13 categories for butterfly, backstroke and freestyle para-swimming disciplines since 2012.

TOP 10 QUICKEST MALE PARALYMPIANS

The below is not to be viewed as a definitive chart, because different classifications cannot be compared. This chart is just to reveal the fastest times recorded...

	SPORT	DISTANCE	FASTEST ATHLETE	CLASS	COUNTRY	YEAR	TIME	SPEED (MPH)	(KPH)
1	RUNNING	200 M	ALAN FONTELES CARDOSO OLIVEIRA	T43	BRAZIL	2013	0:20.66	21.65	34.85
2	RUNNING	100 M	JASON SMYTH	T13	IRELAND	2012	0:10.46	21.39	34.42
3	WHEELCHAIR RACING	400 M	LIXIN ZHANG	T54	CHINA	2008	0:45.07	19.85	31.95
4	WHEELCHAIR RACING	800 M	MARCEL HUG	T54	SWITZERLAND	2010	1:31.12	19.64	31.61
5	WHEELCHAIR RACING	1500 M	MARCEL HUG	T53 / 54	SWITZERLAND	2010	2:54.51	19.23	30.94
6	SWIMMING: Freestyle	50 M	ANDRE BRASIL	S10	BRAZIL	2009	0:22.44	4.98	8.02
7	SWIMMING: Freestyle	100 M	ANDRE BRASIL	S10	BRAZIL	2009	0:48.70	4.59	7.39
8	SWIMMING: Butterfly	50 M	TIMOTHY ANTALFY	S13	AUSTRALIA	2014	0:24.60	4.55	7.32
9	SWIMMING: Backstroke	50 M	SEAN RUSSO	S13	AUSTRALIA	2013	0:27.30	4.1	6.59
10	SWIMMING: Butterfly	100 M	ANDRE BRASIL	S10	BRAZIL	2009	0:54.76	4.08	6.57

^{TOP}10 QUICKEST **SPORTSMEN**

Looking at all of the different sports where a burst of acceleration is employed, these 10 athletes are the fastest in the world...

	SPORT	DISTANCE	FASTEST ATHLETE	COUNTRY	YEAR	TIME	AVERAGE SPEED (MPH)	(KPH)
1	RUNNING	100 M	USAIN BOLT	JAMAICA	2009	0:09.58	23.35	37.58
2	RUNNING	200 M	USAIN BOLT	JAMAICA	2009	0:19.19	23.31	37.52
3	RUNNING	400 M	WAYDE VAN NIEKERK	SOUTH AFRICA	2016	0:43.03	20.79	33.47
4	RUNNING	800 M	DAVID RUDISHA	KENYA	2012	1:40.91	17.73	28.54
5	RUNNING	1000 M	NOAH NGENY	KENYA	1999	2:11.96	16.95	27.28
6	SWIMMING: Freestyle	50 M	FLORENT MANAUDOU	FRANCE	2014	0:20.26	5.52	8.88
7	SWIMMING: Butterfly	50 M	STEFFEN DEIBLER	GERMANY	2009	0:21.80	5.13	8.26
8	SWIMMING: Backstroke	50 M	FLORENT MANAUDOU	FRANCE	2014	0:22.22	5.03	8.1
9	SWIMMING: Freestyle	100 M	AMAURY LEVEAUX	FRANCE	2008	0:44.94	4.98	8.01
10	SWIMMING: Butterfly	100 M	CHAD LE CLOS	SOUTH AFRICA	2016	0:48.08	4.65	7.49

3 WAYDE VAN NIEKERK

His world record 400 m time was achieved at the 2016 Summer Olympics in Rio de Janeiro, Brazil. It surpassed American Michael Johnson's record time of 43.18, which he had held since 1999. The South African runner holds a total of four gold, two silver, and one bronze medal from international championships.

SPEED MASTERS

TOP 10 FASTEST 100M **MALE SPRINTERS**

Jamaican Usain Bolt has been the fastest man on Earth for nearly a decade. Here are the other runners who have come closest to taking his crown...

	ATHLETE	COUNTRY	YEAR	TIME (SECS)	AVERAGE SPEED (MPH)	(KPH)
1	USAIN BOLT	JAMAICA	2009	9.58	23.35	37.58
2	TYSON GAY	USA	2009	9.69	23.08	37.14
=	YOHAN BLAKE	JAMAICA	2012	9.69	23.08	37.14
4	ASAFA POWELL	JAMAICA	2008	9.72	23.01	37.03
5	JUSTIN GATLIN	USA	2015	9.74	22.97	36.96
6	NESTA CARTER	JAMAICA	2010	9.78	22.87	36.81
7	MAURICE GREENE	USA	1999	9.79	22.85	36.77
8	STEVE MULLINGS	JAMAICA	2011	9.80	22.83	36.74
9	RICHARD THOMPSON	TRINIDAD & TOBAGO	2014	9.82	22.78	36.66
10	DONOVAN BAILEY / TRAYVON BROMELL / BRUNY SURIN	CANADA / USA / CANADA	1996 / 2015 / 1999	9.84	22.73	36.58

TOP 10 FASTEST 100M **FEMALE SPRINTERS**

This chart details not only the fastest women of all time, it also reveals the average speed their sprinting achieves...

	ATHLETE	COUNTRY	YEAR	TIME (SECS)	AVERAGE SPEED (MPH)	(KPH)
1	FLORENCE GRIFFITH JOYNER	USA	1988	10.49	21.32	34.31
2	CARMELITA JETER	USA	2009	10.64	21.02	33.83
3	MARION JONES	USA	1998	10.65	21.00	33.80
4	SHELLY-ANN FRASER-PRYCE	JAMAICA	2012	10.70	20.91	33.65
=	ELAINE THOMPSON	JAMAICA	2016	10.70	20.91	33.65
6	CHRISTINE ARRON	FRANCE	1998	10.73	20.85	33.56
7	ENGLISH GARDNER	USA	2016	10.74	20.83	33.52
=	MERLENE OTTEY	JAMAICA	1996	10.74	20.83	33.52
9	KERRON STEWART	JAMAICA	2009	10.75	20.81	33.49
10	EVELYN ASHFORD / VERONICA CAMPBELL-BROWN	USA / JAMAICA	1984 / 2011	10.76	20.79	33.46

1 USAIN BOLT

Jamaican running legend Usain St Leo Bolt was born in the town of Sherwood Content on August 21, 1986. His 100 m and 200 m world records were set at the 2009 Berlin World Championships. Bolt has won 23 gold medals (including eight from Olympic events), five silver medals, and has been awarded Athlete of the Year multiple times.

7 ENGLISH GARDNER

The Philadelphia-born sprinter was 24 years old when she achieved her fastest 100 m time at the 2016 Rio Olympics. At these Games' 4 x 100 m relay event, Gardner won gold alongside her team members Tianna Bartoletta, Tori Bowie, and Allyson Felix. In the same event, Gardner won silver at the International Association of Athletics Federations World Championships in 2013 and 2015.

TOP 10 DIVING CHAMPION NATIONS (SUMMER OLYMPICS)

The balletic, free-falling skills displayed in competitive diving became an Olympic event for the first time in 1904...

	COUNTRY	GOLD	SILVER	BRONZE	TOTAL
1	USA	49	44	45	138
2	CHINA	40	19	10	69
3	RUSSIA (INCL. SOVIET UNION ERA)	8	12	12	32
4	SWEDEN	6	8	7	21
5	GERMANY	2	8	11	21
6	MEXICO	1	7	6	14
7	AUSTRALIA	3	3	7	13
8	CANADA	1	4	8	13
9	ITALY	3	5	3	11
10	UK	1	3	6	10

10 TOM DALEY, UK

Devon-born British diver Tom Daley has a total of nine gold, three silver, and three bronze career medals. These include two Olympic bronze medals from the 2012 and 2016 Summer Games. Daley is a two-time FINA (International Swimming Federation) World Aquatics champion, winning gold in the 10 m platform individual event in Rome, Italy, in 2009, and gold for the team event at Kazan, Russia, in 2015.

6 STEFKA KOSTADINOVA

Still the record-holder
for women's high jump after 31 years,
Kostadinova's career saw her acquire 13 gold
medals between 1985 and 1997, when she
retired. Since 2005, she has been the head
of the Bulgarian Olympic Committee,
a nonprofit organization that
was founded in 1923.

TOP 10 GREATEST MALE & FEMALE HIGH JUMPERS

Although the men's high jump has been featured at the Summer Olympics
since they began in 1896, the women's category debuted in 1928...

	ATHLETE	SEX	COUNTRY	YEAR	HEIGHT (FT)	(M)
1	JAVIER SOTOMAYOR	MALE	CUBA	1993	8.04	2.45
2	MUTAZ ESSA BARSHIM	MALE	QATAR	2014	7.97	2.43
3	PATRIK SJÖBERG	MALE	SWEDEN	1987	7.94	2.42
=	CARLO THRÄNHARDT	MALE	GERMANY	1988	7.94	2.42
=	BOHDAN BONDARENKO / IVAN UKHOV	MALE	UKRAINE / RUSSIA	2014	7.94	2.42
6	STEFKA KOSTADINOVA	FEMALE	BULGARIA	1987	6.86	2.09
7	KAJSA BERGQVIST	FEMALE	SWEDEN	2006	6.82	2.08
=	BLANKA VLASIC	FEMALE	CROATIA	2009	6.82	2.08
9	LYUDMILA ANDONOVA	FEMALE	BULGARIA	1984	6.79	2.07
=	HEIKE HENKEL / ANNA CHICHEROVA	FEMALE	GERMANY / RUSSIA	1992 / 2011	6.79	2.07

TOP 10 MALE & FEMALE **PARALYMPIC SHOT PUTTERS**

The size and weight of the shot can vary, depending on the type of competition, but these are the overall distance champions...

	ATHLETE	SEX	CLASS	COUNTRY	YEAR	DISTANCE (FT)	(M)
1	XIA DONG	MALE	F37	CHINA	2012	57.48	17.52
2	ASSUNTA LEGNANTE	FEMALE	F11	ITALY	2014	56.82	17.32
3	MUHAMMAD ZIYAD ZOLKEFLI	MALE	F20	MALAYSIA	2016	55.25	16.84
4	ROMAN DANYLIUK	MALE	F12	UKRAINE	2015	54.59	16.64
5	HAITAO SUN	MALE	F13	CHINA	2000	54.00	16.46
6	WEI GUO	MALE	F35	CHINA	2008	53.22	16.22
7	SAFIYA BURKHANOVA	FEMALE	F12	UZBEKISTAN	2016	49.38	15.05
8	FRANZISKA LIEBHARDT	FEMALE	F37	GERMANY	2016	45.80	13.96
9	EWA DURSKA	FEMALE	F20	POLAND	2016	45.73	13.94
10	JUN WANG	FEMALE	F35	CHINA	2016	45.64	13.91

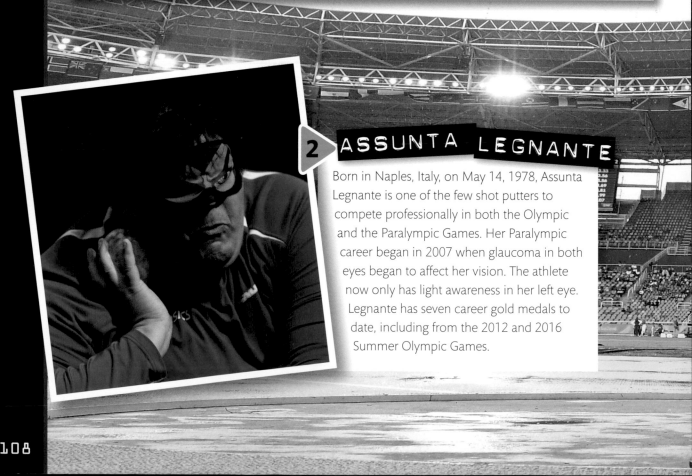

2 ASSUNTA LEGNANTE

Born in Naples, Italy, on May 14, 1978, Assunta Legnante is one of the few shot putters to compete professionally in both the Olympic and the Paralympic Games. Her Paralympic career began in 2007 when glaucoma in both eyes began to affect her vision. The athlete now only has light awareness in her left eye. Legnante has seven career gold medals to date, including from the 2012 and 2016 Summer Olympic Games.

10 ▶ PIOTR MALACHOWSKI

The 6' 4" Polish discus champion won his second Olympic silver medal in Rio de Janeiro, Brazil, in 2016, but he gave it away. Małachowski decided to auction off the medal to raise money for a three-year-old boy's cancer treatment. Olek Szymanski suffered from retinoblastoma, a form of eye cancer, for almost two years. Two Polish billionaires ended up winning the auction for an undisclosed amount that would cover the cost of the surgery.

TOP 10 ▶ MALE & FEMALE **DISCUS CHAMPIONS**

Materials and weights differ between discus competitions, but these are the 10 athletes who have achieved the furthest throws...

	ATHLETE	SEX	COUNTRY	YEAR	DISTANCE (FT)	(M)
1	GABRIELE REINSCH	FEMALE	GERMANY	1988	256.36	78.14
2	ZDENKA ŠILHAVÁ	FEMALE	CZECHOSLOVAKIA	1984	244.62	74.56
3	ILKE WYLUDDA	FEMALE	GERMANY	1989	244.62	74.56
4	DIANA GANSKY	FEMALE	GERMANY	1987	243.04	74.08
=	JÜRGEN SCHULT	MALE	GERMANY	1986	243.04	74.08
6	VIRGILIJUS ALEKNA	MALE	LITHUANIA	2000	242.39	73.88
7	DANIELA COSTIAN	FEMALE	ROMANIA	1988	242.26	73.84
8	GERD KANTER	MALE	ESTONIA	2006	240.75	73.38
9	YURIY DUMCHEV	MALE	RUSSIA	1983	235.76	71.86
10	PIOTR MAŁACHOWSKI	MALE	POLAND	2013	235.70	71.84

TOP 10 MALE PARALYMPIC **JAVELIN MASTERS**

Not a comparison of the different classes, this chart merely collects together the furthest throws by male Paralympic competitors...

	ATHLETE	CLASS	COUNTRY	YEAR	DISTANCE (FT)	(M)
1	BRANIMIR BUDETIC	F13	CROATIA	2016	215.68	65.74
2	ZHU PENGKAI	F12	CHINA	2012	211.22	64.38
3	DEVENDRA JHAJHARIA	F46	INDIA	2016	209.88	63.97
4	GAO MINGJIE	F44	CHINA	2011	196.26	59.82
5	XIA DONG	F37	CHINA	2008	189.67	57.81
6	HELGI SVEINSSON	F42	ICELAND	2015	188.19	57.36
7	AKEEM STEWART	F43	TRINIDAD & TOBAGO	2016	188.06	57.32
8	GUO WEI	F35	CHINA	2008	183.96	56.07
9	BIL MARINKOVIC	F11	AUSTRIA	2010	177.13	53.99
10	OLEKSANDR DOROSHENKO	F38	UKRAINE	2004	168.54	51.37

1 BRANIMIR BUDETIC

Budetic was born on April 20, 1990. He carried the Croatian flag during the opening ceremony of the 15th Paralympic Games, held in Rio in 2016. Prior to becoming a professional javelin thrower, Budetic first practiced handball. In 2013, he was named Sportsperson of the Year by the Croatian Paralympic Committee.

5 ▷ TATYANA KOTOVA

The Uzbekistan-born athlete won her first gold medal in the long jump at the 1997 European U23 Championships held in Turku, Finland. Kotova is a two-time IAAF World Indoor champion, taking gold at the 1999 competition in Maebashi, Japan, and in Birmingham, England, in 2003.

TOP 10 FEMALE **LONG JUMP CHAMPIONS**

The distance leapt by Russia's Galina Chistyakova has not been bested for 30 years, although some sportswomen in this chart have come close...

	ATHLETE	COUNTRY	YEAR	DISTANCE (FT)	(M)
1	GALINA CHISTYAKOVA	RUSSIA	1988	24.67	7.52
2	JACKIE JOYNER-KERSEE	USA	1994	24.57	7.49
3	HEIKE DRECHSLER	GERMANY	1988	24.54	7.48
4	ANISOARA CUSMIR	ROMANIA	1983	24.38	7.43
5 ▷	TATYANA KOTOVA	RUSSIA	2002	24.34	7.42
6	YELENA BELEVSKAYA	RUSSIA	1987	24.25	7.39
7	INESSA KRAVETS	UKRAINE	1992	24.18	7.37
8	TATYANA LEBEDEVA	RUSSIA	2004	24.05	7.33
9	OLENA KHLOPOTNOVA	RUSSIA	1985	23.98	7.31
=	MARION JONES / BRITTNEY REESE	USA	1998 / 2016	23.98	7.31

TOP 10

PARALYMPIC SKIING
CHAMPION NATIONS

Combining all the gold, silver, and bronze winners from Paralympic skiing championships, these countries have won the most medals...

	COUNTRY	TOTAL PARALYMPIC SKIING MEDALS
1	AUSTRIA	253
2	USA	237
3	GERMANY (INCL. EAST & WEST GERMANY ERA)	177
4	SWITZERLAND	104
5	FRANCE	93
6	CANADA	91
7	ITALY	44
8	SPAIN	35
9	SLOVAKIA	33
10	JAPAN	30

3 MARTIN BRAXENTHALER, GERMANY

Often called the most successful Paralympic monoskier, Martin Braxenthaler has several gold and silver medals to his name. These include four gold wins at the 2002 Winter Paralympics, held at Salt Lake City, Utah, USA. These games marked the first time the Winter Paralympic Games had been held in the States.

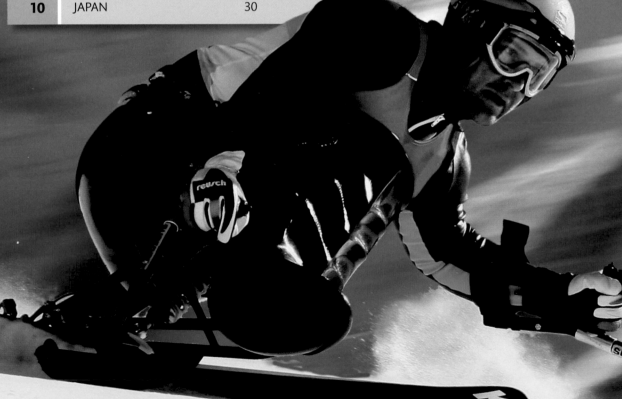

1 ▷ SHAUN WHITE, USA

Born in San Diego, California, USA, on September 3, 1986, by the time Shaun White was just nine years old, he was being mentored by professional skateboarding legend Tony Hawk. He has multiple gold medals in skateboarding as well as snowboarding. At the 2010 Winter Olympic Games in Vancouver, Canada, White set a new snowboarding halfpipe record of 48.4 points.

TOP 10

OLYMPIC **SNOWBOARDING NATIONS**

Focusing on the snowboarding competitions held at the Winter Olympics, here are the 10 nations who have come out on top...

	COUNTRY	TOTAL OLYMPIC SNOWBOARDING MEDALS
1	USA	24
2	SWITZERLAND	12
3	FRANCE	10
4	CANADA	7
5	AUSTRIA	6
6	GERMANY	5
=	RUSSIA	5
8	NORWAY	4
9	FINLAND	3
=	JAPAN	3

TOP 10 | MOST SUCCESSFUL **OLYMPIC NATIONS**

Including all of the games held prior to the 2018 Winter Games in Pyeongchang, South Korea, these nations won the most medals...

	COUNTRY / TEAM	TOTAL SUMMER GAMES MEDALS	TOTAL WINTER GAMES MEDALS	TOTAL MEDALS
1	USA	2,520	282	2,802
2	RUSSIA (INCL. SOVIET UNION ERA)	1,441	318	1,759
3	GERMANY (INCL. EAST & WEST ERA)	1,228	358	1,586
4	GREAT BRITAIN	847	26	873
5	FRANCE	715	109	824
6	ITALY	577	114	691
7	SWEDEN	494	144	638
8	CHINA	544	53	597
9	AUSTRALIA	497	12	509
10	HUNGARY	491	6	497

9 AUSTRALIA

Australia's medals break down as: 152 gold, 166 silver, and 191 bronze, across all Summer and Winter Olympic Games. Although impressive, the nation dwarfs this total with their impressive 1,155 medal wins from every Paralympic Games. Australia have hosted the Summer Olympics twice, in 1956 and 2000.

TOP 10 MOST SUCCESSFUL **PARALYMPIC NATIONS**

Not including results from the Winter Paralympic Games (March 9–8, 2018 in Pyeongchang, South Korea), these countries are the biggest winners...

	COUNTRY / TEAM	TOTAL SUMMER GAMES MEDALS	TOTAL WINTER GAMES MEDALS	TOTAL MEDALS
1	USA	2,054	277	2,331
2	GREAT BRITAIN	1,789	27	1,816
3	GERMANY (INCL. EAST & WEST ERA)	1,323	345	1,668
4	AUSTRALIA	1,125	30	1,155
5	CANADA	976	135	1,111
6	FRANCE	949	152	1,101
7	CHINA	1,033	0	1,033
8	SWEDEN	637	99	736
9	NETHERLANDS	714	10	724
10	SPAIN	661	43	704

5 CANADA

This country has taken part in every Winter Paralympic Games (1976–present) and in the 13 Summer Paralympic Games since 1968. Canada hosted the 1976 Summer Paralympics in Toronto, its city with the highest population of around 2.7 million people. The CPC (Canadian Paralympic Committee) covers more than 40 different sports organizations.

TOP 10 MOST SUCCESSFUL **OLYMPIANS**

Combining all of the winners from 1896 to the 2016 Summer Olympics in
Rio de Janeiro, Brazil, these competitors are the medal champions...

	OLYMPIAN	DISCIPLINE(S)	COUNTRY	YEARS	GOLD	SILVER	BRONZE	TOTAL
1	MICHAEL PHELPS	SWIMMING	USA	2004–16	23	3	2	28
2	LARISA LATYNINA	GYMNASTICS	SOVIET UNION (NOW RUSSIA)	1956–64	9	5	4	18
3	NIKOLAI ANDRIANOV	GYMNASTICS	SOVIET UNION (NOW RUSSIA)	1972–80	7	5	3	15
4	OLE EINAR BJØRNDALEN	BIATHLON	NORWAY	1998–2014	8	4	1	13
5	BORIS SHAKHLIN	GYMNASTICS	SOVIET UNION (NOW RUSSIA)	1956–64	7	4	2	13
6	EDOARDO MANGIAROTTI	FENCING	ITALY	1936–60	6	5	2	13
7	TAKASHI ONO	GYMNASTICS	JAPAN	1952–64	5	4	4	13
8	PAAVO NURMI	ATHLETICS	FINLAND	1920–28	9	3	0	12
9	BJØRN DÆHLIE	CROSS-COUNTRY SKIING	NORWAY	1992–98	8	4	0	12
=	BIRGIT FISCHER	CANOEING	GERMANY	1980–2004	8	4	0	12

2 LARISA LATYNINA

Born on December 27, 1934,
Larisa Latynina holds the world record
of the most Olympic gold medals won
by any gymnast. Olympics wins aside,
during her career, Latynina also won
an additional nine World Artistic
Gymnastics Championships gold
medals, and another seven gold at
European Women's Artistic Gymnastics
Championships.

1 TRISCHA ZORN

In 2012, American athlete Trischa Zorn was inducted into the Paralympic Hall of Fame. By a 24-medal difference, she is the most successful Paralympian of all time. The visually impaired swimmer was the US flag bearer during the closing ceremony of the 2004 Summer Paralympics in Athens, Greece. She was also nominated for *Sports Illustrated* Woman of the Year in 1988.

TOP 10 MOST SUCCESSFUL **PARALYMPIANS**

Not including the 2018 Winter Games winners, these are the 10 Paralympians who have won the most medals...

	PARALYMPIAN	DISCIPLINE(S)	COUNTRY	YEARS	GOLD	SILVER	BRONZE	TOTAL
1	TRISCHA ZORN	SWIMMING	USA	1980–2004	31	9	5	55
2	HEINZ FREI	ATHLETICS, CYCLING, CROSS-COUNTRY SKIING	SWITZERLAND	1984–2000	14	6	11	31
3	JONAS JACOBSSON	SHOOTING	SWEDEN	1980–2012	17	4	9	30
4	RAGNHILD MYKLEBUST	BIATHLON, CROSS-COUNTRY SKIING, ICE SLEDGE RACING	NORWAY	1988–2002	22	3	2	27
5	ROBERTO MARSON	ATHLETICS, FENCING	ITALY	1964–76	16	7	3	26
6	BÉATRICE HESS	SWIMMING	FRANCE	1984–2004	20	5	0	25
7	SARAH STOREY	SWIMMING, CYCLING	UK	1992–2016	14	8	3	25
8	CLAUDIA HENGST	SWIMMING	GERMANY	1988–2004	13	4	8	25
9	DANIEL DIAS	SWIMMING	BRAZIL	2008–16	14	7	3	24
10	FRANK HÖFLE	BIATHLON, CROSS-COUNTRY SKIING, CYCLING	GERMANY	1992–2002	14	5	5	24

MOST HOSTED OLYMPIC & PARALYMPIC NATIONS

Combining all of the Summer and Winter Olympic and Paralympic Games, these countries have played host the most...

	COUNTRY	TOTAL TIMES HOSTED OLYMPIC & PARALYMPIC GAMES
1	USA	11
2	FRANCE	6
3	CANADA	5
=	ITALY	5
=	JAPAN	5
=	UK	5
7	AUSTRIA	4
=	GERMANY	4
=	GREECE	4
=	NORWAY	4

RIO 2016

306 events covering 28 different kinds of sport took place in Rio de Janeiro, Brazil, for the 2016 Summer Olympics. The opening ceremony was on August 5, and the games closed on August 21. A total of 207 different nations with more than 11,000 athletes participated in events held in 38 locations.

The Summer Youth Olympics debuted in 2010 in Singapore, with the first Winter Youth Games taking place in 2012 in Innsbruck, Austria. The 2018 Summer Youth Olympics take place in Buenos Aires, Argentina, October 6–18.

1 CHINA

The 2014 Summer Youth Olympics, the second ever of their kind, were held in Nanjing, China. In August (16–28), 222 events took place, covering 28 sports (just like the adult Summer Olympics). These Summer Youth Olympics had their own bespoke, multicolored mascot called Lele.

TOP 10 MOST MEDALS WON
BY YOUTH OLYMPIC NATIONS

Since the Youth Olympic Games' debut in 2010, these 10 countries have been the most successful on the podiums...

	COUNTRY / TEAM	GOLD	SILVER	BRONZE	TOTAL
1	CHINA	78	38	25	141
2	RUSSIA	57	45	38	140
3	MIXED NOCs*	29	27	33	89
4	GERMANY	21	31	34	86
5	USA	26	23	18	67
6	AUSTRALIA	14	22	30	66
7	SOUTH KOREA	31	16	14	61
8	JAPAN	19	23	17	59
9	UKRAINE	17	18	23	58
10	FRANCE	18	8	24	50

*MIXED NATIONAL OLYMPIC COMMITTEES

1 PHILIPPINE ARENA

This four-story, 213 ft (64.9 m) structure had its grand opening on July 21, 2014. The roof, featuring 9,000 tons of steel, was inspired by the Nipa hut, an iconic symbol of the Philippines. The lower section includes 1,988 retractable seats that are primarily used by choirs for religious events. The arena is regularly used for basketball matches, as well as gymnastics and boxing.

TOP 10 LARGEST INDOOR ARENAS

These impressive structures are home to major sporting events as well as music shows and religious gatherings too...

	ARENA	LOCATION	CAPACITY CROWD
1	PHILIPPINE ARENA	BOCAUE (PHILIPPINES)	55,000
2	SAITAMA SUPER ARENA	SAITAMA (JAPAN)	37,000
3	SC OLIMPIYSKIY	MOSCOW (RUSSIA)	35,000
4	GWANGMYEONG VELODROME	GWANGMYEONG (SOUTH KOREA)	30,000
5	TELENOR ARENA	BÆRUM (NORWAY)	26,000
6	KOMBANK ARENA	BELGRADE (SERBIA)	25,000
=	MINEIRINHO	BELO HORIZONTE (BRAZIL)	25,000
=	SMART ARANETA COLISEUM	QUEZON CITY (PHILIPPINES)	25,000
=	BAKU CRYSTAL HALL	BAKU (AZERBAIJAN)	25,000
=	SCC PETERBURGSKIY	ST PETERSBURG (RUSSIA)	25,000

BIGGEST **STADIUMS**

Some of the entries in this chart can seat more than four times the crowd
capacity listed in the arena top 10 opposite...

	STADIUM	LOCATION	CAPACITY CROWD
1	RUNGRADO 1ST OF MAY STADIUM	PYONGYANG (NORTH KOREA)	150,000
2	MICHIGAN STADIUM	MICHIGAN (USA)	107,601
3	BEAVER STADIUM	PENNSYLVANIA (USA)	107,572
4	OHIO STADIUM	OHIO (USA)	104,944
5	KYLE FIELD	TEXAS (USA)	102,733
6	NEYLAND STADIUM	TENNESSEE (USA)	102,455
7	TIGER STADIUM	LOUISIANA (USA)	102,321
8	BRYANT–DENNY STADIUM	ALABAMA (USA)	101,821
9	DARRELL K ROYAL–TEXAS MEMORIAL STADIUM	TEXAS (USA)	100,119
10	MELBOURNE CRICKET GROUND	MELBOURNE (AUSTRALIA)	100,024

4
SPORTS

7 TIGER STADIUM

Owned by the Louisiana State University
(LSU), this Baton Rouge-based outdoor
stadium was first opened on November
25, 1924. Its most recent expansion came
in 2014. Although it is the home of the
LSU Tigers football team, nonsporting
events have included Taylor Swift's 1989
World Tour in 2015.

Epic
STRUCTURES

1 432 PARK AVENUE

This skyscraper is in the heart of Manhattan, which is New York City's most populous of its five boroughs. Foundation work began in 2011 and the building was completed just before Christmas of 2015. It has a total floor area of 412,637 square ft (38,335.2 square m). The building includes a private theater with a 220 in (558.8 cm) screen. The first apartment was bought for $18.116 million.

TOP 10 LARGEST **ALL-RESIDENTIAL BUILDINGS**

The skyscrapers in this chart serve a singular purpose: to provide homes for people. The 10 buildings here have a total of 841 floors...

	BUILDING	CITY / REGION	COUNTRY	YEAR COMPLETED	FLOORS	HEIGHT (FT)	(M)
1	432 PARK AVENUE	NEW YORK CITY	USA	2015	85	1,396	425.5
2	PRINCESS TOWER	DUBAI	UNITED ARAB EMIRATES	2012	101	1,356	413.4
3	23 MARINA	DUBAI	UNITED ARAB EMIRATES	2012	88	1,287	392.4
4	BURJ MOHAMMED BIN RASHID TOWER	ABU DHABI	UNITED ARAB EMIRATES	2014	88	1,251	381.2
5	ELITE RESIDENCE	DUBAI	UNITED ARAB EMIRATES	2012	87	1,248	380.5
6	THE TORCH	DUBAI	UNITED ARAB EMIRATES	2011	86	1,155	352
7	Q1 TOWER	GOLD COAST	AUSTRALIA	2005	78	1,058	322.5
8	HHHR TOWER	DUBAI	UNITED ARAB EMIRATES	2010	72	1,042	317.6
9	OCEAN HEIGHTS	DUBAI	UNITED ARAB EMIRATES	2010	83	1,017	310
10	CAYAN TOWER	DUBAI	UNITED ARAB EMIRATES	2013	73	1,005	306.4

TOP 10 BUILDINGS WITH **THE MOST FLOORS**

The structural height of these constructions is not the focus of this top 10.
Instead, it's measured by the number of stops the elevators have...

	BUILDING	CITY	COUNTRY	YEAR COMPLETED	TOTAL FLOORS
1	BURJ KHALIFA	DUBAI	UNITED ARAB EMIRATES	2010	163
2	SHANGHAI TOWER	SHANGHAI	CHINA	2015	128
3	MAKKAH ROYAL CLOCK TOWER HOTEL	MECCA	SAUDI ARABIA	2012	120
4	GUANGZHOU CTF FINANCE CENTRE	GUANGZHOU	CHINA	2016	111
5	INTERNATIONAL COMMERCE CENTRE	HONG KONG	CHINA	2010	108
=	WILLIS TOWER	CHICAGO	USA	1974	108
7	GUANGZHOU INTERNATIONAL FINANCE CENTER	GUANGZHOU	CHINA	2010	103
8	EMPIRE STATE BUILDING	NEW YORK CITY	USA	1931	102
9	TAIPEI 101	TAIPEI	TAIWAN/CHINA	2004	101
=	SHANGHAI WORLD FINANCIAL CENTER / PRINCESS TOWER	SHANGHAI / DUBAI	CHINA / UNITED ARAB EMIRATES	2008/ 2012	101

4 GUANGZHOU CTF FINANCE CENTRE

Classified as
a "mixed-use" tower, this building
has 273 hotel rooms, 414 apartments and 1,705 parking
spaces. Its 86 elevators travel at a top speed of 20 meters
per second, which translates to 44.7 mph (71.9 kph).
Initially proposed in 2009, it officially opened in October
2016 and is China's third tallest building.

10 LARGEST **ALL-HOTEL BUILDINGS**

Some buildings combine office space with residential and hotel rooms, but these 10 are exclusively hoteliers...

	BUILDING	COUNTRY	YEAR COMPLETED	FLOORS	HEIGHT (FT)	(M)
1	JW MARRIOTT MARQUIS HOTEL DUBAI TOWERS	UNITED ARAB EMIRATES	2012 & 2013	82	1,166	355.4
2	ROSE RAYHAAN BY ROTANA	UNITED ARAB EMIRATES	2007	71	1,093	333
3	BURJ AL ARAB	UNITED ARAB EMIRATES	1999	56	1,053	321
4	EMIRATES TOWER TWO	UNITED ARAB EMIRATES	2000	56	1,014	309
5	BAIYOKE TOWER II	THAILAND	1997	85	997	304
6	WUXI MAOYE CITY MARRIOTT HOTEL	CHINA	2014	68	997	303.8
7	KHALID AL ATTAR TOWER 2	UNITED ARAB EMIRATES	2011	66	965	294
8	ABRAJ AL BAIT ZAMZAM TOWER	SAUDI ARABIA	2012	58	915	279
9	ABRAJ AL BAIT HAJAR TOWER	SAUDI ARABIA	2012	54	906	276
10	FOUR SEASONS HOTEL	BAHRAIN	2015	50	885	269.4

10 FOUR SEASONS HOTEL

The tallest building in the city of Manama, Bahrain, this Four Seasons hotel is the 42nd highest construction in the Middle East, and ranks 201st tallest in the world. Its main Al Bahrain Ballroom is 9,935 square ft (923 square m) and can hold 900 people. It also has two additional ballrooms and five swimming pools. On February 22, 2017, at the Food and Travel Bahrain Awards, this building was named Hotel of the Year.

 SHANGHAI TOWER

In Shanghai's new Lujiazui Finance and Trade Zone, this tower is part of a colossal trio that includes Shanghai World Financial Center and Jin Mao Tower. The Shanghai Tower has a mix of hotel rooms, office space, shops, and restaurants placed throughout the structure. It also utilizes a number of renewable energy sources, making it one of the most sustainable towers in the world.

TOP 10 BIGGEST BUILDINGS **THAT INCLUDE HOTELS**

Even the smallest of the constructions in this list is approaching a third of a mile (half a kilometer) in height...

	BUILDING	COUNTRY	YEAR COMPLETED	FLOORS	ROOMS	HEIGHT (FT)	(M)
1	BURJ KHALIFA	UNITED ARAB EMIRATES	2010	163	304	2,717	828
2	SHANGHAI TOWER	CHINA	2015	128	258	2,073	632
3	MAKKAH ROYAL CLOCK TOWER HOTEL	SAUDI ARABIA	2012	120	858	1,972	601
4	GUANGZHOU CTF FINANCE CENTRE	CHINA	2016	111	273	1,739	530
5	SHANGHAI WORLD FINANCIAL CENTER	CHINA	2008	101	174	1,614	492
6	INTERNATIONAL COMMERCE CENTRE	CHINA	2010	108	312	1,588	484
7	ZIFENG TOWER	CHINA	2010	66	450	1,476	450
8	KK100	CHINA	2011	100	249	1,449	441.8
9	GUANGZHOU INTERNATIONAL FINANCE CENTER	CHINA	2010	103	374	1,439	438.6
10	TRUMP INTERNATIONAL HOTEL & TOWER	USA	2009	98	339	1,389	423.2

TOP 10 BIGGEST LIBRARIES

The British Library in London, England, has around 2,000 staff members who help run the complex that receives two million people each year...

	LIBRARY	CITY	COUNTRY	NUMBER OF BOOKS (MILLIONS)
1	THE BRITISH LIBRARY	LONDON	UK	170
2	LIBRARY OF CONGRESS	WASHINGTON, D.C.	USA	162
3	LIBRARY AND ARCHIVES	OTTAWA	CANADA	54
4	NEW YORK PUBLIC LIBRARY	NEW YORK CITY	USA	53.1
5	RUSSIAN STATE LIBRARY	MOSCOW	RUSSIA	44.4
6	BIBLIOTHÈQUE NATIONALE DE FRANCE	PARIS	FRANCE	40
7	NATIONAL LIBRARY OF RUSSIA	ST PETERSBURG	RUSSIA	36.5
8	NATIONAL DIET LIBRARY	TOKYO / KYOTO	JAPAN	35.6
9	ROYAL DANISH LIBRARY	COPENHAGEN	DENMARK	35.1
10	NATIONAL LIBRARY OF CHINA	BEIJING	CHINA	33.8

4 NEW YORK PUBLIC LIBRARY

Established in 1895, the main branch of this library system in Bryant Park, Manhattan, has been featured in dozens of major feature films, including: *Escape from New York* (1981), *Ghostbusters* (1984), and *Breakfast at Tiffany's* (1961), as well as countless TV series such as *Seinfeld* (1989–98) and *Person of Interest* (2011–16). With a total of 93 different branches / buildings, across the Bronx, Manhattan, and Staten Island, more than 3,000 staff are employed by the New York Public Library system.

TOP 10 AIRPORTS WITH THE MOST PASSENGERS

There are nearly 50,000 airports in the world. These 10 see a total of 769.8 million passengers passing through them every year...

	AIRPORT	LOCATION	COUNTRY	TOTAL PASSENGERS PER YEAR (MILLIONS)
1	HARTSFIELD–JACKSON ATLANTA INTERNATIONAL AIRPORT	GEORGIA	USA	101.49
2	BEIJING CAPITAL INTERNATIONAL AIRPORT	BEIJING	CHINA	89.94
3	DUBAI INTERNATIONAL AIRPORT	DUBAI	UNITED ARAB EMIRATES	78.01
4	O'HARE INTERNATIONAL AIRPORT	ILLINOIS	USA	76.94
5	TOKYO HANEDA AIRPORT	TOKYO	JAPAN	75.32
6	LONDON HEATHROW AIRPORT	LONDON	UK	74.99
7	LOS ANGELES INTERNATIONAL AIRPORT	CALIFORNIA	USA	74.94
8	HONG KONG INTERNATIONAL AIRPORT	HONG KONG	CHINA	68.28
9	PARIS-CHARLES DE GAULLE AIRPORT	ÎLE-DE-FRANCE	FRANCE	65.77
10	DALLAS-FORT WORTH INTERNATIONAL AIRPORT	TEXAS	USA	64.07

1 HARTSFIELD–JACKSON ATLANTA INTERNATIONAL AIRPORT

With 200 gates, and more than 55,000 employees, Atlanta Airport's origins go back to 1926 when a mail aircraft landed on its (originally) less than 300-acres field. As of 2018, it has runways that exceed 10,000 ft (3,048 m) and a total area of 6,800,000 square ft (630,000 square m).

BIGGEST BUILDS

TOP 10 LARGEST **ALL-OFFICE BUILDINGS**

For the biggest business-only constructions, these 10 (including an 87-year-old tower) remain the record-holders for height...

	BUILDING	CITY	COUNTRY	YEAR COMPLETED	FLOORS	HEIGHT (FT)	(M)
1	ONE WORLD TRADE CENTER	NEW YORK CITY	USA	2014	104	1,776	541
2	TAIPEI 101	TAIPEI	TAIWAN/CHINA	2004	101	1,667	508
3	PETRONAS TWIN TOWERS	KUALA LUMPUR	MALAYSIA	1998	88	1,483	451.9
4	WILLIS TOWER	CHICAGO	USA	1974	108	1,451	442.1
5	AL HAMRA TOWER	KUWAIT CITY	KUWAIT	2011	80	1,354	412.6
6	TWO INTERNATIONAL FINANCE CENTRE	HONG KONG	CHINA	2003	88	1,352	412
7	CITIC PLAZA	GUANGZHOU	CHINA	1996	80	1,280	390.2
8	SHUN HING SQUARE	SHENZHEN	CHINA	1996	69	1,260	384
9	EMPIRE STATE BUILDING	NEW YORK CITY	USA	1931	102	1,250	381
10	CENTRAL PLAZA	HONG KONG	CHINA	1992	78	1,227	373.9

DECADES OF COMPLETION

Here is how the above chart ranks by the decade of opening...

'30s	'70s	'90s	'00s	'10s
1	1	4	2	2

9 EMPIRE STATE BUILDING

This structure can be found at 350 5th Avenue, New York City. It was designed by architectural company Shreve, Lamb, and Harmon and was built in less than 14 months from its March 17, 1930, start date. It is the fifth tallest building in the US, and 28th tallest building in the world. Its 73 elevators can travel at 7.1 meters per second.

1 NETHERLANDS

Maastoren, the tallest building in the Netherlands, can be found in Rotterdam. At 541 ft (164.8 m) high, this 44-floor office block was completed in 2010. It ranks as the 114th tallest building in Europe. 2017 saw construction begin of Woontoren Zalmhaven, a 617 ft (188 m) residential concrete tower that is planned to be finished in 2020.

TOP 10 COUNTRIES WITH THE MOST TELECOM TOWERS

The word "telecom" comes from the "telecommunications" purposes of these buildings...

	COUNTRY	NUMBER OF TELECOM TOWERS
1	NETHERLANDS	88
2	CHINA	28
3	USA	18
4	GERMANY	13
5	UK	10
6	JAPAN	9
7	CANADA	6
8	RUSSIA	4
=	ITALY	4
=	KUWAIT	4

1 ▷ GREAT WALL OF CHINA

Its name of Chángchéng means "long wall." This Northern China structure is more than 2,300 years old and was constructed by many different dynasties. Due to man-made damage and natural erosion, around 30 percent of the Great Wall is gone. The Chinese government has invested in funding and passed laws to protect the Great Wall.

TOP **10**

LONGEST **BUILDINGS**

When it comes to constructing something that goes on for miles, these 10 efforts more than qualify...

	CONSTRUCTION	COUNTRY	LENGTH (FT)	(M)
1 ▷	GREAT WALL OF CHINA	CHINA	29,041,338.5	8,851,800
2	RANIKOT FORT	PAKISTAN	28,215	8,600
3	WALLS OF STON	CROATIA	18,045	5,500
4	KLYSTRON GALLERY	USA	10,084	3,073.7
5	MODLIN FORTRESS	POLAND	7,381.9	2,250
6	MOSCOW KREMLIN WALL	RUSSIA	7,332.7	2,235
7	DUBAI INTERNATIONAL AIRPORT CARGO GATEWAY	UNITED ARAB EMIRATES	5,820.2	1,774
8	SOBORNOSTI AVENUE / MOLODYOZHI STREET APARTMENT	UKRAINE	5,741.5	1,750
9	KANSAI INTERNATIONAL AIRPORT	JAPAN	5,577.4	1,700
=	RED DOG MINE ENCLOSURE	USA	5,577.4	1,700

TOP 10 BIGGEST AQUARIUMS

How much do you know about your nearest aquarium? Find out what its total water capacity is and then compare it to these 10...

	AQUARIUM	LOCATION	TOTAL WATER (MILLIONS) (US GAL)	(LTR)
1	S.E.A. AQUARIUM	SINGAPORE	12	45
2	GEORGIA AQUARIUM	USA	6.3	23.85
3	DUBAI AQUARIUM & UNDERWATER ZOO	DUBAI	2.64	10
4	OKINAWA CHURAUMI AQUARIUM	JAPAN	1.98	7.5
5	L'OCEANOGRÀFIC OF THE CITY OF ARTS AND SCIENCES	SPAIN	1.85	7
6	TURKUAZOO	TURKEY	1.32	5
7	MONTEREY BAY AQUARIUM	USA	1.2	4.54
8	USHAKA MARINE WORLD	SOUTH AFRICA	0.98	3.71
9	SHANGHAI OCEAN AQUARIUM	CHINA	0.92	3.48
10	AQUARIUM OF GENOA	ITALY	0.87	3.29

2 GEORGIA AQUARIUM

Georgia Aquarium first opened its doors on November 23, 2005. Their extensive conservation work includes the research and rescue of dolphins in northeast Florida waters, and the rehabilitation of loggerhead sea turtles so they can be released back into the wild. More than 2 million people visit every year.

TALLEST **COMPLETED BUILDINGS**

As you read this, there are countless projects underway to build towers that exceed some of these giants, but for now, these are the 10 tallest...

	BUILDING	CITY	COUNTRY	YEAR COMPLETED	FLOORS	HEIGHT (FT)	(M)
1	BURJ KHALIFA	DUBAI	UNITED ARAB EMIRATES	2010	163	2,717	828
2	SHANGHAI TOWER	SHANGHAI	CHINA	2015	128	2,073	632
3	MAKKAH ROYAL CLOCK TOWER HOTEL	MECCA	SAUDI ARABIA	2012	120	1,972	601
4	ONE WORLD TRADE CENTER	NEW YORK CITY	USA	2014	104	1,776	541
5	GUANGZHOU CTF FINANCE CENTRE	GUANGZHOU	CHINA	2016	111	1,739	530
6	TAIPEI 101	TAIPEI	TAIWAN/CHINA	2004	101	1,667	508
7	SHANGHAI WORLD FINANCIAL CENTER	SHANGHAI	CHINA	2008	101	1,614	492
8	INTERNATIONAL COMMERCE CENTRE	HONG KONG	CHINA	2010	108	1,588	484
9	PETRONAS TWIN TOWERS	KUALA LUMPUR	MALAYSIA	1998	88	1,483	451.9
10	ZIFENG TOWER	NANJING	CHINA	2010	66	1,476	450

1 BURJ KHALIFA

This combination of 900 residential apartments, office space, and 304 hotel rooms has 58 elevators to serve its occupants. It has just one floor below ground and 2,957 parking spaces. Construction began in 2004, with Burj Khalifa opening on January 4, 2010, as part of downtown Dubai.

TOP 10 COUNTRIES WITH THE MOST SKYSCRAPERS

To be called a "skyscraper" the building has to be a minimum of 330 ft (100 m) tall, and these are the countries that are home to the most...

	COUNTRY	TOTAL SKYSCRAPERS
1	USA	4,550
2	CHINA	2,549
3	CANADA	1,017
4	AUSTRALIA	832
5	INDONESIA	571
6	JAPAN	559
7	RUSSIA	540
8	NETHERLANDS	503
9	UNITED ARAB EMIRATES	392
10	SOUTH KOREA	358

1 USA

There are several new skyscrapers being developed all across the US. These include New York City's Central Park Tower (proposed to be 1,550 ft / 472.4 m tall), and Chicago's Vista Tower (1,186 ft / 361.6 m), both set to be completed in 2020. Of the USA's skyscrapers, 2,465 exceed 330 ft (100 m).

COUNTRIES WITH
THE MOST 300 M+ BUILDINGS

These nations' skylines are full of glass, steel, and concrete structures. But the number listed below all exceed 984 ft in height...

COUNTRY	NUMBER OF 300 M+ BUILDINGS
1 CHINA	47
2 UNITED ARAB EMIRATES	22
3 USA	17
4 RUSSIA	4
5 MALAYSIA	3
= SAUDI ARABIA	3
7 SOUTH KOREA	2
= THAILAND	2
= TAIWAN/CHINA	2
= KUWAIT	2

1 CHINA

China tops several of the Epic Structures top 10 charts. Of its skyscrapers, 1,828 exceed 330 ft (100 m). The proposed H700 Shenzhen Tower is planned to be 2,425 ft (739 m) tall, making it the tallest (future) building in China. Nearly 1.4 billion people live in China. Its most populated city, Shanghai, has more than 24 million residents. China's capital, Beijing, is home to 21.6 million.

The tallest building in South Korea is Seoul's Lotte World Tower. Completed in 2017, it stands 1,819 ft (554.5 m) tall with 123 floors, combining offices and hotel rooms. South Korea has a total of 360 skyscrapers, 286 of which are more than 330 ft (100 m) high. Busan's LCT Landmark Tower is due to be completed by 2020, and will have a total height of 1,350 ft (411.6 m).

TOP 10

COUNTRIES WITH **THE MOST 200 M+ BUILDINGS**

For the towers to count in this chart, they have to be 656.2 ft tall or more. Compare this chart with the one opposite...

	COUNTRY	NUMBER OF 200 M+ BUILDINGS
1	CHINA	490
2	USA	175
3	UNITED ARAB EMIRATES	89
4	SOUTH KOREA	57
5	JAPAN	36
6	AUSTRALIA	30
=	INDONESIA	30
=	SINGAPORE	30
9	PHILIPPINES	24
10	CANADA	21

LONGEST **ROLLER COASTERS**

When it comes to measuring these rides, instead of examining their height, this top 10 collects the ones with the longest tracks...

	ROLLER COASTER	LOCATION	COUNTRY	LENGTH (FT)	(M)
1	STEEL DRAGON 2000	NAGASHIMA SPA LAND	JAPAN	8,133	2,479
2	THE ULTIMATE	LIGHTWATER VALLEY	UK	7,442	2,268
3	THE BEAST	KINGS ISLAND	USA	7,359	2,243
4	FUJIYAMA	FUJI-Q HIGHLAND	JAPAN	6,709	2,045
5	FURY 325	CAROWINDS	USA	6,602	2,012
6	MILLENNIUM FORCE	CEDAR POINT	USA	6,595	2,010
7	FORMULA ROSSA	FERRARI WORLD	UNITED ARAB EMIRATES	6,562	2,000
8	THE VOYAGE	HOLIDAY WORLD & SPLASHIN' SAFARI	USA	6,442	1,964
9	CALIFORNIA SCREAMIN'	DISNEY CALIFORNIA ADVENTURE	USA	6,072	1,851
10	DESPERADO	BUFFALO BILL'S	USA	5,843	1,781

7 FORMULA ROSSA

This, the fastest roller coaster in the world, first opened on November 4, 2010. It gives riders a one-minute-32 experience featuring a 169 ft (51.5 m) drop, and accelerates to its top speed of 149.1 mph (240 kph) in five seconds. Manufacturer Intamin has created 70 different roller coasters for parks all over the world.

TOP 10 LONGEST BRIDGES

To convey the massive scale of these constructions, even the bridge at the number 10 spot is 22.3 mi (35.8 km) long...

	BRIDGE	COUNTRY	LENGTH (FT)	(M)
1	DANYANG–KUNSHAN GRAND BRIDGE	CHINA	540,700	164,800
2	THSR CHANGHUA–KAOHSIUNG VIADUCT	TAIWAN / CHINA	516,132	157,317
3	TIANJIN GRAND BRIDGE	CHINA	373,000	113,700
4	WEINAN WEIHE GRAND BRIDGE	CHINA	261,588	79,732
5	BANG NA EXPRESSWAY	THAILAND	177,000	54,000
6	HONG KONG–ZHUHAI–MACAU BRIDGE	CHINA	160,000	50,000
7	BEIJING GRAND BRIDGE	CHINA	157,982	48,153
8	LAKE PONTCHARTRAIN CAUSEWAY	USA	126,122	38,442
9	MANCHAC SWAMP BRIDGE	USA	120,440	36,710
10	YANGCUN BRIDGE	CHINA	117,493	35,812

1 DANYANG–KUNSHAN GRAND BRIDGE

Four years in the making, the longest bridge in the world has kept its crown since it opened for use on June 30, 2011. It is located in the eastern Jiangsu province, one of China's 23 provinces, part of 34 divisions. It carries the Beijing–Shanghai High-Speed Railway.

TOP 10 OLDEST **OPERATIONAL MUSEUMS**

Find out how old your local museum is, and then compare it to the ones in this top 10, two of which opened more than 500 years ago...

	MUSEUM	CITY	COUNTRY	YEAR OFFICIALLY OPENED TO THE PUBLIC
1	CAPITOLINE MUSEUMS	ROME	ITALY	1471
2	VATICAN MUSEUMS	VATICAN CITY	VATICAN CITY	1506
3	ROYAL ARMOURIES MUSEUM, THE TOWER OF LONDON	LONDON	UK	1660
4	KUNSTMUSEUM BASEL (FORMERLY AMERBACH CABINET)	BASEL	SWITZERLAND	1671
5	MUSÉE DES BEAUX-ARTS ET D'ARCHÉOLOGIE DE BESANÇON	BESANÇON	FRANCE	1694
6	KUNSTKAMERA	ST PETERSBURG	RUSSIA	1727
7	BRITISH MUSEUM	LONDON	UK	1759
8	UFFIZI GALLERY	FLORENCE	ITALY	1769
9	MUSEUM OF THE HISTORY OF RIGA AND NAVIGATION	OLD RIGA	LATVIA	1773
10	TEYLERS MUSEUM	HAARLEM	NETHERLANDS	1784

TOP 10 MOST **POPULAR MUSEUMS**

Home to ancient artifacts, prehistoric fossils, and art from across the centuries, these buildings preserve the planet's history and our creativity...

	MUSEUM	CITY	COUNTRY	ANNUAL ATTENDANCE (MILLIONS)
1	LOUVRE	PARIS	FRANCE	8.6
2	NATIONAL MUSEUM OF CHINA	BEIJING	CHINA	7.29
3	NATIONAL MUSEUM OF NATURAL HISTORY	WASHINGTON, D.C.	USA	6.9
=	NATIONAL AIR & SPACE MUSEUM	WASHINGTON, D.C.	USA	6.9
5	BRITISH MUSEUM	LONDON	UK	6.82
6	THE METROPOLITAN MUSEUM OF ART	NEW YORK CITY	USA	6.53
7	VATICAN MUSEUMS	VATICAN CITY	VATICAN CITY	6
8	SHANGHAI SCIENCE & TECHNOLOGY MUSEUM	SHANGHAI	CHINA	5.95
9	NATIONAL GALLERY	LONDON	UK	5.9
10	NATIONAL PALACE MUSEUM	TAIPEI	TAIWAN / CHINA	5.3

8 UFFIZI GALLERY

The origins of this museum lie in the translation of its name. "Uffizi" is Italian for "offices," and was ordered by the second Duke of Florence, Cosimo I de' Medici, to be built for the city's administrative and judiciary work. Up to 2 million people visit the Uffizi each year to see its art collection.

3 NATIONAL MUSEUM OF NATURAL HISTORY

First open to the public in 1910, this is part of the world-renowned Smithsonian Institution. It houses more than 126 million artifacts and specimens. These include more than 4 million pressed plants and 3.5 million preserved natural science specimens that are loaned to other museums every year.

TOP **10**

FASTEST **ROLLER COASTERS**

This chart is for anyone who is a thrill-seeker, as all of these rides exceed the speed you experience on a freeway...

	ROLLER COASTER	LOCATION	COUNTRY	TOP SPEED (MPH)	(KPH)
1	FORMULA ROSSA	FERRARI WORLD	UNITED ARAB EMIRATES	149.1	240
2	KINGDA KA	SIX FLAGS	USA	128	206
3	TOP THRILL DRAGSTER	CEDAR POINT	USA	120	193.1
4	FERRARI VERTICAL ACCELERATOR	FERRARI LAND	SPAIN	112	180
5	DODONPA	FUJI-Q HIGHLAND	JAPAN	106.9	172
6	SUPERMAN: ESCAPE FROM KRYPTON	SIX FLAGS	USA	100.8	162.2
7	TOWER OF TERROR II	DREAMWORLD	AUSTRALIA	100	160.9
8	STEEL DRAGON 2000	NAGASHIMA SPA LAND	JAPAN	95	152.9
=	FURY 325	CAROWINDS	USA	95	152.9
10	MILLENNIUM FORCE	CEDAR POINT	USA	93	149.7

5  DODONPA

This 55-second ride accelerates its passengers from zero to 106.9 mph (172 kph) in just 1.6 seconds, using compressed air to propel the roller coaster from its launch position. Riders experience a G-force stronger than astronauts do during take-off. The track is 3,901 ft (1,189 m) long.

TOP 10 MOST POPULAR **THEME PARKS**

Combining the number of visitors to every park owned by these companies, these are the franchises that attract the most visitors each year...

	PARK CORPORATION	(PRIME) LOCATION	ANNUAL ATTENDANCE (MILLIONS)
1	WALT DISNEY PARKS & RESORTS	USA	137.9
2	MERLIN ENTERTAINMENTS GROUP	UK	62.9
3	UNIVERSAL STUDIOS RECREATION GROUP	USA	44.8
4	OCT PARKS CHINA	CHINA	30.2
5	SIX FLAGS INC.	USA	28.6
6	CEDAR FAIR ENTERTAINMENT COMPANY	USA	24.5
7	CHIMELONG GROUP	CHINA	23.6
8	FANTAWILD GROUP	CHINA	23.1
9	SEAWORLD PARKS & ENTERTAINMENT	USA	22.5
10	SONGCHENG WORLDWIDE	CHINA	22.3

3 UNIVERSAL STUDIOS

On July 15, 1964, the working film studio conducted its first tour for the public, marking its first steps toward developing its integrated Universal Studios Hollywood theme park. On April 7, 2016, The Wizarding World of Harry Potter opened in its upper lot.

TOP 10

OLDEST **OPERATIONAL THEME PARKS**

If you thought that amusement parks were a modern creation, take a look at when these 10 first opened to the public...

	THEME PARK	LOCATION	COUNTRY	FIRST OPENED	TOTAL YEARS OPERATIONAL
1	DYREHAVSBAKKEN	KLAMPENBORG	DENMARK	1583	435
2	WURSTELPRATER	VIENNA	AUSTRIA	1766	252
3	BLACKGANG CHINE	ISLE OF WIGHT	UK	1843	175
=	TIVOLI GARDENS	COPENHAGEN	DENMARK	1843	175
5	LAKE COMPOUNCE	CONNECTICUT	USA	1846	172
6	HANAYASHIKI	TOKYO	JAPAN	1853	165
7	CEDAR POINT	OHIO	USA	1870	148
=	SIX FLAGS NEW ENGLAND	MASSACHUSETTS	USA	1870	148
9	IDLEWILD PARK	PENNSYLVANIA	USA	1878	140
10	SEABREEZE AMUSEMENT PARK	ROCHESTER	USA	1879	139

3 BLACKGANG CHINE

"Chine," meaning a ravine in the coastline, is a word still commonly used in the South of England. The Blackgang Chine (which this park gets its name from) has now been completely eroded away. One of the park's oldest attractions, the skeleton of a whale, is still on display today. Other features include a giant maze, animatronic dinosaurs, and a butterfly walk.

MOST POPULAR **WATER PARKS**

All over the world, water slides and wave pools provide entertainment to millions of families every year...

5 Epic STRUCTURES

	WATER PARK	LOCATION	COUNTRY	ANNUAL ATTENDANCE (MILLIONS)
1	CHIMELONG WATER PARK	GUANGZHOU	CHINA	2.35
2	TYPHOON LAGOON (WALT DISNEY WORLD RESORT)	FLORIDA	USA	2.29
3	BLIZZARD BEACH (WALT DISNEY WORLD RESORT)	FLORIDA	USA	2.1
4	BAHAMAS AQUAVENTURE WATER PARK	PARADISE ISLAND	BAHAMAS	1.87
5	THERMAS DOS LARANJAIS	OLÍMPIA	BRAZIL	1.76
6	AQUATICA	FLORIDA	USA	1.6
7	OCEAN WORLD	GANGWON-DO	SOUTH KOREA	1.51
8	CARIBBEAN BAY (EVERLAND RESORT)	GYEONGGI-DO	SOUTH KOREA	1.43
9	WET 'N WILD ORLANDO	FLORIDA	USA	1.31
10	HOT PARK RIO QUENTE	CALDAS NOVAS	BRAZIL	1.29

2 TYPHOON LAGOON

This Disney-owned water park first opened on June 1, 1989. Its features include a state-of-the-art wave pool, with 6 ft (1.8 m) high waves, where you can take surfing lessons. Castaway Creek is the park's 2,000 ft (609.6 m) long slow-moving river that attendees can float down.

Mechanical CREATIONS

ZONE

6

TOP 10 LONGEST **SUBMARINES**

Huge budgets, years of planning, and cutting-edge technology go into the construction of these military vehicles...

	CLASS	COUNTRY	LENGTH (FT)	(M)
1	TYPHOON	RUSSIA	574.14	175
2	BOREI	RUSSIA	557.74	170
=	OHIO	USA	557.74	170
4	DELTA III	RUSSIA	544.62	166
5	OSCAR II	RUSSIA	508.53	155
6	VANGUARD	UK	491.8	149.9
7	TRIOMPHANT	FRANCE	452.76	138
8	YASEN	RUSSIA	393.7	120
9	VIRGINIA	USA	377.3	115
10	SIERRA II	RUSSIA	364.17	111

9 VIRGINIA

A US Navy Virginia-class submarine costs $2.7 billion. It weighs 2,240 long tons, which is equal to 17,472,000 lb (79,251,65.9 kg). They are made by a collaboration between 119-year-old Connecticut shipbuilding experts General Dynamics Electric Boat and Virginia-based Newport News Shipbuilding. To date, 13 vessels of this class have been built.

LONGEST SUBMARINES BY NATION

- UK 1
- FRANCE 1
- USA 2
- RUSSIA 6

TOP 10 MOST AIRCRAFT CARRIERS

The cost of an individual aircraft carrier exceeds tens of billions of dollars, but the programs to design, develop, and test them cost even more...

	COUNTRY	NUMBER IN SERVICE	TOTAL NUMBER EVER BUILT
1	USA	10	67
2	UK	0	40
3	JAPAN	0	20
4	FRANCE	1	8
5	RUSSIA	1	7
6	INDIA	1	5
7	CANADA	0	5
8	AUSTRALIA	0	3
9	SPAIN	1	3
10	ITALY	2	2

3 JAPANESE AIRCRAFT CARRIER

The Japan Maritime Self-Defense Force was founded in 1954, and was preceded by the Imperial Japanese Navy (1868–1945). The *Izumo* is a $1.3 billion aircraft carrier (specifically, a helicopter carrier) that entered service in 2013. Two are currently active. The second, JS *Kaga*, was launched in 2017.

TOP 10 FASTEST ON WATER **RECORD-HOLDERS**

Four decades on, no one has even come close to besting the number
one entry on this chart...

	SKIPPER	VESSEL	COUNTRY	YEAR	BEST SPEED ACHIEVED (MPH)	(KPH)
1	KEN WARBY	SPIRIT OF AUSTRALIA	AUSTRALIA	1978	317.6	511.12
2	LEE TAYLOR	HUSTLER	USA	1967	285.22	459.02
3	DONALD CAMPBELL	BLUEBIRD K7	UK	1964	276.33	444.71
4	STANLEY SAYRES, ELMER LENINSCHMIDT	SLO-MO-SHUN IV	USA	1952	178.5	287.26
5	MALCOLM CAMPBELL	BLUEBIRD K4	UK	1939	141.74	228.11
6	GAR WOOD	MISS AMERICA X	USA	1932	124.86	200.94
7	KAYE DON	MISS ENGLAND III	ITALY	1932	119.81	192.82
8	HENRY SEGRAVE	MISS ENGLAND II	UK	1930	98.76	158.94
9	GEORGE WOOD	MISS AMERICA II	USA	1928	92.84	149.41
10	JULES FISHER	FARMAN HYDROGLIDER	USA	1924	87.39	140.64

TOP 10 MOST SUCCESSFUL **WORLD CUP SAILING NATIONS**

When you consider that windy weather is common in Britain, especially
in its coastal towns, it's no surprise this nation's sailors top this chart...

	COUNTRY	TOTAL GOLD	TOTAL SILVER	TOTAL BRONZE	TOTAL MEDALS
1	GREAT BRITAIN	96	91	76	263
2	AUSTRALIA	91	74	71	236
3	FRANCE	49	53	48	150
4	USA	34	29	46	109
5	NETHERLANDS	45	29	32	106
6	NEW ZEALAND	26	36	22	84
7	CHINA	28	23	26	77
8	SPAIN	25	23	24	72
9	GERMANY	26	18	17	61
10	CROATIA	16	20	18	54

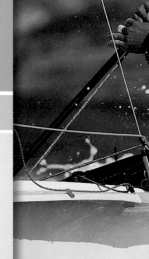

3 ▸ DONALD CAMPBELL

Born in Surrey, England, on March 23, 1921, Donald Campbell is the only person to achieve a world record for speed on land and on water in the same year. He died on January 4, 1967, while attempting to achieve 300 mph (483 kph) in the *Bluebird K7*. He lost control of the vehicle as it sped across Coniston Water, a lake in Cumbria.

10 ▸ CROATIA

Croatian sailing champions Šime Fantela and Igor Marenic have 16 gold medals between them. At the 2016 Summer Olympic Games in Rio de Janeiro, Brazil, the pair took home the first ever Olympic sailing gold for Croatia in the 470-class race. The two-sailor vessel in this class features the same size boat for men's and women's races.

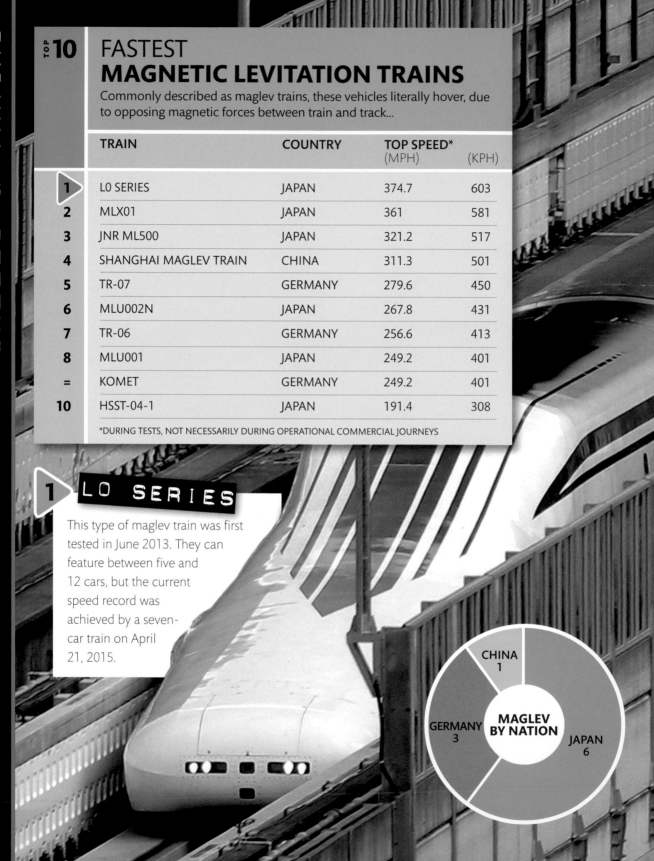

TOP **10**

FASTEST
MAGNETIC LEVITATION TRAINS

Commonly described as maglev trains, these vehicles literally hover, due to opposing magnetic forces between train and track...

	TRAIN	COUNTRY	TOP SPEED* (MPH)	(KPH)
1	L0 SERIES	JAPAN	374.7	603
2	MLX01	JAPAN	361	581
3	JNR ML500	JAPAN	321.2	517
4	SHANGHAI MAGLEV TRAIN	CHINA	311.3	501
5	TR-07	GERMANY	279.6	450
6	MLU002N	JAPAN	267.8	431
7	TR-06	GERMANY	256.6	413
8	MLU001	JAPAN	249.2	401
=	KOMET	GERMANY	249.2	401
10	HSST-04-1	JAPAN	191.4	308

*DURING TESTS, NOT NECESSARILY DURING OPERATIONAL COMMERCIAL JOURNEYS

1 L0 SERIES

This type of maglev train was first tested in June 2013. They can feature between five and 12 cars, but the current speed record was achieved by a seven-car train on April 21, 2015.

CHINA
1

GERMANY
3

MAGLEV BY NATION

JAPAN
6

1 ▸ TGV POS

A total of 19 TGV POS trains have been in service since 2006. These models are built by French manufacturer Alstom and operated by SNCF, France's national railway company. The world-record speed was set on April 3, 2007, on the high-speed LGV Est line. A standard in-service TGV POS is comprised of two power cars and eight carriages.

TOP **10**

FASTEST
WHEEL-AND-TRACK TRAINS

Although traditional-style trains have the forces of friction that maglevs do not, this doesn't compromise their ability to achieve extreme speeds...

	TRAIN	COUNTRY	TOP SPEED* (MPH)	(KPH)
1	TGV POS	FRANCE	357.2	574.8
2	TGV ATLANTIQUE	FRANCE	320.2	515.3
3	CRH380BL	CHINA	302.8	487.3
4	CRH380A	CHINA	302	486.1
5	AVE CLASS 103	SPAIN	250.8	403.7
6	CRH3	CHINA	244.9	394.2
7	ETR.400	ITALY	244.7	393.8
8	ZEFIRO 380	CHINA	236.1	380
9	ICE 3	GERMANY / NETHERLANDS	228.7	368
10	AVE CLASS 102	SPAIN	226.8	365

*DURING TESTS, NOT NECESSARILY DURING OPERATIONAL COMMERCIAL JOURNEYS

TOP 10 FASTEST CARS

To convey the true masters of automobile speed, this top 10 features both concept cars and production cars...

	MODEL	TOP SPEED (MPH)	(KPH)
1	BUGATTI CHIRON	288*	463.5
2	KOENIGSEGG ONE:1	273*	439.35
3	HENNESSEY VENOM GT	270.49*	435.31
4	KOENIGSEGG AGERA R	270	434.5
5	KOENIGSEGG AGERA S	268	431.3
6	BUGATTI VEYRON 16.4 SUPER SPORT WORLD RECORD EDITION	267.85*	431.07
7	KOENIGSEGG AGERA RS	267	429.7
8	KOENIGSEGG AGERA	260	418.42
9	SSC ULTIMATE AERO	257.44	414.31
10	9FF GT9-R	257	413.59

*WITH LIMITERS DISENGAGED

1 BUGATTI CHIRON

Only 500 units of this French-made supercar will ever be built, and the first 200 sold before it debuted on the market. The Bugatti Chiron was unveiled to the public on March 1, 2016 at the annual International Geneva Motor Show in Switzerland. It has a seven-speed, automatic gearbox.

TOP **10** ΓASTEST **MOTORCYCLES**

Like the car-based top 10 opposite, the below chart includes experimental, concept bikes, alongside models that are available for purchase / used in racing...

	MODEL	TOP SPEED (MPH)	(KPH)
1	TOP 1 ACK ATTACK	394.1	634.2
2	BUB SEVEN STREAMLINER	367.4	591.2
3	LIGHTNING BOLT	333.1	536.1
4	EASYRIDERS	322.9	519.6
5	SILVER BIRD	303.8	488.9
6	GYRONAUT X-1	279.6	450
7	YAMAHA BIG RED	265.5	427.3
8	HARLEY-DAVIDSON GODZILLA SPORTSTER	255	410.4
9	DUCATI DESMOSEDICI GP16	218.2	351.15
10	DUCATI DESMOSEDICI GP9	216.86	348

10 DUCATI DESMOSEDICI GP9

Bike fans got their first look at the GP9 on June 9, 2008, at Spain's Circuit de Barcelona-Catalunya race track. What makes this Ducati motorcycle unique is its carbon-fibre body. Eight years later, Ducati debuted the GP16, following the GP9, GP10, GP11, and GP12.

FASTEST **MANNED AIRCRAFT**

There are specialized, remote-controlled planes that do not require a pilot, but this chart is dedicated to those that do...

	AIRCRAFT	PILOT(S)	DATE	TOP SPEED (MPH)	(KPH)
1	NORTH AMERICAN X-15	WILLIAM J. "PETE" KNIGHT	OCT 3, 1967	4,519	7,273
2	LOCKHEED SR-71 BLACKBIRD	ELDON W. JOERSZ & GEORGE T. MORGAN	JUL 28, 1976	2,193.2	3,529.6
3	LOCKHEED YF-12A	ROBERT L. STEPHENS & DANIEL ANDRE	MAY 1, 1965	2,070.1	3,331.5
4	MIKOYAN GUREVICH YE-166	GEORGII MOSOLOV	JUL 7, 1962	1,665.9	2,681
5	MCDONNELL-DOUGLAS F-4 PHANTOM II	ROBERT G. ROBERTSON	NOV 22, 1961	1,606.3	2,585.1
6	CONVAIR F-106 DELTA DART	JOSEPH ROGERS	DEC 15, 1959	1,525.9	2,455.7
7	LOCKHEED F-104C STARFIGHTER	W. W. IRWIN	MAY 16, 1958	1,404	2,259.5
8	MCDONNELL F-101A VOODOO	ADRIAN DREW	DEC 12, 1957	1,207.6	1,943.5
9	FAIREY DELTA 2	PETER TWISS	MAR 10, 1956	1,139.2	1,833.31
10	F-100C SUPER SABRE	HORACE A. HANES	AUG 20, 1955	822.1	1,323

HIGHEST ALTITUDES IN **HANG GLIDING & PARAGLIDING**

These solo contraptions rely purely on the aerodynamics, the wind, and expert control by their human pilots...

	PILOT	COUNTRY	HEIGHT (FT)	(M)
1	ROBBIE WHITTALL	UK	14,849.1	4,526
2	RICHARD WESTGATE	UK	14,370.1	4,380
3	ANTON RAUMAUF	AUSTRIA	14,301.2	4,359
4	LARRY TUDOR	USA	14,248.7	4,343
5	KAT THURSTON	UK	14,189.6	4,325
6	JUDY LEDEN	UK	13,024.9	3,970
7	RAINER M. SCHOLL	GERMANY	12,532.8	3,820
8	TOMÁS SUCHÁNEK	CZECHOSLOVAKIA	11,482.9	3,500
9	BURKHARD MARTENS	GERMANY	11,381.2	3,469
10	ROBERT SCHICK	USA	6,561.7	2,000

2 LOCKHEED SR-71 BLACKBIRD

Before it became public knowledge, the Lockheed SR-71 *Blackbird* was a military "black project" developed in the 1960s at a "black site." These phrases refer to highly classified, top-secret government projects. This aircraft's debut flight was on December 22, 1964, and 32 of them were built.

6 JUDY LEDEN

Three-time world champion Judy Leden was awarded an MBE (Member of the Order of the British Empire) in 1989. That year, she succeeded in being the first woman ever to cross the English Channel by hang glider.

TOP 10 PLANES WITH THE **LARGEST WINGSPANS**

When you consider that a skyscraper is defined as such because it is a minimum of 330 ft (100 m) high, these wingspans are truly astounding...

	PLANE	COUNTRY	DEBUT FLIGHT	WINGSPAN (FT)	(M)
1	HUGHES H-4 SPRUCE GOOSE	USA	NOV 2, 1947	319.8	97.5
2	ANTONOV AN-225 MRIYA	RUSSIA (SOVIET UNION ERA)	NOV 21, 1988	290	88.4
3	AIRBUS A380-800	EUROPE (VARIOUS)	APR 21, 2005	261.8	79.8
4	ANTONOV AN-124	RUSSIA (SOVIET UNION ERA)	DEC 26, 1982	240.5	73.3
5	CONVAIR B-36J-III	USA	AUG 8, 1946	230	70.1
=	CONVAIR XC-99	USA	NOV 23, 1947	230	70.1
7	BOEING 747-8F	USA	FEB 8, 2010	224.7	68.5
8	LOCKHEED C-5B	USA	JUN 30, 1968	222.7	67.9
9	BOEING 747-400	USA	FEB 9, 1969	211.3	64.4
=	ANTONOV AN-22	RUSSIA (SOVIET UNION ERA)	FEB 27, 1965	211.3	64.4

2 ANTONOV AN-225 MRIYA

This, the heaviest plane ever constructed (with a total payload of 559,580 lb / 253,821.2 kg), was created to transport the Russian space shuttle *Buran*. To date, only one An-225 has been built. Its maiden flight was on November 21, 1988, and it remains in service. A possible second unit may be developed and completed by 2019.

NATIONS' FIRST
ORBITAL LAUNCHES

Modern technological advances in the 21st century mean space exploration is easier than it was 60 years ago, when satellites were first sent up...

	COUNTRY	SATELLITE	DATE LAUNCHED
1	RUSSIA (SOVIET UNION ERA)	SPUTNIK 1	OCT 4, 1957
2	USA	EXPLORER 1	FEB 1, 1958
3	FRANCE	ASTÉRIX	NOV 26, 1965
4	JAPAN	OSUMI	FEB 11, 1970
5	CHINA	DONG FANG HONG I	APR 24, 1970
6	UK	PROSPERO	OCT 28, 1971
7	INDIA	ROHINI D1	JUL 18, 1980
8	ISRAEL	OFEQ 1	SEP 19, 1988
9	IRAN	OMID	FEB 2, 2009
10	NORTH KOREA	KWANGMYONGSONG-3 UNIT 2	DEC 12, 2012

2 EXPLORER 1

This, America's first ever satellite, achieved 111 days of orbit. It weighed just 30.8 lb (13.37 kg) and measured 80.8 in (205.1 cm) in length. Explorer 1 was able to transmit scientific data back to Earth via two radio antennas.

Some $13 billion was projected to be spent on making 28 of these presidential executive transport helicopters. However, the program was canceled in 2007. The nine that were built, costing nearly $4.5 billion, were sold to Canada and were used for spare parts.

TOP 10 MOST EXPENSIVE MILITARY HELICOPTERS

The roots of the helicopter go back to a spinning-top toy from China more than 2,000 years ago...

	HELICOPTER	COUNTRY OF MANUFACTURE	COST ($ MILLIONS)
1	LOCKHEED MARTIN VH-71 KESTREL	USA	400
2	SIKORSKY CH-53K KING STALLION	USA	92.8
3	BELL BOEING V-22 OSPREY	USA	72.1
4	BOEING AH-64D APACHE	USA	64
5	NHINDUSTRIES NH90	GERMANY	59
6	EC 665 TIGER	FRANCE / GERMANY / SPAIN	48
7	SIKORSKY SH-60 SEAHAWK	USA	42.9
8	BOEING CH-47F CHINOOK	USA	38.6
9	BELL AH-1Z VIPER	USA	31
10	KAMAN SH-2G SUPER SEASPRITE	USA	26

TOP **10**

FASTEST **HELICOPTERS**

As well as being designed for precision maneuverability, some helicopters can also achieve incredible speeds...

	HELICOPTER	COUNTRY	SPEED (MPH)	(KPH)
1	EUROCOPTER X³	FRANCE	293.3	472
2	MI-24LL PSV	RUSSIA	251.7	405
3	MIL MI-28 HAVOC	RUSSIA	201.3	324
4	KAMOV KA-50 BLACK SHARK	RUSSIA	195.7	315
=	BOEING CH-47 CHINOOK	USA	195.7	315
6	AGUSTAWESTLAND AW139	UK / ITALY	192.6	310
7	AGUSTAWESTLAND AW101	UK / ITALY	192	309
8	NHINDUSTRIES NH90	FRANCE / GERMANY / ITALY / NETHERLANDS	186.4	300
9	MIL MI-26 HALO	RUSSIA	183.3	295
10	BOEING AH-64 APACHE	USA	182.1	293

1 EUROCOPTER X³

The only copy of this high-speed helicopter has been on display in Le Bourget, France's *Musée de l'air et de l'espace*, since 2014. It weighs 11,464 lb (5,200 kg). In 2012, it won the American Helicopter Society's Howard Hughes Award, given for "outstanding improvement in fundamental vertical flight technology."

6 RICHARD MEREDITH-HARDY

The British microlight pilot (born August 23, 1957) holds multiple speed records as well as two World Microlight Championship titles. Meredith-Hardy has flown microlights for nearly 25 years. His interest in flying was piqued by a neighbor who had a two-seater microlight.

TOP 10

FASTEST **MICROLIGHT & PARAMOTOR CHAMPIONS**

These aerial vehicles weigh around 660–1,000 lb (300–455 kg) and are designed to hold no more than two people...

	PILOT	COUNTRY	SPEED (MPH)	(KPH)
1	ALBERTO RODOLFO PORTO	ITALY	201.2	323.82
2	ERIC DE BARBERIN-BARBERINI	FRANCE	186.7	300.51
3	PAVEL SKARYTKA	CZECHOSLOVAKIA	120.7	194.2
4	JEAN-LUC SOULLIER	BELGIUM	118	189.87
5	GORDON DOUGLAS	UK	106.8	171.86
6	RICHARD MEREDITH-HARDY	UK	79.5	128
7	ALBERT UKENA	FRANCE	63.5	102.25
8	RYAN D. SHAW	USA	50.1	80.55
9	THOMAS KELLER	GERMANY	49.5	79.6
10	DAVID ROTUREAU	FRANCE	39.9	64.17

TOP 10

FASTEST 0-60 MPH CARS

Especially in competitive racing, acceleration is everything, and these 10 cars are faster from a dead stop than any others...

	MODEL	TIME FROM 0 TO 60 MPH (SECS)
1	AMZ GRIMSEL ELECTRIC RACE CAR	1.5
2	INFINITI FORMULA 1 RED BULL RB11	1.7
3	FORD SVT BOSS MUSTANG 10.0L CONCEPT	1.9
4	LINGENFELTER CORVETTE 427	1.97
5	PORSCHE 918 SPYDER	2.2
=	HENNESSEY DODGE VIPER VENOM 1000TT	2.2
7	ARIEL ATOM 500	2.3
=	BUGATTI CHIRON	2.3
9	FERRARI LAFERRARI	2.4
=	BUGATTI VEYRON 16.4 GRAND SPORT VITESSE	2.4

2 INFINITI FORMULA 1 RED BULL RB11

This 1,548 lb (702 kg) race car was designed by English engineer Adrian Newey. He serves the Red Bull Racing F1 team as their Chief Technical Officer. In 2012, Newey was awarded an OBE (Officer of the Order of the British Empire) for his work in the motorsport industry.

INNOVATIONS

6 ▶ USS JOHN F. KENNEDY

Pictured is the only vessel in this class, the USS *John F. Kennedy* (CV-67). It was commissioned on September 7, 1968, and was taken out of service on August 1, 2007. With a full load, it weighed 182,171,620 lb (82,631,656.9 kg / 82,655 tons).

TOP 10 LONGEST **BATTLESHIPS**

From all-wooden ships, to the first classes of ironclad battleships, to these, the most colossal vessels to currently sail the seven seas...

	BATTLESHIP / CLASS	COUNTRY	LENGTH (FT)	(M)
1	USS ENTERPRISE	USA	1,122	342
2	GERALD R. FORD	USA	1,105.6	337
3	NIMITZ	USA	1,092.5	333
4	KITTY HAWK	USA	1,072.8	327
5	FORRESTAL CLASS	USA	1,066.3	325
6	USS JOHN F. KENNEDY	USA	1,049.9	320
7	MIDWAY	USA	1,003.9	306
8	ADMIRAL KUZNETSOV	RUSSIA	990.8	302
9	QUEEN ELIZABETH	UK	931.8	284
10	KIEV	RUSSIA	928.5	283

4468

164

TOP 10 FASTEST **STEAM LOCOMOTIVES**

Don't be fooled into thinking that these coal-stoked engines mean that steam power equals slow speeds...

	TRAIN	COUNTRY	YEAR	TOP SPEED (MPH)	(KPH)
1	LNER CLASS A4 4468 MALLARD	UK	1938	126	202.6
2	BORSIG DRG SERIES 05 002	GERMANY	1936	125	200.4
3	PENNSYLVANIA RAILROAD E2 #7002	USA	1905	115	185.07
4	BR 18 201	GERMANY	1972	113	182.4
5	MILWAUKEE ROAD CLASS A	USA	1935	112.5	181.1
6	LNER CLASS A4 2509 SILVER LINK	UK	1935	112	180.3
7	LNER CLASS A3 2750 PAPYRUS	UK	1935	105	168.5
8	MILWAUKEE ROAD CLASS F6	USA	1934	104	166.6
9	GWR 3700 CLASS 3440 CITY OF TRURO	UK	1904	102	164
10	LNER CLASS A3 4472 FLYING SCOTSMAN	UK	1934	100	161

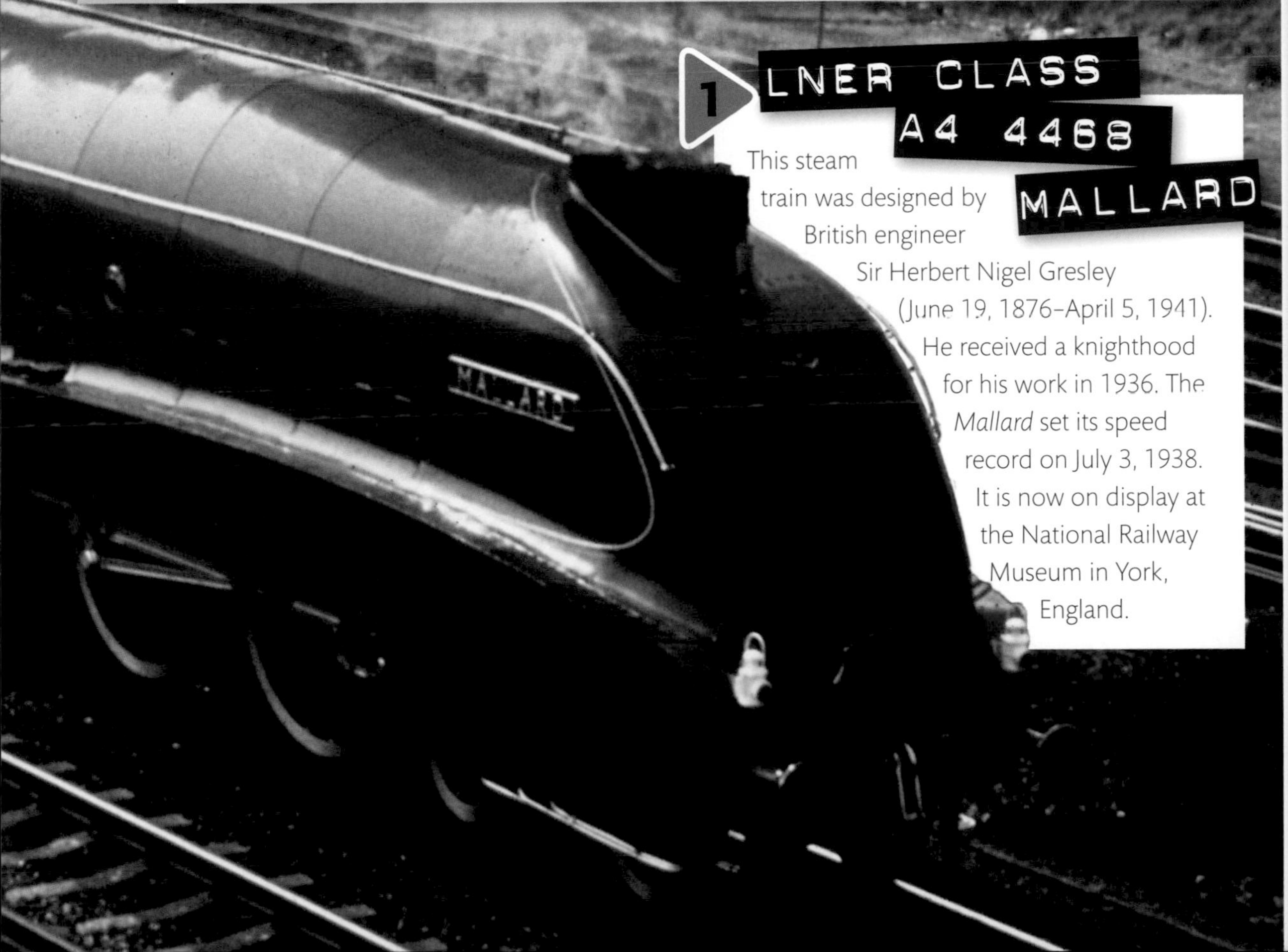

1 LNER CLASS A4 4468 MALLARD

This steam train was designed by British engineer Sir Herbert Nigel Gresley (June 19, 1876–April 5, 1941). He received a knighthood for his work in 1936. The *Mallard* set its speed record on July 3, 1938. It is now on display at the National Railway Museum in York, England.

TOP 10 | BIGGEST **VEHICLES OF ALL**

Combining every vehicle that travels across the ground, on or under the waves, and through the skies, these are the biggest ever constructed...

	TYPE	NAME	COUNTRY	SIZE (FT)	(M)
1	TRAIN	BHP IRON ORE	AUSTRALIA	24,124	7,353
2	LAND TRANSPORTER	F60 OVERBURDEN CONVEYOR	GERMANY	1,647	502.01
3	SHIP	SEAWISE GIANT OIL TANKER	JAPAN	1,504.1	458.46
4	AIRCRAFT CARRIER	USS ENTERPRISE	USA	1,122	342
5	AIRSHIP	HINDENBURG & GRAF ZEPPELIN II	GERMANY	803.8	245
6	SUBMARINE	TYPHOON-CLASS	RUSSIA	574.15	175
7	SPACE STATION	INTERNATIONAL SPACE STATION	USA / CANADA / RUSSIA / JAPAN / EUROPE	356*	108.5*
8	PLANE	HUGHES H4 HERCULES	USA	319.92**	97.51**
9	HELICOPTER	MIL V-12	RUSSIA (SOVIET UNION ERA)	121.39	37
10	TANK	CHAR 2C / FCM 2C	FRANCE	33.69	10.27

ALL MEASUREMENTS ARE VEHICLE LENGTHS EXCEPT: *WIDTH AND **WINGSPAN

1 BHP IRON ORE

A single driver led the 682 wagons loaded with iron ore on this record-setting train journey on June 21, 2001. The total weight of cargo and train approached 220,400,000 lb (99,971,758.3 kg / 100,000 tons). Its length displayed in the above chart equates to 4.6 mi (7.4 km).

TOP 10

FASTEST **VEHICLES OF ALL**

Comparing every kind of vehicle, if extreme speed is the objective, these are the 10 that come out on top...

	TYPE	NAME	COUNTRY	TOP SPEED (MPH)	(KPH)
1	ROCKET	APOLLO 10	USA	24,791	39,897
2	HYPERSONIC CRUISE VEHICLE	FALCON HTV-2	USA	13,000	20,921.47
3	ROCKET PLANE	NORTH AMERICAN X-15	USA	4,520	7,274.24
4	PLANE	LOCKHEED SR-71 BLACKBIRD	USA	2,193.6	3,529.6
5	JET-ENGINE CAR	THRUSTSSC	UK	763.04	1,227.98
6	UNMANNED AERIAL VEHICLE	BARRACUDA	GERMANY / SPAIN	647	1,041.3
7	CAR	BLUEBIRD CN7	AUSTRALIA	440	710
8	MOTORCYCLE	TOP 1 ACK ATTACK	USA	376.36	605.7
9	TRAIN	L0 SERIES SCMAGLEV	JAPAN	375	603.5
10	BOAT	SPIRIT OF AUSTRALIA	AUSTRALIA	345	555.21

5  THRUSTSSC

The British-made ThrustSSC's land-speed record has not been beaten in over two decades, since it was set on October 15, 1997, in Nevada, USA's Black Rock Desert. It was driven by Andy Green, a wing commander with the Royal Air Force.

Outer
SPACE

TOP 10

FIRST 10 **WOMEN IN SPACE**

On April 24, 2017, Peggy Whitson of the USA broke the record for the most cumulative time spent in space of any NASA astronaut. These are the first 10 female astronauts...

	ASTRONAUT	COUNTRY	MISSION	LAUNCH DATE
1	VALENTINA TERESHKOVA	RUSSIA (SOVIET UNION ERA)	VOSTOK 6	JUN 16, 1963
2	SVETLANA SAVITSKAYA	RUSSIA (SOVIET UNION ERA)	SOYUZ T-5	JUL 19, 1982
3	SALLY RIDE	USA	STS-7	JUN 18, 1983
4	JUDITH RESNIK	USA	STS-41-D	AUG 30, 1984
5	KATHRYN D. SULLIVAN	USA	STS-41-G	OCT 5, 1984
6	ANNA LEE FISHER	USA	STS-51-A	NOV 8, 1984
7	MARGARET RHEA SEDDON	USA	STS-51-D	APR 12, 1985
8	SHANNON LUCID	USA	STS-51-G	JUN 17, 1985
9	BONNIE J. DUNBAR	USA	STS-61-A	OCT 30, 1985
10	MARY L. CLEAVE	USA	STS-61-B	NOV 26, 1985

3 SALLY RIDE

Los Angeles-born physicist Sally Ride (May 26, 1951–July 23, 2012) became the first American woman to travel into space as part of NASA's STS-7 mission. This was the second flight of *Challenger*, the seventh Space Shuttle mission for the US agency. During her NASA career she helped develop the SRMS (Shuttle Remote Manipulator System) robotic arm.

2 ALAN SHEPARD

The first American in space was Alan Shepard (November 18, 1923–July 21, 1998). Born in Derry, New Hampshire, prior to becoming an astronaut with NASA, Shepard served in the US Navy during World War II. His first space flight lasted 15 minutes and 28 seconds, his capsule splashing down in the North Atlantic Ocean.

TOP 10 FIRST 10 **MEN IN SPACE**

Russia and the USA's space race began in the mid-1950s, and carried through to the following decade...

	ASTRONAUT	COUNTRY	MISSION	LAUNCH DATE
1	YURI GAGARIN	RUSSIA (SOVIET UNION ERA)	VOSTOK 1	APR 12, 1961
2	ALAN SHEPARD	USA	MERCURY 3	MAY 5, 1961
3	GUS GRISSOM	USA	MERCURY 4	JUL 21, 1961
4	GHERMAN TITOV	RUSSIA (SOVIET UNION ERA)	VOSTOK 2	AUG 6, 1961
5	JOHN GLENN	USA	MERCURY 6	FEB 20,1962
6	SCOTT CARPENTER	USA	MERCURY 7	MAY 24, 1962
7	ANDRIYAN NIKOLAYEV	RUSSIA (SOVIET UNION ERA)	VOSTOK 3	AUG 11, 1962
8	PAVEL POPOVICH	RUSSIA (SOVIET UNION ERA)	VOSTOK 4	AUG 12, 1962
9	WALTER SCHIRRA	USA	MERCURY 8	OCT 3, 1962
10	GORDON COOPER	USA	MERCURY 9	MAY 15, 1963

TOP 10

LONGEST HUMAN **SPACE FLIGHTS**

Not to be confused with "cumulative" days in space, this chart examines astronauts who have had the longest single-trip missions...

	ASTRONAUT	COUNTRY	CONSECUTIVE DAYS IN SPACE
1	VALERI POLYAKOV	RUSSIA	437.7
2	SERGEI AVDEYEV	RUSSIA	379.6
3	VLADIMIR TITOV	RUSSIA (SOVIET UNION ERA)	365
=	MUSA MANAROV	RUSSIA (SOVIET UNION ERA)	365
5	SCOTT KELLY	USA	340.4
=	MIKHAIL KORNIENKO	RUSSIA	340.4
7	YURI ROMANENKO	RUSSIA (SOVIET UNION ERA)	326.5
8	SERGEI KRIKALEV	RUSSIA (INCL. SOVIET UNION ERA)	311.8
9	VALERI POLYAKOV	RUSSIA (SOVIET UNION ERA)	240.9
10	LEONID KIZIM / VLADIMIR SOLOVYOV / OLEG ATKOV	RUSSIA (SOVIET UNION ERA)	237

5 SCOTT KELLY

Not only a record-breaking astronaut, Scott Kelly's career also saw him serve as a US Navy captain. He retired from the navy in June 2012, and retired from NASA in April 2016. His consecutive-days record was from the year-long mission on board the ISS, a project that provided key data for what happens to the human body after long periods of being in space.

1 GENNADY PADALKA

As well as Gennady Padalka's number one record on this chart, his career also includes 10 EVAs (spacewalks) culminating in nearly 39 hours of outside-the-craft activity. Padalka has been awarded several medals for his work, including the highest honor a Russian civilian can receive, the title of Hero of the Russian Federation.

TOP 10 MOST TIME **SPENT IN SPACE (MULTIPLE MISSIONS)**

Although NASA astronauts have set many different records, it is Russia's space agency that dominates this particular top 10...

	ASTRONAUT	COUNTRY	TOTAL FLIGHTS	TOTAL TIME IN SPACE (DAYS)
1	GENNADY PADALKA	RUSSIA	5	879.5
2	YURI MALENCHENKO	RUSSIA	6	827.4
3	SERGEI KRIKALEV	RUSSIA*	6	803.4
4	ALEKSANDR KALERI	RUSSIA	5	769.3
5	SERGEI AVDEYEV	RUSSIA*	3	747.6
6	VALERI POLYAKOV	RUSSIA*	2	678.7
7	ANATOLY SOLOVYEV	RUSSIA*	5	651.1
8	VIKTOR AFANASYEV	RUSSIA*	4	555.8
9	YURY USACHEV	RUSSIA	4	552.8
10	PAVEL VINOGRADOV	RUSSIA	3	546.9

*INCLUDES MISSION(S) DURING SOVIET UNION ERA

TOP 10 FIRST **SPACEWALKS**

When an astronaut has to carry out a task outside the safety of their craft or station, it is described as a spacewalk...

	ASTRONAUT	COUNTRY	MISSION	SPACEWALK TIME (MINS)	DATE
1	ALEXEY LEONOV	RUSSIA (SOVIET UNION ERA)	VOSKHOD 2	15	MAR 18, 1965
2	EDWARD WHITE	USA	GEMINI 4	20	JUN 3, 1965
3	EUGENE CERNAN	USA	GEMINI 9A	127	JUN 5, 1966
4	MICHAEL COLLINS	USA	GEMINI 10	49	JUL 19, 1966
5	MICHAEL COLLINS	USA	GEMINI 10	39	JUL 20, 1966
6	RICHARD GORDON	USA	GEMINI 11	33	SEP 13, 1966
7	RICHARD GORDON	USA	GEMINI 11	128	SEP 14, 1966
8	BUZZ ALDRIN	USA	GEMINI 12	149	NOV 12, 1966
9	BUZZ ALDRIN	USA	GEMINI 12	126	NOV 13, 1966
10	BUZZ ALDRIN	USA	GEMINI 12	55	NOV 14, 1966

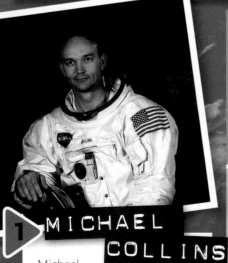

1 MICHAEL COLLINS

Michael Collins was the first American astronaut to complete more than one EVA. His total time in space is just over 11 days, as part of Gemini 10 (1966) and then Apollo 11 (1969), the Moon-landing mission.

TOP 10 NATIONS WITH THE **MOST SPACEWALKERS**

If you've seen the 2013 film *Gravity*, you will be familiar with what spacewalk tasks can look like...

	NATION	TOTAL SPACEWALKERS
1	USA	129
2	RUSSIA (INCL. SOVIET UNION ERA)	63
3	CANADA	3
=	JAPAN	3
=	FRANCE	3
6	CHINA	2
=	GERMANY	2
8	SWEDEN	1
=	ITALY	1
=	SWITZERLAND / UK	1

2 EDWARD WHITE

Edward White's successful
Gemini 4 mission, with fellow crew member
James McDivitt, lasted just over four
days. Tragically, White, along with fellow
astronauts Virgil "Gus" Grissom and
Roger B. Chaffee, died in a fire that broke
out during Apollo 1's pre-launch test on
January 27, 1967.

1 INTA

INTA, Spain's National Institute of Aerospace Technology, launched its first satellite on November 15, 1974. Its headquarters are located in Torrejón de Ardoz, near Madrid. The Intasat was launched from a NASA Delta rocket. OPTOS is INTA's latest satellite, functional since 2013.

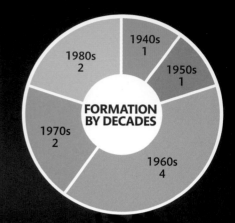

FORMATION BY DECADES

- 1940s: 1
- 1950s: 1
- 1960s: 4
- 1970s: 2
- 1980s: 2

TOP 10 LONGEST-RUNNING OPERATIONAL SPACE AGENCIES

Several nations' space agencies have existed in different forms before their current ones. However, these are the longest-running ones that are operational now...

	AGENCY	COUNTRY	YEAR FOUNDED
1	INTA (INSTITUTO NACIONAL DE TÉCNICA AEROESPACIAL)	SPAIN	1942
2	NASA (NATIONAL AERONAUTICS & SPACE ADMINISTRATION)	USA	1958
3	CNES (CENTRE NATIONAL D'ÉTUDES SPATIALES)	FRANCE	1961
=	SUPARCO (SPACE AND UPPER ATMOSPHERE RESEARCH COMMISSION)	PAKISTAN	1961
5	DLR (GERMAN AEROSPACE CENTER)	GERMANY	1969
=	ISRO (INDIAN SPACE RESEARCH ORGANISATION)	INDIA	1969
7	SNSB (SWEDISH NATIONAL SPACE BOARD)	SWEDEN	1972
8	ESA (EUROPEAN SPACE AGENCY)	(EUROPEAN SYNDICATION)	1975
9	ASI (ITALIAN SPACE AGENCY)	ITALY	1988
10	CSA (CANADIAN SPACE AGENCY)	CANADA	1989

TOP 10 MOST ASTRONAUTS LAUNCHED BY A NATION

In total, how many people would you guess have been launched into space? The results of the countries that have sent the most people up in rockets are below...

	COUNTRY	TOTAL PEOPLE SENT INTO SPACE
1	USA	336
2	RUSSIA (INCL. SOVIET UNION ERA)	122
3	GERMANY	11
=	CHINA	11
=	JAPAN	11
6	FRANCE	10
7	CANADA	9
8	ITALY	7
9	BELGIUM / NETHERLANDS	2
=	BULGARIA / UK	2

1 USA

In April 2017, NASA revealed its five-phase plan to lead toward sending astronauts to Mars by 2033. However, Elon Musk's SpaceX (Space Exploration Technologies Corporation) and American aviation company Boeing are attempting to reach the red planet by 2022.

TOP 10 LONGEST AMOUNT OF **TIME SPENT IN SPACE**

Ranking this subject by nation, instead of by individual astronauts, these are the 10 countries that have notched up the most humans-in-space time...

	COUNTRY	TOTAL HUMAN DAYS IN SPACE
1	RUSSIA (INCL. SOVIET UNION ERA)	26,111.78
2	USA	18,451.5
3	JAPAN	1,186.54
4	GERMANY	658.97
5	ITALY	627.22
6	CANADA	506.15
7	FRANCE	432.19
8	NETHERLANDS	210.69
9	BELGIUM	207.66
10	UK	193.81

MIR

Russia's *Mir* was the first ever human-made space station. It was built in orbit between the years of 1986 and 1996, and was staffed by a crew for more than 12 years. Due to a lack of funding, *Mir* was destroyed via a controlled re-entry into the Earth's atmosphere on March 23, 2001. Fragments could be witnessed burning up in the skies over the South Pacific region.

INTERNATIONAL SPACE STATION

The *International Space Station* is a project born out of the collaboration of five different space agencies: ESA (Europe), CSA (Canada), JAXA (Japan), NASA (USA), and Roscosmos (Russia). It weighs around 925,000 lb (419,572.9 kg), and has a solar array wingspan of 240 ft (73.2 m). The *ISS* is four times the size the *Mir* space station was, and has eight miles of wires for its power system.

TOP **10**

MOST ISS VISITS BY NATION

The *International Space Station* is a joint venture between nations but the astronauts from just two countries have visited it more than any others...

	NATION	INDIVIDUAL(S)	ISS CREW MEMBER(S)
1	USA	142	49
2	RUSSIA	46	39
3	JAPAN	8	6
4	CANADA	7	2
5	ITALY	5	3
6	GERMANY	3	2
7	FRANCE	3	1
8	BELGIUM	1	1
=	NETHERLANDS	1	1
=	UK	1	1

TOP 10 BIGGEST SPACE PROGRAMS

Space exploration, while exciting and beneficial to our understanding of our place in the universe, is an extremely costly venture...

	AGENCY	COUNTRY	BUDGET ($ MILLIONS)
1	NASA (NATIONAL AERONAUTICS & SPACE ADMINISTRATION)	USA	19,300
2	ROSCOSMOS (RUSSIAN FEDERAL SPACE AGENCY)	RUSSIA	5,600
3	ESA (EUROPEAN SPACE AGENCY)	(EUROPEAN SYNDICATION)	5,510
4	CNES (CENTRE NATIONAL D'ÉTUDES SPATIALES)	FRANCE	2,500
5	JAXA (JAPAN AEROSPACE EXPLORATION AGENCY)	JAPAN	2,460
6	DLR (GERMAN AEROSPACE CENTER)	GERMANY	2,000
7	ASI (ITALIAN SPACE AGENCY)	ITALY	1,800
8	CNSA (CHINA NATIONAL SPACE ADMINISTRATION)	CHINA	1,780
9	ISRO (INDIAN SPACE RESEARCH ORGANISATION)	INDIA	1,200
10	CSA (CANADIAN SPACE AGENCY)	CANADA	488.7

3 ESA

ESA was first established on May 30, 1975. Its headquarters are in Paris, France. Its 22 member nations amount to a worldwide staff of more than 2,000 people. Canada is also an associated member. ESA is not affiliated with the EU (European Union).

TOP 10 NATIONS' FIRST
LAUNCHED SATELLITES

Going back to where the development of space probes began, these represent the first satellites that these countries put up there...

	COUNTRY	SATELLITE	DATE
1	SOVIET UNION (NOW RUSSIA)	SPUTNIK 1	OCT 4, 1957
2	USA	EXPLORER 1	FEB 1, 1958
3	UK	ARIEL 1	APR 26, 1962
4	CANADA	ALOUETTE 1	SEP 29, 1962
5	ITALY	SAN MARCO 1	DEC 15, 1964
6	FRANCE	ASTÉRIX	NOV 26, 1965
7	AUSTRALIA	WRESAT	NOV 29, 1967
8	GERMANY	AZUR	NOV 8, 1969
9	JAPAN	OSUMI	FEB 11, 1970
10	CHINA	DONG FANG HONG 1	APR 24, 1970

1 SPUTNIK 1

This was the first human-made artificial satellite successfully put into orbit above the Earth. Its construction was led by Mikhail S. Khomyakov at OKB-1, a Russian spacecraft parts manufacturer. It completed 1,440 orbits during its 21-day mission.

TOP 10
PLANETS / DWARF PLANETS
WITH THE LARGEST SURFACE AREA

If Earth sometimes feels like a massive place to live, check out the sizes of our neighboring planets higher up on this chart...

	NAME	TYPE	SURFACE AREA (SQUARE MI)	(SQUARE KM)
1	JUPITER	PLANET	23,713,907,537.2	61,418,738,571
2	SATURN	PLANET	16,452,636,641.4	42,612,133,285
3	URANUS	PLANET	3,120,894,516	8,083,079,690
4	NEPTUNE	PLANET	2,941,431,558.2	7,618,272,763
5	EARTH	PLANET	196,936,993.6	510,064,472
6	VENUS	PLANET	177,697,463.2	460,234,317
7	MARS	PLANET	55,742,105.7	144,371,391
8	MERCURY	PLANET	28,879,283.2	74,797,000
9	ERIS	DWARF PLANET	6,562,533.2	16,996,883.3
10	PLUTO	DWARF PLANET	6,427,805.6	16,647,940

MAKEMAKE

This dwarf planet was discovered on March 31, 2005. Ten years later, NASA's Hubble Space Telescope first observed Makemake's moon, currently nicknamed MK2.

3 SATURN

This planet's famous rings are
made up of billions of particles.
Some of these are as big as mountains, but
others resemble specks of dust. Saturn has
53 confirmed moons, but a further nine are
classified as "provisional" at this time.

TOP 10
CELESTIAL BODIES
WITH THE LARGEST VOLUME

Although Jupiter heads both of the charts on these pages in terms of
planets, take a close look at how much bigger the Sun is...

	NAME	TYPE	VOLUME (CUBIC MI)	(CUBIC KM)
1	THE SUN	STAR	338,102,469,632,763,000	1,409,272,569,059,860,000
2	JUPITER	PLANET	343,382,767,518,322	1,431,281,810,739,360
3	SATURN	PLANET	198,439,019,647,006	827,129,915,150,897
4	URANUS	PLANET	16,394,283,780,641	68,334,355,695,584
5	NEPTUNE	PLANET	15,000,714,125,712	62,525,703,987,421
6	EARTH	PLANET	259,875,159,532	1,083,206,916,846
7	VENUS	PLANET	222,738,686,740	928,415,345,893
8	MARS	PLANET	39,133,515,914	163,115,609,799
9	GANYMEDE	MOON	18,306,424,766	76,304,506,998
10	TITAN	MOON	17,152,879,380	71,496,320,086

9 CERES

Ceres was first observed by Italian astronomer and priest Giuseppe Piazzi (July 16, 1746–July 22, 1826) on January 1, 1801. It was classified as an asteroid until 2006. NASA's *Dawn* spacecraft (launched September 27, 2007) orbited Ceres in 2015, making it the first dwarf planet a man-made craft has reached.

TOP 10 PLANETS / DWARF PLANETS
WITH THE GREATEST ORBIT

Some planets / dwarf planets have a shorter orbital journey around the Sun than others, but these 10 travel immense distances...

	NAME	TYPE	ORBIT SIZE AROUND THE SUN (MI)	(KM)
1	ERIS	DWARF PLANET	6,325,635,074	10,180,122,852
2	MAKEMAKE	DWARF PLANET	4,214,975,546	6,783,345,606
3	HAUMEA	DWARF PLANET	3,996,666,630	6,432,011,461
4	PLUTO	DWARF PLANET	3,670,092,055	5,906,440,628
5	NEPTUNE	PLANET	2,795,173,960	4,498,396,441
6	URANUS	PLANET	1,783,744,300	2,870,658,186
7	SATURN	PLANET	886,489,415	1,426,666,422
8	JUPITER	PLANET	483,638,564	778,340,821
9	CERES	DWARF PLANET	257,055,204	413,690,250
10	MARS	PLANET	141,637,725	227,943,824

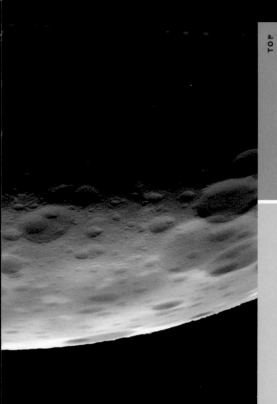

TOP 10

FASTEST PLANETS / DWARF PLANETS
ORBITING OUR SUN

We have determined that the time it takes Earth to complete one full orbit of the Sun is one year, but other planets have very different timescales...

	NAME	DAYS FOR ONE ORBIT OF THE SUN
1	MERCURY	87.97
2	VENUS	224.7
3	EARTH	365.26
4	MARS	686.98
5	CERES	1,680.19
6	JUPITER	4,332.82
7	SATURN	10,755.7
8	URANUS	30,687.15
9	NEPTUNE	60,190.03
10	PLUTO	90,553.02

1 MERCURY

Mercury has an orbit distance of 35,983,125 mi (57,909,227 km). During the arc of its orbit when it is closest to the Sun, it is still 29 million mi (47 million km) away from it. Mercury moves through space at around 31 mi (49.9 km) per second.

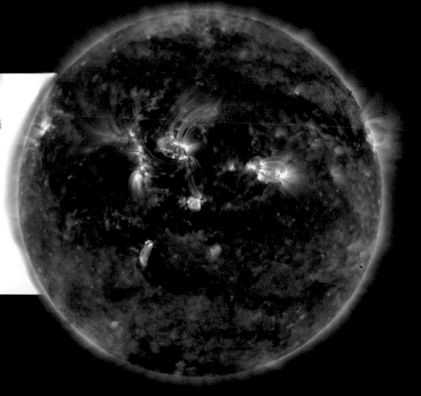

TOP 10 BIGGEST MASSES **IN OUR SOLAR SYSTEM**

The masses below are featured in pounds and kilograms so you can compare them to other weights elsewhere in this book. Earth is 13 septillion (24 zeroes) lb compared to the Sun's 4.3 nonillion (30 zeroes) lb...

	NAME	TYPE	WEIGHT (LB)	(KG)
1	THE SUN	STAR	4,385,214,857,119,400,000,000,000,000,000	1,989,100,000,000,000,000,000,000,000,000
2	JUPITER	PLANET	4,184,660,337,117,234,000,000,000,000	1,898,130,000,000,000,000,000,000,000
3	SATURN	PLANET	1,252,928,923,798,754,200,000,000,000	568,319,000,000,000,000,000,000,000
4	NEPTUNE	PLANET	225,775,402,698,538,000,000,000,000	102,410,000,000,000,000,000,000,000
5	URANUS	PLANET	191,383,951,185,244,540,000,000,000	86,810,300,000,000,000,000,000,000
6	EARTH	PLANET	13,166,425,175,687,742,000,000,000	5,972,190,000,000,000,000,000,000
7	VENUS	PLANET	10,730,603,779,539,576,000,000,000	4,867,320,000,000,000,000,000,000
8	MARS	PLANET	1,414,690,904,050,707,400,000,000	641,693,000,000,000,000,000,000
9	MERCURY	PLANET	727,754,745,946,667,200,000,000	330,104,000,000,000,000,000,000
10	GANYMEDE	MOON	326,693,870,251,330,477,251,333.6	148,185,846,875,052,000,000,000

4 PLUTO

Since its discovery on February 18, 1930, Pluto was originally called a planet for 76 years. However, in 2006 the International Astronomical Union reclassified how a "planet" should be defined, leading Pluto to be described as a dwarf planet.

SUN VS. EARTH

This visual comparison shows just how colossal the Sun is...

SUN

• EARTH

5 URANUS

To date, Uranus has 27 moons and 13 rings (albeit, very faint ones). The latest two rings were discovered on December 22, 2005. Uranus is known as an "ice giant" because it is composed mostly of ammonia, methane, and water. Uranus and Venus are the only planets that rotate east to west.

TOP 10

SMALLEST PLANETS / DWARF PLANETS **IN OUR SOLAR SYSTEM**

If you are unfamiliar with some of the names of the dwarf planets in this top 10, find out more about these members of our solar system...

	NAME	TYPE	EQUATORIAL RADIUS (MI)	(KM)
1	CERES	DWARF PLANET	295.9	476.2
2	MAKEMAKE	DWARF PLANET	445.523	717
3	HAUMEA	DWARF PLANET	471.621 TO 608.944*	759 TO 980*
4	PLUTO	DWARF PLANET	715.2	1,151
5	ERIS	DWARF PLANET	722.7	1,163
6	MERCURY	PLANET	1,516	2,439.7
7	MARS	PLANET	2,106.1	3,389.5
8	VENUS	PLANET	3,760.4	6,051.8
9	EARTH	PLANET	3,958.75	6,371
10	NEPTUNE	PLANET	15,299.4	24,622

*DUE TO ITS ELONGATED SHAPE

HOTTEST **PLANETS / DWARF PLANETS**

Even if we had the technology to travel great distances to other planets, the temperatures on them are vastly different to Earth...

	NAME	TYPE	HOTTEST EFFECTIVE TEMPERATURE RECORDED	
			(°F)	(°C)
1	VENUS	PLANET	863.6	462
2	MERCURY	PLANET	800.6	427
3	EARTH	PLANET	136.4	58
4	MARS	PLANET	70	20
5	CERES	DWARF PLANET	-157	-105
6	JUPITER	PLANET	-234	-148
7	SATURN	PLANET	-288	-178
8	NEPTUNE	PLANET	-353	-214
9	URANUS	PLANET	-357	-216
10	PLUTO	DWARF PLANET	-369	-223

3 EARTH

The name of our planet dates back at least 1,000 years. As well as data about space, NASA's satellites also relay back key information to help us understand things affecting our planet such as pollution and climate change. Another 30 planets the size of ours could fit between Earth and the Moon.

9 ▶ MARS

The "red planet" has two moons, Phobos and Deimos. Its distinct coloring comes from the iron in the soil oxidizing, creating its rusty hue. NASA's *MAVEN* (Mars Atmosphere and Volatile Evolution Mission) craft has detected iron, magnesium, and sodium ions present in Mars' atmosphere since 2015.

TOP 10 COLDEST PLANETS / DWARF PLANETS

It's not just extreme heat that would be an issue for us to deal with on the surface of celestial objects in our solar system...

	NAME	TYPE	COLDEST EFFECTIVE TEMPERATURE RECORDED (°F)	(°C)
1	HAUMEA	DWARF PLANET	-401.8	-241
2	MAKEMAKE	DWARF PLANET	-398.2	-239
3	PLUTO	DWARF PLANET	-387	-233
4	ERIS	DWARF PLANET	-383.8	-231
5	URANUS	PLANET	-357	-216
6	NEPTUNE	PLANET	-353	-214
7	SATURN	PLANET	-288	-178
8	JUPITER	PLANET	-234	-148
9	MARS	PLANET	-225	-143
10	CERES	DWARF PLANET	-157	-105

TOP 10 PLANETS / DWARF PLANETS WITH LONGEST DAYS

Using what we determine a day to be (sunrise to the following sunrise the next morning), living on Mercury would feel like a very, very long day...

	NAME	TYPE	HOURS
1	MERCURY	PLANET	4,222.6
2	VENUS	PLANET	2,802
3	PLUTO	PLANET	153.28
4	ERIS	DWARF PLANET	25.9
5	MARS	PLANET	24.66
6	EARTH	PLANET	23.93
7	MAKEMAKE	DWARF PLANET	22.48
8	URANUS	PLANET	17.24
9	NEPTUNE	PLANET	16.11
10	SATURN	PLANET	10.66

9 NEPTUNE

Voyager 2 is the only craft to have visited Neptune, back in 1989. The space probe was launched on August 20, 1977, and achieved a distance of 3,080 mi (4,956.8 km) above the planet's north pole on August 25, 1989. In 2013, a study of archival images captured by NASA's Hubble Space Telescope revealed an as-yet unnamed 14th moon orbiting this dark, extremely windy planet. For now, this moon has been logged as "S/2004 N 1."

1 JUPITER

Being the biggest planet in our solar system, it's appropriate that Jupiter is named after the king of the Roman gods of the same name. A day on Jupiter lasts just 9.93 hours. It has an equatorial circumference of 272,945.9 mi (439,263.8 km). It could have a solid core approximately the size of Earth, but it is mostly comprised of hydrogen and helium gas.

TOP 10

PLANETS / DWARF PLANETS
WITH STRONGEST GRAVITY

The stronger the gravity, the more things weigh. If you weighed 100 lb on Earth, you would weigh more than 250 lb on Jupiter...

	NAME	TYPE	EQUATORIAL GRAVITY (m/s^2)
1	JUPITER	PLANET	23.12
2	NEPTUNE	PLANET	11
3	SATURN	PLANET	10.44
4	EARTH	PLANET	9.81
5	VENUS	PLANET	8.87
6	URANUS	PLANET	8.69
7	MARS	PLANET	3.71
8	MERCURY	PLANET	3.7
9	HAUMEA	DWARF PLANET	0.63
10	PLUTO	DWARF PLANET	0.62

TOP 10 TALLEST MOUNTAINS **IN OUR SOLAR SYSTEM**

If you think that the mountains on Earth are large, look at the size of the ones that are found elsewhere in space...

NAME	LOCATION	TYPE	HIGHEST POINT (MI)	(BASE TO PEAK) (KM)
1 OLYMPUS MONS	MARS	PLANET	16.2	26
2 RHEASILVIA	VESTA	MINOR PLANET	15.5	25
3 ARSIA MONS	MARS	PLANET	12.4	20
= EQUATORIAL RIDGE	LAPETUS	MOON	12.4	20
5 ASCRAEUS MONS	MARS	PLANET	11.3	18.2
= SOUTH BOÖSAULE	IO	MOON	11.3	18.2
7 ELYSIUM MONS	MARS	PLANET	9.9	16
8 PAVONIS MONS	MARS	PLANET	8.7	14
9 EUBOEA MONTES	IO	MOON	8.3	13.4
10 IONIAN MONS	IO	MOON	7.9	12.7

TOP 10 BIGGEST **MOONS**

Jupiter's moon Ganymede is almost four times bigger than Earth's, whereas Uranus' Oberon is 10 times smaller than ours...

NAME	ORBITS	VOLUME (CUBIC MI)	(CUBIC KM)
1 GANYMEDE	JUPITER	18,306,424,766	76,304,506,998
2 TITAN	SATURN	17,152,879,380	71,496,320,086
3 CALLISTO	JUPITER	14,071,981,516	58,654,577,603
4 IO	JUPITER	6,074,366,707	25,319,064,907
5 THE MOON	EARTH	5,271,283,736	21,971,669,064
6 EUROPA	JUPITER	3,821,058,818	15,926,867,918
7 TRITON	NEPTUNE	2,491,268,118	10,384,058,491
8 TITANIA	URANUS	493,409,858	2,056,622,001
9 RHEA	SATURN	448,676,716	1,870,166,133
10 OBERON	URANUS	443,588,799	1,848,958,769

1 ▷ OLYMPUS MONS

This mountain, a shield volcano, is situated in Mars' Tharsis Montes region, and has a diameter of 374 mi (601.9 km). This area of Mars features three other shield volcanoes: Arsia Mons, Ascraeus Mons, and Pavonis Mons. As a comparison, Olympus Mons is two-and-a-half times higher than Mount Everest.

MOST MOONS

Of the planets featured in the Biggest Moons chart, here's how many moons they have...

67	62	14	27	1
JUPITER	SATURN	NEPTUNE	URANUS	EARTH

4 ▷ IO

Of Jupiter's 67 moons (14 of which have yet to be given official names), Io was first discovered in 1610 by Italian astronomer and physicist Galileo Galilei (February 15, 1564– January 8, 1642). It has been classified as the most volcanically active celestial body in our solar system.

LUNAR VS. SOLAR ECLIPSES

The main difference between these two kinds of eclipses is that lunars occur at nighttime and solars during the day. When the Earth is between its Moon and the Sun, a lunar eclipse occurs. A solar eclipse (the more well known of the two) is when the Moon is between the Sun and Earth, blocking the Sun from view.

TOP 10

NEXT 10 LUNAR & SOLAR ECLIPSES

If you're fascinated by eclipses, this next top 10 is for you. Grab your diary and make a note of these events coming up over the next two years...

	TIME (UTC*)	DATE	TYPE OF ECLIPSE
1	10:51:13	JAN 31, 2018	LUNAR (TOTAL)
2	18:55	FEB 15, 2018	SOLAR (PARTIAL)
3	01:48	JUL 13, 2018	SOLAR (PARTIAL)
4	17:14	JUL 27, 2018	LUNAR (TOTAL)
5	08:02	AUG 11, 2018	SOLAR (PARTIAL)
6	23:34	JAN 5, 2019	SOLAR (PARTIAL)
7	02:36	JAN 20, 2019	LUNAR (TOTAL)
8	16:55	JUL 2, 2019	SOLAR (TOTAL)
9	18:43	JUL 16, 2019	LUNAR (PARTIAL)
10	02:29	DEC 26, 2019	SOLAR (ANNULAR)

*UTC (COORDINATED UNIVERSAL TIME) IS THE TIME BY WHICH ALL OF THE TIME ZONES AROUND THE WORLD ARE REGULATED

TOP 10

FIRST HUMANS **TO WALK ON THE MOON**
Not that many people have stepped foot onto our Moon.
These 10 were the first...

	ASTRONAUT	COUNTRY	MISSION	DATE WALKED ON THE MOON
1	NEIL ARMSTRONG	USA	APOLLO 11	JUL 21, 1969
2	BUZZ ALDRIN	USA	APOLLO 11	JUL 21, 1969
3	PETE CONRAD	USA	APOLLO 12	NOV 19–20, 1969
4	ALAN BEAN	USA	APOLLO 12	NOV 19–20, 1969
5	ALAN SHEPARD	USA	APOLLO 14	FEB 5–6, 1971
6	EDGAR MITCHELL	USA	APOLLO 14	FEB 5–6, 1971
7	DAVID SCOTT	USA	APOLLO 15	JUL 31–AUG 2, 1971
8	JAMES IRWIN	USA	APOLLO 15	JUL 31 –AUG 2, 1971
9	JOHN W. YOUNG	USA	APOLLO 16	APR 21–23, 1972
10	CHARLES DUKE	USA	APOLLO 16	APR 21–23, 1972

1 NEIL ARMSTRONG

Born in Wapakoneta, Ohio, Neil Armstrong (August 5, 1930–August 25, 2012) served as a naval aviator from 1949 to 1952. He was part of NASA's predecessor NACA (National Advisory Committee for Aeronautics) from 1955, before NASA's formation in 1958. He first became an astronaut in 1962.

Video
GAMES

ZONE
8

TOP 10 BIGGEST **CONSOLE GAMES OF ALL TIME**

The chart examines total game sales from every video game platform ever made. These are the 10 bestsellers of all time...

	GAME	GENRE	RELEASED	PLATFORM	UNIT SALES (MILLIONS)
1	WII SPORTS	SPORTS	2006	WII	82.57
2	SUPER MARIO BROS.	PLATFORM	1985	NES	40.24
3	MARIO KART WII	RACING	2008	WII	35.52
4	WII SPORTS RESORT	SPORTS	2009	WII	32.78
5	POKÉMON RED / BLUE / GREEN	RPG	1996	GAME BOY	31.37
6	TETRIS	PUZZLE	1989	GAME BOY	30.26
7	NEW SUPER MARIO BROS.	PLATFORM	2006	DS	29.8
8	WII PLAY	PARTY	2006	WII	28.94
9	NEW SUPER MARIO BROS. WII	PLATFORM	2009	WII	28.32
10	DUCK HUNT	SHOOTER	1984	NES	28.31

2 SUPER MARIO BROS.

Nintendo's NES Classic Edition (released on November 10, 2016) is a miniature version of the original 1980s NES (Nintendo Entertainment System) console. The Classic Edition has 30 built-in games, including *Mario Bros.*, *Super Mario Bros. 1, 2* and *3*, *Castlevania*, and *Donkey Kong*.

7 NINTENDOGS

The *Nintendogs* franchise has seen multiple releases, including 2005's *Chihuahua & Friends*, *Shiba & Friends*, and *Dachshund & Friends*. The Nintendo 3DS handheld console has three versions of *Nintendogs + Cats*, all released in 2011: *Toy Poodle & New Friends*, *French Bulldog & New Friends*, and *Golden Retriever & New Friends*.

TOP 10 BIGGEST-SELLING GAMES OF THE 21ST CENTURY

Gaming in this century has seen a giant leap forward in technology, but the most popular titles are more than 10 years old...

	GAME	GENRE	RELEASED	PLATFORM	UNIT SALES (MILLIONS)
1	WII SPORTS	SPORTS	2006	WII	82.57
2	MARIO KART WII	RACING	2008	WII	35.52
3	WII SPORTS RESORT	SPORTS	2009	WII	32.78
4	NEW SUPER MARIO BROS.	PLATFORM	2006	DS	29.8
5	WII PLAY	PARTY	2006	WII	28.94
6	NEW SUPER MARIO BROS. WII	PLATFORM	2009	WII	28.32
7	NINTENDOGS	SIMULATION	2005	DS	24.67
8	MARIO KART DS	RACING	2005	DS	23.21
9	WII FIT	SPORTS	2007	WII	22.7
10	KINECT ADVENTURES!	PARTY	2010	XBOX 360	21.81

RANKS BY DECADE

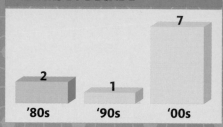

2	1	7
'80s	'90s	'00s

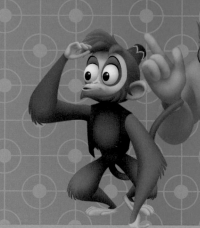

BIGGEST-SELLING **GAMING PLATFORMS**

From the PS4 through to every handheld console, these are the gaming systems that have sold more copies than their rivals...

	PLATFORM	MADE BY	RELEASED	UNIT SALES (MILLIONS)
1	PLAYSTATION 2	SONY	2000	157.68
2	NINTENDO DS	NINTENDO	2004	154.88
3	GAME BOY / GAME BOY COLOR	NINTENDO	1989 / 1998	118.69
4	PLAYSTATION	SONY	1994	104.25
5	WII	NINTENDO	2006	101.18
6	PLAYSTATION 3	SONY	2006	86.69
7	XBOX 360	MICROSOFT	2005	85.63
8	GAME BOY ADVANCE	NINTENDO	2001	81.51
9	PLAYSTATION PORTABLE	SONY	2004	80.82
10	NINTENDO ENTERTAINMENT SYSTEM	NINTENDO	1983	61.91

1 PLAYSTATION 2

Sony's PlayStation 2 was first released in Japan on March 4, 2000, and in the US on October 26, 2000. Of its total sales, 53.65 million are from the US, and 23.18 million come from Japan. Sony announced that production of the PS2 had stopped on January 4, 2013, marking almost 13 years of manufacture.

TOP 10 PLATFORMS WITH **THE MOST GAME SALES**

Determining the most popular brands and systems for gaming is one thing, but these platforms have sold the most games...

	PLATFORM	MADE BY	RELEASED	UNIT SALES OF ALL GAMES (MILLIONS)
1	PLAYSTATION 2	SONY	2000	1,661.95
2	XBOX 360	MICROSOFT	2005	1,002.73
3	PLAYSTATION 3	SONY	2006	970.96
4	WII	NINTENDO	2006	965.73
5	PLAYSTATION	SONY	1994	962.01
6	NINTENDO DS	NINTENDO	2004	844.72
7	NINTENDO ENTERTAINMENT SYSTEM	NINTENDO	1983	501.48
8	GAME BOY / GAME BOY COLOR	NINTENDO	1989 / 1998	501.11
9	SUPER NINTENDO ENTERTAINMENT SYSTEM	NINTENDO	1990	379.06
10	GAME BOY ADVANCE	NINTENDO	2001	377.41

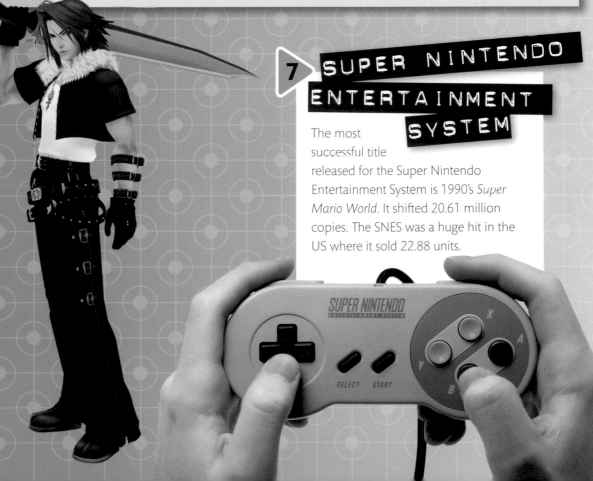

7 SUPER NINTENDO ENTERTAINMENT SYSTEM

The most successful title released for the Super Nintendo Entertainment System is 1990's *Super Mario World*. It shifted 20.61 million copies. The SNES was a huge hit in the US where it sold 22.88 units.

2 NINTENDO 3DS

This successor to Nintendo's original DS console debuted on February 26, 2011. The latest iteration of this handheld system is the New Nintendo 3DSI XL, which was released on February 13, 2015. The 10 most popular games for the 3DS are all published by Nintendo.

TOTAL YEARS OF THE 3 COMPANIES

Microsoft 43 YEARS (1975)

Nintendo 129 YEARS (1889)

Sony 73 YEARS (1946)

TOP 10 LONGEST-RUNNING PLATFORMS

The life cycle of many gaming systems is around six years before the manufacturer decides to release a new console, but these have endured far longer...

	PLATFORM	MADE BY	YEARS IN PRODUCTION	TOTAL YEARS
1	NINTENDO ENTERTAINMENT SYSTEM	NINTENDO	1983–2003	20
2	NINTENDO DS / DS LITE / 3DS / 3DSI XL	NINTENDO	2004–PRESENT	14
=	GAME BOY / GAME BOY COLOR	NINTENDO	1989–2003	14
4	PLAYSTATION	SONY	1994–2006	12
=	PLAYSTATION 2	SONY	2000–12	12
=	PLAYSTATION 3	SONY	2006–PRESENT	12
7	XBOX 360	MICROSOFT	2005–16	11
8	PLAYSTATION PORTABLE	SONY	2004–14	10
=	SUPER NINTENDO ENTERTAINMENT SYSTEM	NINTENDO	1993–2003	10
10	WII	NINTENDO	2006–13	7

TOP 10 BIGGEST-SELLING **NINTENDO PLATFORMS**

Japanese company Nintendo is responsible for some of the most successful games and gaming systems of all time...

	PLATFORM	YEARS IN PRODUCTION	UNIT SALES (MILLIONS)
1	NINTENDO DS / DS LITE / DSI	2004–16	154.88
2	GAME BOY / GAME BOY COLOR	1989–2003	118.69
3	WII	2006–13	101.18
4	GAME BOY ADVANCE	2001–09	81.51
5	NINTENDO ENTERTAINMENT SYSTEM	1983–2003	61.91
6	NINTENDO 3DS / 3DSI XL	2011–PRESENT	61.37
7	SUPER NINTENDO ENTERTAINMENT SYSTEM	1983–2003	49.1
8	NINTENDO 64	1996–2003	32.93
9	GAMECUBE	2001–07	21.74
10	WII U	2012–PRESENT	13.63

9 GAMECUBE

Unlike Nintendo's consoles up to this system, which utilized cartridges for their games, the GameCube had tiny DVD-style discs instead. The GameCube's controller was similar to its predecessor, the N64.

NINTENDO CONSOLES
WITH THE MOST GAMES SOLD

If you have a favorite *Mario* or *Zelda* game, check which platform it was released on in this revealing chart about Nintendo game popularity...

	PLATFORM	YEARS IN PRODUCTION	UNIT SALES OF ALL GAMES (MILLIONS)
1	WII	2006–13	908.59
2	NINTENDO DS / DS LITE / DSI	2004–16	808.44
3	GAME BOY ADVANCE	2001–09	318.89
4	NINTENDO 3DS / 3DSI XL	2011–PRESENT	259.45
5	GAME BOY / GAME BOY COLOR	1989–2003	255.49
6	NINTENDO ENTERTAINMENT SYSTEM	1983–2003	251.07
7	NINTENDO 64	1996–2003	218.88
8	SUPER NINTENDO ENTERTAINMENT SYSTEM	1983–2003	199.97
9	GAMECUBE	2001–07	199.35
10	WII U	2012–17	82.21

WII VS. WII U

Launched on November 18, 2012, the Wii U's short lifespan saw production cease on January 31, 2017. Only 370 games were released for Nintendo's sixth home console. Its predecessor, the Wii, was in production for seven years, with 2,798 releases. March 3, 2017, saw the release of Nintendo's latest system, the Switch.

BASIC SET | 8GB

7 SUPER MARIO MAKER

This is a game-creation title. Players can create their own levels from components found in *Super Mario Bros.* (1985), *Super Mario Bros. 3* (1988), *Super Mario World* (1990), and *New Super Mario Bros. U* (2012).

TOP 10 BIGGEST **WII U GAMES**

Nintendo's Wii U first appeared on the market in November 2012, and since then its Mario-themed titles remain its most popular...

	GAME	GENRE	RELEASED	UNIT SALES (MILLIONS)
1	MARIO KART 8	RACING	2014	7.09
2	NEW SUPER MARIO BROS. U	ACTION	2012	5.22
3	SUPER SMASH BROS. FOR WII U AND 3DS	FIGHTING	2014	4.87
4	SPLATOON	SHOOTER	2015	4.43
5	NINTENDO LAND	ACTION	2012	4.42
6	SUPER MARIO 3D WORLD	PLATFORM	2013	4.32
7	SUPER MARIO MAKER	PLATFORM	2015	3.21
8	NEW SUPER LUIGI U	PLATFORM	2013	2.24
9	THE LEGEND OF ZELDA: THE WIND WAKER	ACTION	2013	1.79
10	WII PARTY U	PARTY	2013	1.75

4 ▶ HALO 5: GUARDIANS

The *Halo* series features 13 titles to date. The 12th, *Halo 5: Guardians*, debuted on October 27, 2015, exclusively on Microsoft's Xbox One. The latest, *Halo Wars 2*, debuted worldwide on February 21, 2017.

TOP 10 BIGGEST-SELLING **XBOX ONE GAMES**

"First-person shooter" is still the most popular genre of gaming for players who prefer the Xbox One...

	GAME	GENRE	RELEASED	UNIT SALES (MILLIONS)
1	CALL OF DUTY: BLACK OPS 3	SHOOTER	2015	7.39
2	GRAND THEFT AUTO V	ACTION	2014	5.48
3	CALL OF DUTY: ADVANCED WARFARE	SHOOTER	2014	5.27
4	HALO 5: GUARDIANS	SHOOTER	2015	4.48
5	FALLOUT 4	RPG	2015	4.22
6	STAR WARS BATTLEFRONT	SHOOTER	2015	3.66
7	ASSASSIN'S CREED: UNITY	ACTION	2014	3.5
8	DESTINY	ACTION	2014	3.37
9	GEARS OF WAR: ULTIMATE EDITION	SHOOTER	2015	3.28
10	FIFA 16	SPORTS	2015	3.25

TOP 10

BIGGEST-SELLING **PS4 GAMES**

The battle of the PS4 versus Xbox One still rages, but Sony's platform has sold twice as many units of games popular on both systems...

	GAME	GENRE	RELEASED	UNIT SALES (MILLIONS)
1	CALL OF DUTY: BLACK OPS 3	SHOOTER	2015	14.63
2	GRAND THEFT AUTO V	ACTION	2014	12.61
3	FIFA 16	SPORTS	2015	8.57
4	STAR WARS BATTLEFRONT	SHOOTER	2015	7.98
5	CALL OF DUTY: ADVANCED WARFARE	SHOOTER	2014	7.66
6	FIFA 17	SPORTS	2016	7.59
7	FALLOUT 4	RPG	2015	7.16
8	FIFA 15	SPORTS	2014	6.08
9	DESTINY	SHOOTER	2014	5.64
10	UNCHARTED 4: A THIEF'S END	ACTION	2016	5.38

PS4 RANKS BY GENRE

RPG 1
ACTION 2
SPORTS 3
SHOOTER 4

10 UNCHARTED 4: A THIEF'S END

This franchise, launched in 2007 with *Uncharted: Drake's Fortune*, has sold 33.82 million copies across nine releases. *Uncharted 4: A Thief's End* debuted as a PS4 exclusive on May 10, 2016. *Uncharted: The Lost Legacy*, with a new lead protagonist in Chloe Frazer, was launched on August 22, 2017.

BIGGEST-SELLING
HANDHELD CONSOLES / PLATFORMS

After the Nintendo Game Boy stormed the market in 1989, portable, handheld platforms have sold millions of units around the world...

	PLATFORM	GENRE	RELEASED	UNIT SALES (MILLIONS)
1	NINTENDO DS / DS LITE / DSI	NINTENDO	2004	154.88
2	GAME BOY / GAME BOY COLOR	NINTENDO	1989 / 1998	118.69
3	GAME BOY ADVANCE	NINTENDO	2001	81.51
4	PLAYSTATION PORTABLE	SONY	2004	80.82
5	NINTENDO 3DS / 3DSI XL	NINTENDO	2011	61.37
6	PLAYSTATION VITA	SONY	2011	14.69
7	GAME GEAR	SEGA	1990	10.62
8	LEAPSTER	LEAPFROG ENTERPRISES	2008	4
9	NEO GEO POCKET / POCKET COLOR	SNK	1998 / 1999	2
10	TURBOEXPRESS	NEC	1990	1.5

1 NINTENDO DS

Launched on November 21, 2004, the Nintendo DS was the original version of the DS line that has evolved up to 2017's New Nintendo 2DS XL. The DS's biggest hit game was *New Super Mario Bros.*, which sold more than 29 million copies.

Now with a BRIGHTER backlit screen!

GAME BOY
ADVANCE

3 GAME BOY ADVANCE

The most popular release for the Game Boy Advance was 2002's *Pokémon Ruby / Sapphire*, with more than 15 million copies sold. The Game Boy Advance was the fifth iteration of Nintendo's handheld line.

TOP **10**

HANDHELD CONSOLES
WITH THE MOST GAME SALES

It's not just the sales of the games system that are key to a platform's success, as this top 10 reveals...

	PLATFORM	MADE BY	RELEASED	UNIT SALES OF ALL GAMES (MILLIONS)
1	NINTENDO DS / DSI LITE	NINTENDO	2004	844.72
2	GAME BOY / GAME BOY COLOR	NINTENDO	1989 / 1998	501.11
3	GAME BOY ADVANCE	NINTENDO	2001	377.41
4	PLAYSTATION PORTABLE	SONY	2004	303.98
5	NINTENDO 3DS / 3DSI XL	NINTENDO	2011	263.54
6	PLAYSTATION VITA	SONY	2011	63.68
7	GAME GEAR	SEGA	1990	38.26
8	LEAPSTER	LEAPFROG ENTERPRISES	2008	12
9	WONDERSWAN	BANDAI	1999	1.5
10	NEO GEO POCKET / POCKET COLOR	SNK	1998 / 1999	1.44

TOP 10 BIGGEST-SELLING **3DS GAMES**

Nintendo's most successful handheld console may be 14 years old, but new games are still being released for it to great acclaim...

	GAME	GENRE	RELEASED	UNIT SALES (MILLIONS)
1	POKÉMON X / Y	RPG	2013	14.6
2	MARIO KART 7	RACING	2011	12.66
3	POKÉMON OMEGA RUBY / ALPHA SAPPHIRE	RPG	2014	11.68
4	SUPER MARIO 3D LAND	PLATFORM	2011	10.81
5	NEW SUPER MARIO BROS. 2	PLATFORM	2012	9.9
6	ANIMAL CROSSING: NEW LEAF	ACTION	2012	9.16
7	SUPER SMASH BROS. FOR WII U AND 3DS	FIGHTING	2014	7.55
8	POKÉMON SUN / MOON	RPG	2016	7.14
9	TOMODACHI LIFE	SIMULATION	2013	5.23
10	LUIGI'S MANSION: DARK MOON	ADVENTURE	2013	4.59

8  POKÉMON SUN / MOON

The release of *Pokémon Sun* and *Pokémon Moon* marked the 20th anniversary of the *Pokémon* franchise's first game. Season 20 of the *Pokémon* TV series (1997–present) echoes characters and events from the *Sun* and *Moon* video games.

1 MINECRAFT

31 million copies sold of all *Minecraft* console titles have made this gaming franchise a worldwide hit since it first appeared on November 18, 2011. This "sandbox" game has no rules for the players and allows them to explore and create at will.

TOP 10 BIGGEST-SELLING **PS VITA GAMES**

Sony's successor to their PlayStation Portable hasn't had runaway sales for the device or games, but it still has a dedicated fanbase...

	GAME	GENRE	RELEASED	UNIT SALES (MILLIONS)
1	MINECRAFT	ADVENTURE	2014	1.96
2	UNCHARTED: GOLDEN ABYSS	ACTION	2011	1.53
3	CALL OF DUTY BLACK OPS: DECLASSIFIED	ACTION	2012	1.47
4	ASSASSIN'S CREED III: LIBERATION	ACTION	2012	1.32
5	LITTLEBIGPLANET PS VITA	PLATFORM	2012	1.25
6	PERSONA 4: THE GOLDEN	RPG	2012	1.12
7	NEED FOR SPEED: MOST WANTED	RACING	2012	1.01
8	KILLZONE: MERCENARY	SHOOTER	2013	0.8
=	FINAL FANTASY X / X-2 HD REMASTER	RPG	2013	0.8
10	FREEDOM WARS	RPG	2014	0.65

GENRE **BESTSELLERS**

There are many different kinds of video games made, but these 10 are the market leaders for each of the different genres...

	GENRE	GAME	RELEASED	PLATFORM	UNIT SALES (MILLIONS)
1	SPORTS	WII SPORTS	2006	WII	82.57
2	PLATFORM	SUPER MARIO BROS.	1985	NES	40.24
3	RACING	MARIO KART WII	2008	WII	35.52
4	RPG	POKÉMON RED / BLUE / GREEN	1996	GAME BOY	31.37
5	PUZZLE	TETRIS	1989	GAME BOY	30.26
6	PARTY	WII PLAY	2006	WII	28.94
7	SHOOTER	DUCK HUNT	1984	NES	28.31
8	SIMULATION	NINTENDOGS	2005	DS	24.69
9	ACTION	GRAND THEFT AUTO V	2013	PS3	21.04
10	FIGHTING	SUPER SMASH BROS. BRAWL	2008	WII	12.84

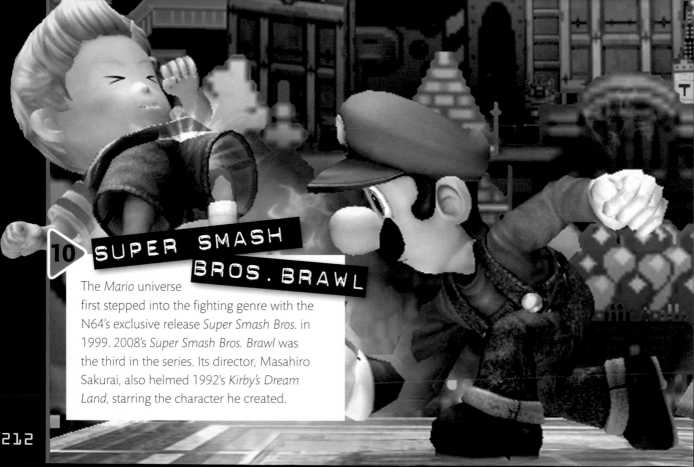

10 SUPER SMASH BROS. BRAWL

The *Mario* universe first stepped into the fighting genre with the N64's exclusive release *Super Smash Bros.* in 1999. 2008's *Super Smash Bros. Brawl* was the third in the series. Its director, Masahiro Sakurai, also helmed 1992's *Kirby's Dream Land*, starring the character he created.

HOLD

NEXT

LEVEL

15

LINES TO CLEAR   9

SCORE
307401

NEXT BEST
q-9138f124-US-en
0

TETRIS

Not just the biggest-selling puzzle game ever, *Tetris* has inspired endless imitators since it debuted on the NES in 1984. All of the official *Tetris*-related releases amount to more than 93 million units sold. 86 different *Tetris* releases have been made for every major platform, both home console and handheld.

YOSHI
22 MILLION

LUIGI
20 MILLION

RELEASES BY CHARACTER

WARIO
22.9 MILLION

TOP **10**

MOST SUCCESSFUL GENRES

If you're a gamer, which type do you enjoy the most? This chart reveals the genres which have achieved the greatest sales...

	GENRE	ALL PLATFORMS' UNIT SALES (MILLIONS)
1	ACTION	1,746.89
2	SPORTS	1,332.55
3	SHOOTER	1,053.16
4	RPG	934.91
5	PLATFORM	828.31
6	PARTY	803.83
7	RACING	729.44
8	FIGHTING	447.71
9	SIMULATION	391.04
10	PUZZLE	243.52

TOP 10 BIGGEST **PLATFORM GAMES**

For those of you who play platformers, it will come as no surprise that this top 10 is dominated by a pair of magical plumbers...

	GAME	PLATFORM	RELEASED	UNIT SALES (MILLIONS)
1	SUPER MARIO BROS.	NES	1985	40.24
2	NEW SUPER MARIO BROS.	DS	2006	29.8
3	NEW SUPER MARIO BROS. WII	WII	2009	28.32
4	SUPER MARIO WORLD	SNES	1990	20.61
5	SUPER MARIO LAND	GAME BOY	1989	18.14
6	SUPER MARIO BROS. 3	NES	1988	17.28
7	SUPER MARIO 64	N64	1996	11.89
8	SUPER MARIO GALAXY	WII	2007	11.35
9	SUPER MARIO LAND 2: 6 GOLDEN COINS	GAME BOY	1992	11.18
10	SUPER MARIO 3D LAND	3DS	2011	10.81

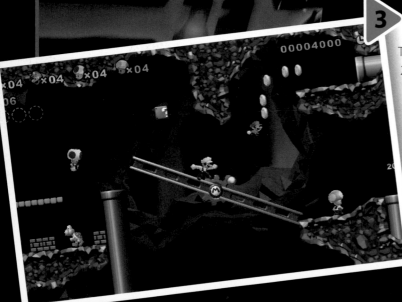

3 NEW SUPER MARIO BROS. WII

This 2009 title marked the first time four players could play a side-scrolling *Super Mario* platformer. The success of this game led to an arcade-only spin-off called *New Super Mario Bros. Wii Coin World*. It was only released in games arcades in Japan.

TOTAL SALES OF EACH GTA GAME

GTA V 60 million | GTA IV 22.4 million | GTA III 17.3 million

1 GRAND THEFT AUTO V

The bestseller of the *GTA* series took $1 billion during its first week of release. Across all platforms, its total sales exceed 60 million units. The franchise began in 1997 when *Grand Theft Auto* was released for the PlayStation and Game Boy Color.

TOP 10 BIGGEST ACTION GAMES

The action genre often caters to "open world" games where players can choose to do whatever they like, instead of following a storyline...

	GAME	PLATFORM	RELEASED	UNIT SALES (MILLIONS)
1	GRAND THEFT AUTO V	PS3	2013	21.04
2	GRAND THEFT AUTO: SAN ANDREAS	PS2	2004	20.81
3	GRAND THEFT AUTO V	XBOX 360	2013	16.27
4	GRAND THEFT AUTO: VICE CITY	PS2	2002	16.15
5	GRAND THEFT AUTO III	PS2	2001	13.1
6	GRAND THEFT AUTO V	PS4	2014	12.61
7	GRAND THEFT AUTO IV	XBOX 360	2008	11.01
8	GRAND THEFT AUTO IV	PS3	2008	10.5
9	GRAND THEFT AUTO: LIBERTY CITY STORIES	PSP	2005	7.69
10	THE LEGEND OF ZELDA: OCARINA OF TIME	N64	1998	7.6

WII SPORTS

Its spin-offs *Wii Sports Resort* (2009) and *Wii Sports Club* (2014) make the total units sold for this franchise 115.71 million, with 50.1 percent of *Wii Sports'* sales coming from its US fans. It is the third biggest-selling video game of all time, and has won many awards, including Best Sports Game at the 2006 E3 Game Critics Awards.

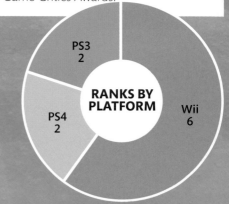

RANKS BY PLATFORM

PS3
2

PS4
2

Wii
6

TOP **10** BIGGEST **SPORTS GAMES**

More than 5,000 sports-themed video games have been released, but none can come close to a 12-year-old, family-centric title...

	GAME	PLATFORM	RELEASED	UNIT SALES (MILLIONS)
1	WII SPORTS	WII	2006	82.57
2	WII SPORTS RESORT	WII	2009	32.78
3	WII FIT	WII	2007	22.7
4	WII FIT PLUS	WII	2009	21.84
5	FIFA 16	PS4	2015	8.57
6	MARIO & SONIC AT THE OLYMPIC GAMES	WII	2007	8
7	FIFA 17	PS4	2016	7.59
8	ZUMBA FITNESS	WII	2010	6.71
9	FIFA SOCCER 12	PS3	2011	6.65
10	FIFA 14	PS3	2013	6.47

TOP 10 BIGGEST RACING GAMES

The *Super Mario Bros.* universe is not just the dominant force in the platform genre, as this surprising top 10 reveals...

	GAME	PLATFORM	RELEASED	UNIT SALES (MILLIONS)
1	MARIO KART WII	WII	2008	35.52
2	MARIO KART DS	DS	2005	23.21
3	GRAN TURISMO 3: A-SPEC	PS2	2001	14.98
4	MARIO KART 7	3DS	2011	12.66
5	GRAN TURISMO 5	PS2	2004	11.66
6	GRAN TURISMO	PS	1997	10.95
7	GRAN TURISMO 5	PS3	2010	10.7
8	MARIO KART 64	N64	1996	9.87
9	GRAN TURISMO 2	PS	1999	9.49
10	SUPER MARIO KART	SNES	1992	8.76

1 MARIO KART WII

The hit *Mario Kart* series started with 1992's *Super Mario Kart*, released for the SNES. That title sold 8.76 million copies. *Mario Kart Wii* is the king of sales for now, but April 28, 2017, saw the release of *Mario Kart 8 Deluxe* for Nintendo's new console, the Switch.

TOP 10 BIGGEST ADVENTURE GAMES

Modern adventure gaming is a very involving experience, with intricate puzzles, tactics, and complex villains to overcome...

	GAME	PLATFORM	RELEASED	UNIT SALES (MILLIONS)
1	MINECRAFT	XBOX 360	2013	9.18
2	THE LEGEND OF ZELDA: OCARINA OF TIME	N64	1998	7.6
3	THE LEGEND OF ZELDA: TWILIGHT PRINCESS	WII	2006	7.15
4	THE LEGEND OF ZELDA	NES	1986	6.51
5	RED DEAD REDEMPTION	PS3	2010	6.49
6	ASSASSIN'S CREED III	PS3	2012	6.45
7	RED DEAD REDEMPTION	XBOX 360	2010	6.32
8	METAL GEAR SOLID 2: SONS OF LIBERTY	PS2	2001	6.05
9	METAL GEAR SOLID	PS	1998	6.03
10	METAL GEAR SOLID 4: GUNS OF THE PATRIOTS	PS3	2008	6

10 METAL GEAR SOLID 4: GUNS OF THE PATRIOTS

Set in 2014 (four years before the events of *Metal Gear Rising: Revengeance*), *Metal Gear Solid 4: Guns of the Patriots* features a stealth-style adventure gameplay that is strong throughout this series. The song that ends the game is sung by Lisbeth Scott, an artist whose work has appeared on the soundtracks for *Iron Man 2* and TV series *True Blood*.

BIGGEST RPG GAMES

There are many different role-playing games titles out there, but one franchise wipes the board with all of them...

	GAME	PLATFORM	RELEASED	UNIT SALES (MILLIONS)
1	POKÉMON RED / BLUE / GREEN VERSION	GAME BOY	1996	31.37
2	POKÉMON GOLD / SILVER VERSION	GAME BOY	1999	23.1
3	POKÉMON DIAMOND / PEARL VERSION	GAME BOY	2006	18.25
4	POKÉMON RUBY / SAPPHIRE VERSION	GAME BOY	2002	15.85
5	POKÉMON BLACK / WHITE VERSION	GAME BOY	2010	15.17
6	POKÉMON YELLOW: SPECIAL PIKACHU EDITION	GAME BOY	1998	14.64
7	POKÉMON X / Y	3DS	2013	14.6
8	POKÉMON HEARTGOLD / SOULSILVER	DS	2009	11.77
9	POKÉMON OMEGA RUBY / ALPHA SAPPHIRE VERSION	3DS	2014	11.68
10	POKÉMON FIRERED / LEAFGREEN VERSION	GBA	2004	10.49

4 POKÉMON RUBY / SAPPHIRE

This is the seventh release in the hit *Pokémon* video game series, a franchise with 265 million copies in sales. *Pokémon Ruby / Sapphire Version* was developed by Game Freak, the team behind 1991's *Yoshi*, 2015's *Tembo the Badass Elephant*, as well as the rest of the *Pokémon* game series.

TOP 10 BIGGEST STRATEGY GAMES

The older platforms, especially the handheld ones of yesteryear, still hold the best sales records for strategy titles...

	GAME	PLATFORM	RELEASED	UNIT SALES (MILLIONS)
1	POKÉMON STADIUM	N64	1999	5.45
2	WARZONE 2100	PS	1999	5.01
3	POKÉMON TRADING CARD GAME	GAME BOY	1998	3.7
4	POKÉMON STADIUM 2	N64	2000	2.73
5	HALO WARS	XBOX 360	2009	2.62
6	YU-GI-OH! THE ETERNAL DUELIST SOUL	GAME BOY	2001	2.07
7	PIKMIN	GAMECUBE	2001	1.63
8	YU-GI-OH! DUEL MONSTERS	GAME BOY	1998	1.61
9	LEGO BATTLES: NINJAGO	DS	2011	1.45
10	POCKET MONSTERS STADIUM	N64	1998	1.37

7 PIKMIN

Six games, and more than 5 million sales later for the series, the first *Pikmin* game for the GameCube remains the most successful. The game challenges the player to collect and utilize different creatures' powers to help rebuild a spacecraft.

3 PAC-MAN

Prior to its 1982 Atari appearance, *Pac-Man*'s roots go back to Namco's 1980 arcade version, created by Japanese video game designer Toru Iwatani. Since then, across all platforms, there have been 97 *Pac-Man* releases.

RANKS BY DECADES

'00s 5
'80s 4
'90s 1

READY

TOP 10 BIGGEST PUZZLE GAMES

If you've ever played a game where falling shapes need to be locked together, then you've played something inspired by the number one here...

	GAME	PLATFORM	RELEASED	UNIT SALES (MILLIONS)
1	TETRIS	GAME BOY	1989	30.26
2	BRAIN AGE 2: MORE TRAINING IN MINUTES A DAY	DS	2005	15.29
3	PAC-MAN	ATARI 2600	1982	7.81
4	TETRIS	NES	1988	5.58
5	DR. MARIO	GAME BOY	1989	5.34
6	PROFESSOR LAYTON AND THE CURIOUS VILLAGE	DS	2007	5.19
7	DR. MARIO	NES	1990	4.85
8	PROFESSOR LAYTON AND THE DIABOLICAL BOX	DS	2007	3.94
9	PROFESSOR LAYTON AND THE UNWOUND FUTURE	DS	2008	3.26
10	PAC-MAN COLLECTION	GBA	2001	2.94

3 TEKKEN 3

This 20-year-old game remains one of the most popular fighting titles ever. The entire *Tekken* franchise has sold 40.74 million copies worldwide. *Tekken 3* first appeared in arcades in 1997, prior to its home console debut on the PlayStation.

TOP 10 BIGGEST **FIGHTING GAMES**

Almost 2,000 games have been released in the fighting genre, but these 10 have outsold all the rest...

	GAME	PLATFORM	RELEASED	UNIT SALES (MILLIONS)
1	SUPER SMASH BROS. BRAWL	WII	2008	12.84
2	SUPER SMASH BROS. FOR WII U AND 3DS	3DS	2014	7.55
3	TEKKEN 3	PS	1998	7.16
4	SUPER SMASH BROS. MELEE	GAMECUBE	2001	7.07
5	STREET FIGHTER II: THE WORLD WARRIOR	SNES	1992	6.3
6	TEKKEN 2	PS	1996	5.74
7	SUPER SMASH BROS.	N64	1999	5.55
8	SUPER SMASH BROS. FOR WII U AND 3DS	WIIU	2014	4.87
9	STREET FIGHTER IV	PS3	2009	4.16
10	STREET FIGHTER II TURBO	SNES	1992	4.1

TOP 10 BIGGEST **SIMULATION GAMES**

Simulation gaming has evolved from the fighter plane and car racing titles to now feature pets, managing a town, and even cooking...

	GAME	PLATFORM	RELEASED	UNIT SALES (MILLIONS)
1	NINTENDOGS	DS	2005	24.67
2	ANIMAL CROSSING: WILD WORLD	DS	2005	12.13
3	ANIMAL CROSSING: NEW LEAF	3DS	2012	9.16
4	COOKING MAMA	DS	2006	5.63
5	TOMODACHI LIFE	3DS	2013	5.23
6	ANIMAL CROSSING: CITY FOLK	WII	2008	4.62
7	NINTENDOGS + CATS	3DS	2011	3.85
8	MYSIMS	DS	2007	3.66
9	POKÉMON SNAP	N64	1999	3.63
10	COOKING MAMA 2: DINNER WITH FRIENDS	DS	2007	3.58

RANKS BY TYPE

COOKING 2

PET 2

GAME 1

LIFE 5

5 TOMODACHI LIFE

This game is classified as a "life simulation" title. You can incorporate any of the Miis (avatars compatible across Nintendo systems since the Wii) into the game. Your characters can then form relationships, perform everyday tasks and go shopping, creating storylines and events.

2 STAR WARS BATTLEFRONT

Rogue One: X-Wing VR Mission was released in December 2016 as a free download for the PS4's version of *Star Wars Battlefront*. The downloadable content was for PlayStation VR, and tied into the story of the 2016 movie *Rogue One: A Star Wars Story*. The sequel, *Star Wars Battlefront II*, was released on November 17, 2017.

TOP 10 BIGGEST MOVIE TIE-IN GAMES

Although LEGO video games that riff on famous movies are hugely popular, a James Bond title remains king...

	GAME	GENRE	PLATFORM	RELEASED	UNIT SALES (MILLIONS)
1	GOLDENEYE 007	SHOOTER	N64	1997	8.09
2	STAR WARS BATTLEFRONT	SHOOTER	PS4	2015	7.98
3	LEGO STAR WARS: THE COMPLETE SAGA	ACTION	WII	2007	5.64
4	LEGO STAR WARS: THE COMPLETE SAGA	ACTION	DS	2007	4.76
5	THE LORD OF THE RINGS: THE TWO TOWERS	ACTION	PS2	2002	4.67
6	SPIDER-MAN: THE MOVIE	ACTION	PS2	2002	4.48
7	LEGO INDIANA JONES: THE ORIGINAL ADVENTURES	ADVENTURE	XBOX 360	2008	3.76
8	HARRY POTTER & THE SORCERER'S STONE	ACTION	PS	2001	3.73
9	STAR WARS BATTLEFRONT	SHOOTER	XBOX ONE	2015	3.66
10	STAR WARS: BATTLEFRONT	SHOOTER	PS2	2004	3.61

TOP 10

BIGGEST **TV TIE-IN GAMES**

It's not just blockbuster movies that have successful tie-in video game titles, and one of the most successful cartoons of all time leads the charge...

	GAME	GENRE	PLATFORM	RELEASED	UNIT SALES (MILLIONS)
1	THE SIMPSONS: HIT & RUN	RACING	PS2	2003	4.7
2	THE SIMPSONS: ROAD RAGE	RACING	PS2	2001	3.61
3	WWF SMACKDOWN!	FIGHTING	PS	2000	3.58
4	WWF WAR ZONE	FIGHTING	PS	1998	3.36
5	RUGRATS: SEARCH FOR REPTAR	ADVENTURE	PS	1998	3.34
6	WWF SMACKDOWN! 2: KNOW YOUR ROLE	FIGHTING	PS	2000	3.2
7	WWE SMACKDOWN! SHUT YOUR MOUTH	FIGHTING	PS2	2002	3.02
8	DRAGON BALL Z: BUDOKAI TENKAICHI 3	FIGHTING	PS2	2007	3
=	WWE SMACKDOWN VS. RAW 2006	FIGHTING	PS2	2005	3
10	WWE SMACKDOWN! VS. RAW	FIGHTING	PS2	2002	2.83

1

THE SIMPSONS: HIT & RUN

The Simpsons TV series has notched up more than 600 episodes since it began in 1989. The first ever *Simpsons* video game was 1991's *The Simpsons: Bart vs. the Space Mutants*. 2013's *The Simpsons: Hit & Run* was released on PS2, GameCube and Xbox. All *Simpsons* games total 23.19 million units sold.

225

2 LEGO STAR WARS: THE COMPLETE SAGA

Across all platforms, *LEGO Star Wars: The Complete Saga* has sold 15.28 million copies. It is the most successful of all 285 LEGO game releases since *LEGO Fun to Build* in 1995. *LEGO Worlds* was released in March 2017, and allows players to create their own levels.

TOP 10 MOST GROSSING **STAR WARS VIDEO GAMES**

The first incarnation of *Star Wars: Battlefront* was released 14 years ago, but now, the PS4 incarnation is the dominant title in this subgenre...

	GAME	GENRE	PLATFORM	RELEASED	UNIT SALES ($ MILLIONS)
1	STAR WARS BATTLEFRONT	SHOOTER	PS4	2015	7.98
2	LEGO STAR WARS: THE COMPLETE SAGA	ACTION	WII	2007	5.64
3	LEGO STAR WARS: THE COMPLETE SAGA	ACTION	DS	2007	4.76
4	STAR WARS BATTLEFRONT	SHOOTER	XBOX ONE	2015	3.66
5	STAR WARS: BATTLEFRONT	SHOOTER	PS2	2004	3.61
6	STAR WARS: BATTLEFRONT II	SHOOTER	PS2	2005	3.59
7	LEGO STAR WARS: THE VIDEO GAME	ACTION	PS2	2005	3.53
8	STAR WARS: EPISODE III – REVENGE OF THE SITH	ACTION	PS2	2005	3.32
9	STAR WARS: EPISODE I RACER	RACING	N64	1999	3.12
10	STAR WARS: THE FORCE UNLEASHED	ACTION	XBOX 360	2008	2.77

TOP 10 BIGGEST **METAL GEAR GAMES**

Japanese video game designer Hideo Kojima created the *Metal Gear* game
series back in the 1980s, with the first title released in 1987...

	GAME	PLATFORM	RELEASED	UNIT SALES (MILLIONS)
1	METAL GEAR SOLID 2: SONS OF LIBERTY	PS2	2001	6.05
2	METAL GEAR SOLID	PS	1998	6.03
3	METAL GEAR SOLID 4: GUNS OF THE PATRIOTS	PS3	2008	5.99
4	METAL GEAR SOLID 3: SNAKE EATER	PS2	2004	4.23
5	METAL GEAR SOLID V: THE PHANTOM PAIN	PS4	2015	3.41
6	METAL GEAR SOLID: PEACE WALKER	PSP	2010	2.06
7	METAL GEAR SOLID: REVENGEANCE	PS3	2013	1.42
8	METAL GEAR SOLID V: GROUND ZEROES	PS4	2014	1.27
9	METAL GEAR SOLID: PORTABLE OPS	PSP	2006	1.18
=	METAL GEAR SOLID: VR MISSIONS	PS	1999	1.18

5 METAL GEAR SOLID V: THE PHANTOM PAIN

Despite its title, this is
actually the 22nd *Metal Gear* release.
It is the sequel to 2014's *Metal Gear
Solid V: Ground Zeroes*, and is the
ninth *Metal Gear* game to be written
and directed by Hideo Kojima. Its
story takes place in 1984, 11 years
prior to the first ever *Metal Gear* title,
set in 1995, but released in 1987.

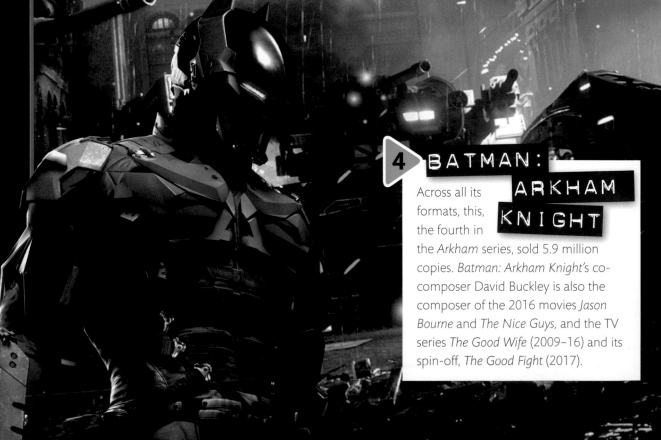

TOP 10 BIGGEST **DC COMICS GAMES**

The DC Comics universe includes Wonder Woman, Superman, the Green Lantern, and a caped crusader who takes almost every spot in this top 10...

	GAME	PLATFORM	RELEASED	UNIT SALES (MILLIONS)
1	BATMAN: ARKHAM CITY	PS3	2011	5.48
2	BATMAN: ARKHAM CITY	XBOX 360	2011	4.73
3	BATMAN: ARKHAM ASYLUM	PS3	2009	4.23
4	BATMAN: ARKHAM KNIGHT	PS4	2015	3.95
5	BATMAN: ARKHAM ASYLUM	XBOX 360	2009	3.48
6	LEGO BATMAN: THE VIDEOGAME	XBOX 360	2008	3.38
7	LEGO BATMAN: THE VIDEOGAME	WII	2008	3.06
8	LEGO BATMAN: THE VIDEOGAME	DS	2008	3.05
9	BATMAN: ARKHAM ORIGINS	PS3	2013	2.29
10	MORTAL KOMBAT VS. DC UNIVERSE	PS3	2008	2

4 BATMAN: ARKHAM KNIGHT

Across all its formats, this, the fourth in the *Arkham* series, sold 5.9 million copies. *Batman: Arkham Knight's* co-composer David Buckley is also the composer of the 2016 movies *Jason Bourne* and *The Nice Guys,* and the TV series *The Good Wife* (2009–16) and its spin-off, *The Good Fight* (2017).

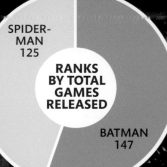

RANKS BY TOTAL GAMES RELEASED

SPIDER-MAN 125

BATMAN 147

10 MARVEL VS. CAPCOM 3: FATE OF TWO WORLDS

This game was also released on the Xbox 360, but only sold 1.07 million copies on that system. The fifth game in the *Marvel vs. Capcom* series, it features characters from both franchises in a tag team-style fighting tournament. The latest in the series, *Marvel vs. Capcom: Infinite*, was released on September 19, 2017.

TOP 10 BIGGEST MARVEL COMICS GAMES

The Marvel Cinematic Universe's movies, along with its comic book titles, have inspired hundreds of game releases...

	GAME	PLATFORM	RELEASED	UNIT SALES (MILLIONS)
1	SPIDER-MAN: THE MOVIE	PS2	2002	4.48
2	SPIDER-MAN 2	PS2	2004	3.41
3	SPIDER-MAN	PS	2000	3.13
4	MARVEL: ULTIMATE ALLIANCE	XBOX 360	2006	2.5
5	LEGO MARVEL SUPER HEROES	XBOX 360	2013	2.22
6	X-MEN LEGENDS	PS2	2004	1.93
7	LEGO MARVEL SUPER HEROES	PS3	2013	1.84
8	LEGO MARVEL SUPER HEROES	PS4	2013	1.62
9	SPIDER-MAN 2: ENTER ELECTRO	PS	2001	1.55
10	MARVEL VS. CAPCOM 3: FATE OF TWO WORLDS	PS3	2011	1.34

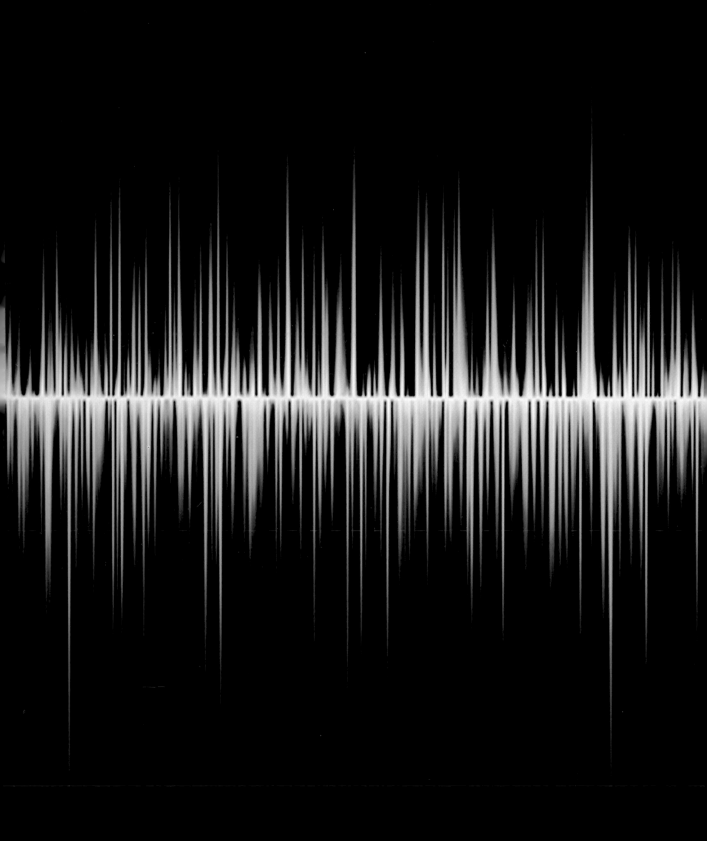

MUSIC ZONE 9

2 RIHANNA

Born in Barbados on February 20, 1988, singer Rihanna consistently released a new studio album every year between 2005–07 and 2009–12. After a four-year break, her eighth album, *Anti*, was released on January 28, 2016. It reached number one in the album charts in the US, Canada, UK, Norway, and Taiwan.

TOP 10 MOST STREAMED ARTISTS (AUDIO & VIDEO) 2016

With streaming now the most popular method of consuming music, the numbers on this chart go into the billions...

	ARTIST	TOTAL STREAMS
1	DRAKE	6,053,703,020
2	RIHANNA	3,297,671,731
3	TWENTY ONE PILOTS	2,635,459,821
4	THE WEEKND	2,524,860,083
5	FUTURE	2,492,554,102
6	KANYE WEST	2,456,355,930
7	JUSTIN BIEBER	2,430,063,560
8	KEVIN GATES	2,096,428,953
9	BEYONCÉ	2,093,171,487
10	EMINEM	1,947,445,547

MOST STREAMED
ALBUMS (AUDIO & VIDEO) 2016

Streaming data covers multiple providers, both music and video based, and the 10 biggest albums of 2016 were...

	ARTIST	ALBUM	TOTAL STREAMS
1	DRAKE	VIEWS	3,104,177,523
2	RIHANNA	ANTI	2,174,863,097
3	JUSTIN BIEBER	PURPOSE	1,916,720,472
4	BRYSON TILLER	TRAPSOUL	1,471,926,526
5	TWENTY ONE PILOTS	BLURRYFACE	1,430,213,711
6	THE CHAINSMOKERS	COLLAGE EP	1,275,089,915
7	KANYE WEST	THE LIFE OF PABLO	1,274,638,793
8	KEVIN GATES	ISIAH	1,253,212,299
9	THE WEEKND	BEAUTY BEHIND THE MADNESS	1,189,212,393
10	FETTY WAP	FETTY WAP	1,110,230,476

5 TWENTY ONE PILOTS

Originally a four-piece band, since the departure of Chris Salih and Nick Thomas, Twenty One Pilots is now duo Tyler Joseph (lead vocals) and Josh Dun (drums). A live version of their *Blurryface* album was released on November 25, 2016.

SOLO ARTISTS VS. BANDS / GROUPS

BANDS / GROUPS 3

SOLO ARTISTS 17

DESIIGNER

Desiigner is songwriter / producer Sidney
Royel Selby III. His debut album, *The Life
of Desiigner*, was released in 2017. "Panda"
was Desiigner's debut single, released on
December 15, 2015. Kanye West sampled the
song on his 2016 album *The Life of Pablo*.

TOP 10

MOST STREAMED
SONGS 2016

The abundance of playlists means that individual songs are
racking up hundreds of millions of streams online...

	ARTIST	SONG	TOTAL STREAMS
1	DESIIGNER	PANDA	736,813,212
2	RIHANNA	WORK	716,636,471
3	THE CHAINSMOKERS	CLOSER	616,482,817
4	DRAKE	ONE DANCE	562,093,409
5	RIHANNA	NEEDED ME	519,758,168
6	THE CHAINSMOKERS	DON'T LET ME DOWN	510,602,192
7	JUSTIN BIEBER	SORRY	479,224,787
8	FIFTH HARMONY	WORK FROM HOME	461,523,305
9	TWENTY ONE PILOTS	STRESSED OUT	454,005,148
10	LUKAS GRAHAM	7 YEARS	436,892,486

GINGER WILDHEART

Ginger Wildheart has more than 30 career albums, including eight studio albums with The Wildhearts. As an independent artist thriving outside of the mainstream streaming platforms, he has experienced huge success via Bandcamp and PledgeMusic. His 2011 triple-album project achieved 555 percent of its funding target, and reached the 100 percent mark in just six hours

TOP 10

STREAMING SERVICES
WITH THE MOST SONGS

For those of you who regularly use some of the most well-known streaming services, this chart may surprise you...

	SERVICE	COUNTRY OF ORIGIN	TOTAL SONGS (MILLIONS)
1	SOUNDCLOUD	GERMANY	100
2	TIDAL	NORWAY	42.5
3	AMAZON PRIME	USA	40
=	APPLE MUSIC	USA	40
=	DEEZER	FRANCE	40
=	GROOVE MUSIC	USA	40
7	GOOGLE PLAY MUSIC	USA	35
8	RHAPSODY	USA	32
=	NAPSTER	USA	32
10	SPOTIFY	SWEDEN	30

TOP 10 MOST POPULAR
GENRES OF ALBUM

For the past few years, the rock genre has been top of this chart, but streaming habits have moved other genres upward...

	GENRE	% OF TOTAL CONSUMPTION
1	POP	14.9
2	HIP-HOP / RAP	14.4
3	R&B	9.5
4	ROCK	8.9
5	COUNTRY	8.7
6	LATIN	6.1
7	ALTERNATIVE	5.5
8	INDIE ROCK	4.8
9	METAL	3.6
10	RELIGIOUS	3.2

ANNEKE VAN GIERSBERGEN

Over the past 23 years, Dutch singer-songwriter Anneke van Giersbergen has been featured on more than 50 albums. This includes six solo albums, 10 studio and live records as the singer of The Gathering, six releases by Devin Townsend, and The Gentle Storm (a collaboration with Arjen Lucassen). Her latest band, Vuur, released their debut album in 2017.

CONSUMPTION: ALBUM SALES

ON-DEMAND STREAMS +82.6%
SONG SALES -24.8%
ALBUM SALES -15.6%

2  DRAKE

Canadian artist Drake (born October 24, 1986) has won 80 international awards from more than 300 nominations. These include three wins and 35 nominations from the Grammys between 2010 and 2017. In the same period of time, Canada's Juno Awards have given Drake six awards from 20 nominations. His hit album *Views* was released on April 29, 2016.

TOP 10 BIGGEST-SELLING ALBUMS (ALL FORMATS) 2016

This top 10 combines sales data from all formats, including digital, CD, vinyl and, in some cases, even the nostalgic cassette format...

	ARTIST	ALBUM	TOTAL SALES
1	ADELE	25	1,550,584
2	DRAKE	VIEWS	1,510,987
3	BEYONCÉ	LEMONADE	1,477,080
4	CHRIS STAPLETON	TRAVELLER	1,016,644
5	PENTATONIX	A PENTATONIX CHRISTMAS	890,533
6	VARIOUS	HAMILTON	786,582
7	TWENTY ONE PILOTS	BLURRYFACE	676,227
8	PRINCE	THE VERY BEST OF PRINCE	644,775
9	RIHANNA	ANTI	515,460
10	GARTH BROOKS	THE ULTIMATE COLLECTION	506,967

2 THE CHAINSMOKERS

Originally a duo of DJs (Alex Pall and Rhett Bixler), Pall ended up collaborating with Andrew Taggart and the current incarnation of The Chainsmokers was formed. "Erase," their debut single in 2012, featured guest vocals from singer and actress Priyanka Chopra, the star of ABC's FBI drama series *Quantico*. The Chainsmokers released their debut full-length album, *Memories...Do Not Open,* on April 7, 2017.

TOP 10 BIGGEST-SELLING SONGS 2016

Compare this chart to the album-related one on the previous page to see how much more popular individual song sales are these days...

	ARTIST	SONG	TOTAL SALES
1	JUSTIN TIMBERLAKE	CAN'T STOP THE FEELING	2,488,419
2	THE CHAINSMOKERS	CLOSER	2,263,573
3	FLO RIDA	MY HOUSE	2,244,602
4	LUKAS GRAHAM	7 YEARS	2,131,715
5	DRAKE	ONE DANCE	2,096,662
6	TWENTY ONE PILOTS	STRESSED OUT	1,943,976
7	JUSTIN BIEBER	LOVE YOURSELF	1,853,732
8	RIHANNA	WORK	1,802,759
9	THE CHAINSMOKERS	DON'T LET ME DOWN	1,795,409
10	TWENTY ONE PILOTS	HEATHENS	1,784,675

10 SIA

Born in Adelaide, Australia, Sia Furler has released seven solo studio albums, 26 singles, and has featured as a guest vocalist on more than 30 other songs. Sia has also written more than 70 songs for other artists, including "Break the Walls" by Fitz & The Tantrums and "Pretty Hurts" by Beyoncé.

TOP **10**

MOST POPULAR
SONGS (SALES & STREAMS) 2016

The significance of streaming is clear from this chart--compare the entries and the numbers to the sales-based top 10 opposite...

	ARTIST	SONG	TOTAL CONSUMPTION
1	DRAKE	ONE DANCE	5,555,380
2	THE CHAINSMOKERS	CLOSER	4,497,430
3	RIHANNA	WORK	4,080,092
4	THE CHAINSMOKERS	DON'T LET ME DOWN	3,849,930
5	DESIIGNER	PANDA	3,601,797
6	JUSTIN TIMBERLAKE	CAN'T STOP THE FEELING	3,596,807
7	LUKAS GRAHAM	7 YEARS	3,544,342
8	FLO RIDA	MY HOUSE	3,458,391
9	TWENTY ONE PILOTS	STRESSED OUT	3,386,331
10	SIA	CHEAP THRILLS	3,348,752

9

MUSIC

PRINCE

Genre-defying artist Prince (June 7, 1958–April 21, 2016) released 39 studio albums. His sixth, *Purple Rain*, was also the soundtrack to the same-named 1984 movie. Prince's 11th album was the original song-soundtrack to the 1989 movie *Batman*.

TOP 10 MOST POPULAR GENRES BY SONG

When it comes to comparing songs, instead of albums, the popularity of genres changes dramatically...

	GENRE	% OF TOTAL STREAMS
1	HIP-HOP / RAP	18.2
2	POP	15.3
3	R&B	10
4	COUNTRY	8.2
5	ROCK	7.5
6	ALTERNATIVE	6
7	INDIE ROCK	5.9
8	LATIN	3.9
=	ELECTRONICA	3.9
10	DANCE	3.5

TOP 10 BIGGEST-SELLING
VINYL ALBUMS 2016

The sales figures may seem small, but vinyl popularity has increased by 25.9 percent over the past few years...

	ARTIST	ALBUM	TOTAL SALES
1	TWENTY ONE PILOTS	BLURRYFACE	49,004
2	AMY WINEHOUSE	BACK TO BLACK	41,087
3	RADIOHEAD	A MOON SHAPED POOL	39,861
4	THE BEATLES	ABBEY ROAD	39,615
5	ADELE	25	39,512
6	DAVID BOWIE	BLACKSTAR	39,334
7	PRINCE & THE REVOLUTION	PURPLE RAIN	35,244
8	BOB MARLEY & THE WAILERS	LEGEND	32,899
9	TWENTY ONE PILOTS	VESSEL	31,006
10	MILES DAVIS	KIND OF BLUE	30,495

3 RADIOHEAD

Radiohead's ninth studio album, *A Moon Shaped Pool*, was released on May 8, 2016, and 2018 marks the 25th anniversary of their debut album, *Pablo Honey*. They have played more than 1,000 live shows and the band's line-up has never changed.

TOP 10 MOST POPULAR **METAL ALBUMS 2016**

One band on this chart made their back catalog available to stream in 2016, resulting in a flurry of activity...

	ARTIST	ALBUM	TOTAL CONSUMPTION
1	METALLICA	HARDWIRED...TO SELF-DESTRUCT	559,469
2	DISTURBED	IMMORTALIZED	481,267
3	METALLICA	METALLICA	358,909
4	FIVE FINGER DEATH PUNCH	GOT YOUR SIX	196,702
5	METALLICA	MASTER OF PUPPETS	180,384
6	METALLICA	RIDE THE LIGHTNING	178,541
7	METALLICA	...AND JUSTICE FOR ALL	176,553
8	LINKIN PARK	HYBRID THEORY	154,452
9	AVENGED SEVENFOLD	THE STAGE	145,123
10	FIVE FINGER DEATH PUNCH	THE WRONG SIDE OF HEAVEN AND THE RIGHTEOUS SIDE OF HELL, VOL. 2	142,705

2 DISTURBED

The American metal band, fronted by singer David Draiman, celebrated their 24th year in 2018. Their fifth studio album, *Immortalized*, debuted at number one in the Billboard chart, like every other album the band has released.

10  DAVID BOWIE

The four-track EP *No Plan* was released on January 8, 2017, on what would have been David Bowie's 70th birthday. Its release came exactly one year after Bowie's final album, *Blackstar*, was released. *No Plan* included four songs from Bowie's 2016 Broadway musical, *Lazarus*.

TOP 10 MOST POPULAR ROCK ALBUMS 2016

From funk, to experimental, to heavy riffs, the rock genre encapsulates a multitude of different subgenres...

	ARTIST	ALBUM	TOTAL CONSUMPTION
1	TWENTY ONE PILOTS	BLURRYFACE	1,661,302
2	PANIC! AT THE DISCO	DEATH OF A BACHELOR	844,844
3	COLDPLAY	A HEAD FULL OF DREAMS	644,125
4	TWENTY ONE PILOTS	VESSEL	593,310
5	METALLICA	HARDWIRED...TO SELF-DESTRUCT	559,469
6	THE LUMINEERS	CLEOPATRA	543,910
7	DISTURBED	IMMORTALIZED	481,267
8	RED HOT CHILI PEPPERS	THE GETAWAY	423,914
9	BLINK-182	CALIFORNIA	408,141
10	DAVID BOWIE	BLACKSTAR	407,661

TOP 10

MOST POPULAR
POP ALBUMS 2016

Female pop artists reign supreme in this top 10, with their combined total consumption figure exceeding 4 million...

	ARTIST	ALBUM	TOTAL CONSUMPTION
1	ADELE	25	2,194,933
2	JUSTIN BIEBER	PURPOSE	1,643,939
3	ARIANA GRANDE	DANGEROUS WOMAN	1,032,184
4	PENTATONIX	A PENTATONIX CHRISTMAS	1,002,001
5	SIA	THIS IS ACTING	903,725
6	MEGHAN TRAINOR	THANK YOU	724,735
7	CHARLIE PUTH	NINE TRACK MIND	716,624
8	VARIOUS	TROLLS (ORIGINAL MOTION PICTURE SOUNDTRACK)	685,194
9	BRUNO MARS	24K MAGIC	683,661
10	ZAYN	MIND OF MINE	647,785

3 ARIANA GRANDE

Before her pop career, Ariana Grande started out on the stage, cast in Jason Robert Brown's 2008 musical *13*. Her debut album, *Yours Truly*, was released on September 3, 2013, three months after Grande's 20th birthday. Three albums into her career, Grande has won 46 international music awards.

▶ 3 HALSEY

Ashley Frangipane's stage name comes from an anagram of her first name. Her second studio album, *Hopeless Fountain Kingdom*, was released on June 2, 2017. Its cowriters include Norwegian producer / rapper Lido and Facing New York's lead singer Ricky Reed.

BIGGEST GROWTH IN ALBUM CONSUMPTION

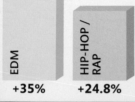

EDM	HIP-HOP / RAP	R&B	LATIN
+35%	+24.8%	+23.9%	+23.6S%

TOP 10 MOST POPULAR EDM ALBUMS 2016

Electronic dance music (EDM) artists cover a broad range of styles, but The Chainsmokers dominate here with two mini-albums...

	ARTIST	ALBUM	TOTAL CONSUMPTION
1	THE CHAINSMOKERS	CLOSER	972,465
2	THE CHAINSMOKERS	CHAINSMOKERS	637,905
▶ 3	HALSEY	BADLANDS	558,097
4	DJ SNAKE	ENCORE	446,726
5	TROYE SIVAN	BLUE NEIGHBOURHOOD	375,224
6	FLUME	SKIN	362,693
7	MAJOR LAZER	PEACE IS THE MISSION	299,985
8	ELLIE GOULDING	DELIRIUM	290,507
9	KYGO	CLOUD NINE	252,874
10	LOGIC	BOBBY TARANTINO	215,249

5 FLORIDA GEORGIA LINE

Florida Georgia Line is country duo Tyler Hubbard and Brian Kelley. Since their self-released EP in 2010, *Anything Like Me*, the singers have released a further two EPs, three albums, and 13 singles. Their 2017 song "God, Your Mama, and Me" featured the Backstreet Boys.

TOP 10 MOST POPULAR
COUNTRY ALBUMS 2016

The country album chart features artists from a broad range of backgrounds, from the four-decade career of Garth Brooks to *The Voice* mentor / judge Blake Shelton...

	ARTIST	ALBUM	TOTAL CONSUMPTION
1	CHRIS STAPLETON	TRAVELLER	1,371,562
2	BLAKE SHELTON	IF I'M HONEST	715,962
3	SAM HUNT	MONTEVALLO	704,767
4	THOMAS RHETT	TANGLED UP	688,310
5	FLORIDA GEORGIA LINE	DIG YOUR ROOTS	643,099
6	KEITH URBAN	RIPCORD	643,073
7	LUKE BRYAN	KILL THE LIGHTS	522,136
8	GARTH BROOKS	THE ULTIMATE COLLECTION	507,105
9	CARRIE UNDERWOOD	STORYTELLER	459,118
10	DIERKS BENTLEY	BLACK	437,416

TOP 10 MOST POPULAR
JAZZ ALBUMS 2016

The classic jazz artists of the previous century are still very popular, but the music that accompanies Charles M. Schulz's creation is still king...

	ARTIST	ALBUM	TOTAL CONSUMPTION
1	VINCE GUARALDI TRIO	A CHARLIE BROWN CHRISTMAS	103,645
2	MILES DAVIS	KIND OF BLUE	74,186
3	JOEY ALEXANDER	MY FAVORITE THINGS	36,246
4	GREGORY PORTER	TAKE ME TO THE ALLEY	27,312
5	JOHN COLTRANE	A LOVE SUPREME EP	26,520
6	KENNY C	SILVER BELLS	26,001
7	NINA SIMONE	THE BEST OF NINA SIMONE	24,790
8	ESPERANZA SPALDING	EMILY'S D+EVOLUTION	23,396
9	LOUIS ARMSTRONG	LOUIS ARMSTRONG	21,976
10	KAMASI WASHINGTON	THE EPIC	19,778

4 GREGORY PORTER

Born in Sacramento, California, jazz artist Gregory Porter won the Grammy Award for Best Jazz Vocal Album in 2017 for *Take Me to the Alley*, and also in 2014 for *Liquid Spirit*. His 2010 debut, *Water*, earned a nomination in the same category. In 2016, Porter performed on the prestigious Pyramid Stage at the UK's Glastonbury Festival.

5 ENRIQUE IGLESIAS

The son of Spanish singer-songwriter Julio Iglesias has released 10 studio albums since 1995. Aside from his music career, Enrique Iglesias has several acting credits, including writer / director Robert Rodriguez's 2003 film *Once Upon a Time in Mexico*, in which he played Lorenzo.

TOP 10 MOST POPULAR **LATIN ALBUMS 2016**

Juan Gabriel makes three appearances on this chart, and Latin music continues to evolve and delve into new territories...

	ARTIST	ALBUM	TOTAL CONSUMPTION
1	J. BALVIN	ENERGÍA	103,066
2	ARIEL CAMACHO Y LOS PLEBES DEL RANCHO	RECUERDEN MI ESTILO	102,512
3	BANDA SINALOENSE MS DE SERGIO LIZÁRRAGA	QUE BENDICIÓN	85,363
4	ARIEL CAMACHO Y LOS PLEBES DEL RANCHO	EL KARMA	80,181
5	ENRIQUE IGLESIAS	SEX AND LOVE	74,542
6	JUAN GABRIEL	LOS DÚO	68,474
7	ROMEO SANTOS	F	63,386
8	JUAN GABRIEL	MIS NÚMERO 1... 40 ANIVERSARIO	61,703
9	JUAN GABRIEL	LOS DÚO 2	58,278
10	SELENA	AMOR PROHIBIDO	47,095

MOST POPULAR
STAGE & SCREEN ALBUMS 2016

Hamilton continues to dominate wherever it goes, but this chart also has a broad range of old and new film soundtracks...

	ARTIST	ALBUM	TOTAL CONSUMPTION
1	VARIOUS	HAMILTON: ORIGINAL BROADWAY CAST RECORDING	1,322,524
2	VARIOUS	THE HAMILTON MIXTAPE	294,337
3	VARIOUS	MOANA (ORIGINAL MOTION PICTURE SOUNDTRACK)	290,463
4	VARIOUS	GUARDIANS OF THE GALAXY: AWESOME MIX VOL. 1 (ORIGINAL MOTION PICTURE SOUNDTRACK)	169,096
5	JOHN WILLIAMS	STAR WARS: THE FORCE AWAKENS (ORIGINAL MOTION PICTURE SOUNDTRACK)	133,033
6	VARIOUS	FROZEN (ORIGINAL MOTION PICTURE SOUNDTRACK)	95,541
7	VARIOUS	EMPIRE: ORIGINAL SOUNDTRACK SEASON 2 VOL. 2	84,114
8	VARIOUS	DIRTY DANCING (ORIGINAL MOTION PICTURE SOUNDTRACK)	59,820
9	TOBY FOX	UNDERTALE (ORIGINAL MOTION PICTURE SOUNDTRACK)	55,850
10	HANS ZIMMER & JUNKIE XL	BATMAN V SUPERMAN: DAWN OF JUSTICE (ORIGINAL MOTION PICTURE SOUNDTRACK)	52,522

1 HAMILTON: ORIGINAL BROADWAY CAST RECORDING

Hamilton is the third stage musical created by Lin-Manuel Miranda, following *21 Chump Street* (2014) and *In the Heights* (1999). As well as writing the music, lyrics, and the book, Miranda also originated the lead role of Alexander Hamilton. It has won 56 awards.

TOP 10 MOST **INSTAGRAM FOLLOWERS (BANDS / GROUPS)**

Since its launch in 2010, Instagram has become one of the most popular methods of sharing photos and videos online...

	ARTIST	HANDLE	FOLLOWING	FOLLOWERS
1	ONE DIRECTION	@ONEDIRECTION	249	17,255,742
2	5 SECONDS OF SUMMER	@5SOS	33	7,295,814
3	COLDPLAY	@COLDPLAY	12	5,879,980
4	LINKIN PARK	@LINKINPARK	16	3,120,606
5	METALLICA	@METALLICA	35	2,931,046
6	SLIPKNOT	@SLIPKNOT	12	2,119,305
7	PARAMORE	@PARAMORE	191	1,605,833
8	AC / DC	@ACDC	16	1,478,922
9	PENTATONIX	@PTXOFFICIAL	34	1,451,004
10	RED HOT CHILI PEPPERS	@CHILIPEPPERS	4	1,444,287

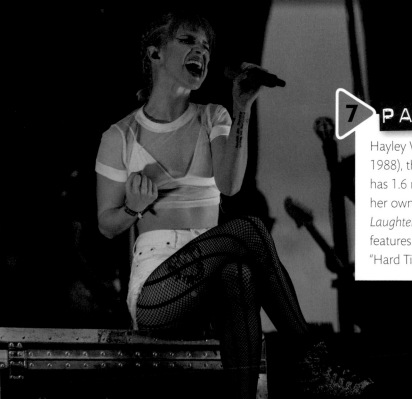

7 PARAMORE

Hayley Williams (born December 27, 1988), the lead singer in Paramore, also has 1.6 million Instagram followers of her own. Paramore's fifth album, *After Laughter*, released on May 12, 2017, features the songs "Told You So" and "Hard Times."

4 ▶ BEYONCÉ

The 2016 concept album *Lemonade* was Beyoncé's second release to be categorized as a "visual album." The songs formed the soundtrack for an HBO-broadcast hour-long film of the same name (included on the second disc of the CD edition). *Lemonade* topped the charts in 17 countries.

TOP 10 MOST **INSTAGRAM FOLLOWERS (SOLO)**

Social media giant Facebook bought Instagram in 2012, and in 2017 the number of registered users passed 700 million...

	ARTIST	HANDLE	FOLLOWING	FOLLOWERS
1	SELENA GOMEZ	@SELENAGOMEZ	254	106,791,691
2	TAYLOR SWIFT	@TAYLORSWIFT	94	96,048,494
3	ARIANA GRANDE	@ARIANAGRANDE	1,306	93,782,973
4	BEYONCÉ	@BEYONCÉ	0	91,516,020
5	NICKI MINAJ	@NICKIMINAJ	577	71,844,228
6	KATY PERRY	@KATYPERRY	278	59,884,788
7	MILEY CYRUS	@MILEYCYRUS	450	58,874,091
8	JENNIFER LOPEZ	@JLO	1,019	56,411,434
9	DEMI LOVATO	@DDLOVATO	226	52,060,475
10	RIHANNA	@BADGALRIRI	1,232	47,910,840

TOP 10 MOST **TWITTER FOLLOWERS (BANDS / GROUPS)**

This social media platform debuted in the summer of 2006. It has grown to have more than 300 million followers...

	ARTIST	HANDLE	FOLLOWING	FOLLOWERS
1	ONE DIRECTION	@ONEDIRECTION	3,983	31,494,228
2	COLDPLAY	@COLDPLAY	1,504	18,497,133
3	MAROON 5	@MAROON5	422	13,612,419
4	5 SECONDS OF SUMMER	@5SOS	32,699	10,529,833
5	LITTLE MIX	@LITTLEMIX	30,544	8,390,317
6	LMFAO	@LMFAO	1,536	8,229,194
7	THE BLACK EYED PEAS	@BEP	46,761	5,265,882
8	LINKIN PARK	@LINKINPARK	52	5,056,389
9	GREEN DAY	@GREENDAY	136	4,501,146
10	PARAMORE	@PARAMORE	182	4,169,181

5 LITTLE MIX

British vocal group Little Mix won the 2011 run of the TV series *The X Factor*. Their first single was a cover version of Irish singer-songwriter Damien Rice's international hit "Cannonball," first released in 2002. Little Mix's fourth album, *Glory Days*, released on November 18, 2016, included the hit "Shout Out to My Ex."

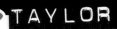

3 TAYLOR SWIFT

Although American singer-songwriter Taylor Swift has a huge social media following, she took a break from it in 2017, with a greatly reduced post-rate. Of her 571 international music award nominations, Swift has won 272, including 10 Grammys.

TOP **10** MOST **TWITTER FOLLOWERS (SOLO)**

This chart is ranked by how many followers these artists have, and the total number of accounts they follow varies considerably...

	ARTIST	HANDLE	FOLLOWING	FOLLOWERS
1	KATY PERRY	@KATYPERRY	186	95,239,982
2	JUSTIN BIEBER	@JUSTINBIEBER	300,997	91,080,405
3	TAYLOR SWIFT	@TAYLORSWIFT13	244	83,002,633
4	RIHANNA	@RIHANNA	1,136	69,095,775
5	LADY GAGA	@LADYGAGA	130,137	64,900,324
6	JUSTIN TIMBERLAKE	@JTIMBERLAKE	227	57,712,081
7	BRITNEY SPEARS	@BRITNEYSPEARS	392,956	49,833,150
8	SELENA GOMEZ	@SELENAGOMEZ	1,278	46,043,841
9	ARIANA GRANDE	@ARIANAGRANDE	66,391	43,455,142
10	SHAKIRA	@SHAKIRA	189	42,314,964

TOP 10 MOST **FACEBOOK LIKES** (BANDS / GROUPS)

Eight of the 10 music acts in this chart are predominantly vocals, guitar, bass, and drums-based bands...

	ARTIST	"LIKES"
1	LINKIN PARK	62,118,693
2	THE BLACK EYED PEAS	44,233,263
3	THE BEATLES	42,267,739
4	COLDPLAY	39,477,204
5	MAROON 5	39,355,499
6	ONE DIRECTION	39,129,286
7	METALLICA	37,638,510
8	GREEN DAY	31,726,388
9	GUNS N' ROSES	30,592,140
10	AC / DC	30,262,779

BANDS / GROUPS 396,801,501

SOLO ARTISTS VS. BANDS / GROUPS

SOLO ARTISTS 791,478,533

1 LINKIN PARK

The six-piece band have run their own fan club, LPU (Linkin Park Underground), since 2001. LPU-only record releases have featured rare and exclusive tracks. The band's seventh studio album, *One More Light*, was released on May 19, 2017. Their debut, *Hybrid Theory* (released October 24, 2000), was named after the band's original name.

TOP 10 MOST **FACEBOOK LIKES (SOLO)**

The number of female and male solo artists in this top 10 is equally split, but most of them were born in the 1980s...

	ARTIST	"LIKES"
1	SHAKIRA	104,502,352
2	EMINEM	91,060,987
3	RIHANNA	81,888,021
4	JUSTIN BIEBER	77,897,693
5	MICHAEL JACKSON	75,516,806
6	WILL SMITH	74,807,822
7	TAYLOR SWIFT	74,681,089
8	BOB MARLEY	74,445,689
9	KATY PERRY	70,760,527
10	ADELE	65,917,547

6 WILL SMITH

Actor and rapper-songwriter Will Smith has won four Grammy Awards. As one half of DJ Jazzy Jeff & The Fresh Prince, the duo released five studio albums including 1993's *Code Red*. Smith has also made four solo albums. In 2017, they reunited to play live festivals together.

VIDEOS

9 ADELE

Fifteen-time Grammy Award-winner Adele has released eight official music videos. "Chasing Pavements," her first, was released on October 24, 2009, and has more than 101 million views. "Send My Love (To My New Lover)," the second official music video for her album 25, has garnered more than 380 million views since its May 22, 2016 premiere.

TOP 10 MOST SUBSCRIBED MUSIC YOUTUBE CHANNELS

YouTube remains the dominant internet channel for fans to follow and watch artists' video-based output...

	ARTIST	SUBSCRIBERS
1	JUSTIN BIEBER	26,643,620
2	RIHANNA	23,863,071
3	ONE DIRECTION	21,378,765
4	TAYLOR SWIFT	20,806,575
5	EMINEM	20,591,510
6	KATY PERRY	20,501,822
7	ARIANA GRANDE	15,012,436
8	SKRILLEX	14,939,245
9	ADELE	13,808,991
10	DAVID GUETTA	12,871,139

4 MARK RONSON FT. BRUNO MARS

"Uptown Funk" is a collaboration between British producer / songwriter Mark Ronson and American singer-songwriter / producer Bruno Mars. This was not their first time working together, as Ronson coproduced Mars' songs "Locked Out of Heaven" and "Gorilla." He also cowrote / produced Mars' "Moonshine."

TOP 10 OFFICIAL MUSIC VIDEOS
WITH THE MOST VIEWS

Although eight of the music videos in the chart were released in the past four years, no one can best South Korean artist Psy's 2012 hit...

	SONG	ARTIST	DATE UPLOADED	VIEWS
1	GANGNAM STYLE	PSY	JUL 15, 2012	2,733,815,253
2	SEE YOU AGAIN	WIZ KHALIFA FT. CHARLIE PUTH	APR 6, 2015	2,340,123,879
3	SORRY	JUSTIN BIEBER	OCT 22, 2015	2,157,836,783
4	UPTOWN FUNK	MARK RONSON FT. BRUNO MARS	NOV 19, 2014	2,113,532,252
5	BLANK SPACE	TAYLOR SWIFT	NOV 10, 2014	1,918,886,617
6	HELLO	ADELE	OCT 22, 2015	1,842,093,274
7	SHAKE IT OFF	TAYLOR SWIFT	AUG 18, 2014	1,838,399,823
8	BAILANDO	ENRIQUE IGLESIAS FT. DESCEMER BUENO & GENTE DE ZONA	APR 11, 2014	1,836,558,490
9	LEAN ON	MAJOR LAZER & DJ SNAKE FT. MØ	MAR 22, 2015	1,825,952,661
10	ROAR	KATY PERRY	SEP 5, 2013	1,728,294,730

Movies & TV

ZONE
10

4 JURASSIC WORLD

The 124-minute, fourth installment in the *Jurassic Park* film franchise starred Chris Pratt as *Velociraptor* expert Owen Grady. This character is the third of Pratt's to become a LEGO mini-figure, following his role of Emmet Brickowski in *The LEGO Movie* (2014), and Peter Quill in the *Guardians of the Galaxy* films (2014 and 2017).

TOP 10 BIGGEST MOVIES OF ALL TIME

Combining every single film ever theatrically released, these are the 10 that have taken the most at box offices worldwide...

	MOVIE	YEAR OF RELEASE	BOX OFFICE ($ WORLDWIDE)
1	AVATAR	2009	2,787,965,087
2	TITANIC	1997	2,186,772,302
3	STAR WARS: EPISODE VII—THE FORCE AWAKENS	2015	2,068,223,624
4	JURASSIC WORLD	2015	1,670,400,637
5	THE AVENGERS	2012	1,519,557,910
6	FURIOUS 7	2015	1,516,045,911
7	AVENGERS: AGE OF ULTRON	2015	1,405,413,868
8	HARRY POTTER AND THE DEATHLY HALLOWS: PART 2	2011	1,341,511,219
9	FROZEN	2013	1,276,480,335
10	IRON MAN 3	2013	1,215,439,994

1 MERYL STREEP

Born in New Jersey, American actress Meryl Streep has 79 acting credits, including *Sophie's Choice* (1982), *Defending Your Life* (1991), *Doubt* (2008), and *Florence Foster Jenkins* (2016). Her three Academy Awards are among more than 160 international film award wins.

TOP 10 ACTORS WITH
THE MOST OSCAR NOMINATIONS

Even just being nominated for an Academy Award is considered one of the most prestigious recognitions of acting talent...

	ACTOR	NATIONALITY	TOTAL OSCAR NOMS
1	MERYL STREEP	USA	20 (INCL. 3 WINS)
2	KATHARINE HEPBURN	USA	12 (INCL. 4 WINS)
3	JACK NICHOLSON	USA	12 (INCL. 3 WINS)
4	BETTE DAVIS	USA	10 (INCL. 2 WINS)
5	LAURENCE OLIVIER	UK	10 (INCL. 1 WIN)
6	SPENCER TRACY	USA	9 (INCL. 2 WINS)
7	PAUL NEWMAN	USA	9 (INCL. 1 WIN)
8	MARLON BRANDO	USA	8 (INCL. 2 WINS)
=	JACK LEMMON	USA	8 (INCL. 2 WINS)
10	AL PACINO / GERALDINE PAGE	USA	8 (INCL. 1 WIN)

BLOCKBUSTERS

1 LILLY & LANA WACHOWSKI

Collectively and creatively known as The Wachowskis, the siblings created, wrote, and directed *The Matrix* trilogy (1999–2003). The three movies made a total of $1,632,989,142 at the box office worldwide. The duo also cocreated (with J. Michael Straczynski) the sci-fi TV series *Sense 8*, which debuted on June 5, 2015.

TOP 10 MOST SUCCESSFUL FEMALE DIRECTORS

Some of the most beloved movies were made by the directors on this list, including *Shrek, Sleepless in Seattle* and *Kung Fu Panda 3*...

	DIRECTOR	TOTAL FILMS DIRECTED (THEATRICALLY RELEASED)	BOX OFFICE ($ WORLDWIDE)
1	LILLY & LANA WACHOWSKI	7	2,045,207,759
2	NANCY MEYERS	6	1,351,752,614
3	JENNIFER LEE	1	1,276,480,335
4	JENNIFER YUH NELSON	2	1,185,573,636
5	BETTY THOMAS	7	1,007,159,961
6	NORA EPHRON	8	879,940,416
7	VICKY JENSON	3	858,098,966
8	BRENDA CHAPMAN	2	759,050,251
9	PHYLLIDA LLOYD	2	724,798,336
10	ANNE FLETCHER	5	685,373,124

3 JAMES CAMERON

The Canadian writer-director is responsible for several modern classics including *The Terminator* (1984), *Aliens* (1986), *The Abyss* (1989), and *Terminator 2: Judgment Day* (1991). His creation *Avatar* (2009) is the biggest movie of all time, and *Avatar 2, 3, 4,* and *5* are all planned for release between 2020 and 2025.

TOP 10 MOST SUCCESSFUL MALE DIRECTORS

These 10 creatives have produced dozens of science fiction and action adventure films that are considered classics...

	DIRECTOR	TOTAL FILMS DIRECTED (THEATRICALLY RELEASED)	BOX OFFICE ($ WORLDWIDE)
1	STEVEN SPIELBERG	30	9,691,930,230
2	PETER JACKSON	14	6,530,713,297
3	JAMES CAMERON	10	6,207,806,867
4	MICHAEL BAY	13	5,845,137,383
5	DAVID YATES	7	5,340,284,639
6	ROBERT ZEMECKIS	18	4,248,997,156
7	CHRISTOPHER NOLAN	10	4,227,531,716
8	CHRIS COLUMBUS	15	4,099,031,132
9	TIM BURTON	18	4,089,305,587
10	GEORGE LUCAS	6	3,997,678,795

COMPOSERS WITH **THE MOST FILM, TV & VIDEO GAME CREDITS**

So many successful composers, and so little space, so we've provided a bonus 11–20 chart to show where a lot of contemporary composers land...

	COMPOSER	NATIONALITY	TOTAL CREDITS
1	ENNIO MORRICONE	ITALY	524
2	GEORGES DELERUE	FRANCE	369
3	JERRY GOLDSMITH	USA	259
4	ELMER BERNSTEIN	USA	249
5	MAX STEINER	AUSTRIA	241
6	ALFRED NEWMAN	USA	230
7	LALO SCHIFRIN	ARGENTINA	211
8	HENRY MANCINI	USA	199
9	MICHEL LEGRAND	FRANCE	197
10	JOHN DEBNEY	USA	183

11	HANS ZIMMER	GERMANY	179
12	NINO ROTA	ITALY	178
13	FRANZ WAXMAN	GERMANY	175
14	ALEXANDRE DESPLAT	FRANCE	169
15	MAURICE JARRE	FRANCE	168
16	JAMES HORNER	USA	158
17	JAMES NEWTON HOWARD	USA	153
18	JOHN WILLIAMS	USA	142
19	PHILIP GLASS	USA	126
20	MICHAEL GIACCHINO	USA	122

1 ENNIO MORRICONE

The Rome, Italy, native has been scoring films since 1946. Born on November 10, 1928, the composer is still writing music for film. His most recent work includes Quentin Tarantino's *The Hateful Eight* (2015), for which he won the Academy Award for Best Original Score.

7 ▶ LIONSGATE

Lionsgate, a production studio and distributor, was founded in 1997. Their movie franchises include *The Hunger Games* (2012–15), *Saw* (2004–17), *The Expendables* (2010–18), and *Twilight* (2008–12).

TOP 10

STUDIOS WITH **THE BIGGEST MARKET SHARE**

Of 100 percent of the total film market, this shows how the most successful studios share it...

	STUDIO	MARKET SHARE
1	BUENA VISTA	23.7
2	WARNER BROS.	17.5
3	20TH CENTURY FOX	13.8
4	UNIVERSAL	12.5
5	SONY / COLUMBIA	8.7
6	PARAMOUNT	7.2
7	LIONSGATE	6.2
8	STX ENTERTAINMENT	1.9
9	FOCUS FEATURES	1.8
10	OPEN ROAD FILMS	1.1

TOP 10 LONGEST-RUNNING **US TV SHOWS**

How long has your favorite TV series been on the air? Compare it to these record-breaking productions...

	SHOW	NETWORK	YEARS ON AIR
1	MEET THE PRESS	NBC	71
2	CBS EVENING NEWS	CBS	70
3	MUSIC & THE SPOKEN WORD	KSL / VARIOUS	69
4	HALLMARK HALL OF FAME	HALLMARK / VARIOUS	67
5	TODAY	NBC	66
6	ABC NEWS / WORLD NEWS	ABC	65
7	THE TONIGHT SHOW	NBC	64
=	FACE THE NATION	CBS	64
9	IT IS WRITTEN	VARIOUS	62
=	THE OPEN MIND	VARIOUS	62

1 MEET THE PRESS

Up to 1992, *Meet the Press* was a 30-minute-long production, at which point it was extended to 52 minutes. The current presenter is Chuck Todd, who began hosting the show in 2014. The person responsible for the theme music for *Meet the Press* is John Williams, the composer behind the likes of the *Star Wars* and *Indiana Jones* movies.

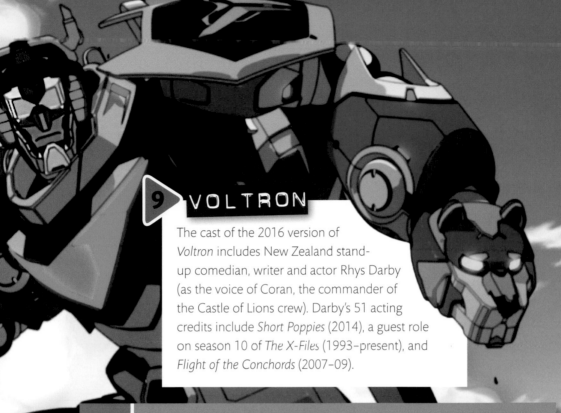

9 ▷ VOLTRON

The cast of the 2016 version of *Voltron* includes New Zealand stand-up comedian, writer and actor Rhys Darby (as the voice of Coran, the commander of the Castle of Lions crew). Darby's 51 acting credits include *Short Poppies* (2014), a guest role on season 10 of *The X-Files* (1993–present), and *Flight of the Conchords* (2007–09).

TOP **10** LONGEST-RUNNING
TV SHOWS SET IN SPACE

Outer space has always been a popular location for drama, comedy, horror, animation, and everything in between...

	SHOW	YEARS ON AIR	TOTAL EPISODES
1	SPACE PATROL	1950–55	1,110
2	DOCTOR WHO	1963–84; 1985–89; 1996; 2005–PRESENT	842
3	STARGATE SG-1	1997–2007	214
4	MYSTERY SCIENCE THEATER 3000	1988–99	197
5	STAR TREK: THE NEXT GENERATION	1987–94	178
6	STAR TREK: DEEP SPACE NINE	1993–99	176
7	STAR TREK: VOYAGER	1995–2001	172
8	THUNDERCATS	1985–89; 2011	156
9	VOLTRON	1984–85; 2016–PRESENT	146
10	FUTURAMA	1999–2003; 2008–2013	141

TOP 10 BIGGEST **STAR WARS MOVIES**

Until we know how successful *Star Wars: Episode VIII—The Last Jedi* is at the box office, these are the biggest *Star Wars* hits to date...

	MOVIE	YEAR OF RELEASE	BOX OFFICE ($ WORLDWIDE)
1	STAR WARS: EPISODE VII—THE FORCE AWAKENS	2015	2,068,223,624
2	ROGUE ONE: A STAR WARS STORY	2016	1,055,494,429
3	STAR WARS: EPISODE I—THE PHANTOM MENACE	1999	1,027,044,677
4	STAR WARS: EPISODE III—REVENGE OF THE SITH	2005	848,754,768
5	STAR WARS: EPISODE IV—A NEW HOPE	1977	775,398,007
6	STAR WARS: EPISODE II—ATTACK OF THE CLONES	2002	649,398,328
7	STAR WARS: EPISODE IV—A NEW HOPE (SPECIAL EDITION)	1997	579,646,015
8	STAR WARS: EPISODE V—THE EMPIRE STRIKES BACK	1980	538,375,067
9	STAR WARS: EPISODE VI—RETURN OF THE JEDI	1983	475,106,177
10	STAR WARS: EPISODE VI—RETURN OF THE JEDI (SPECIAL EDITION)	1997	353,096,720

2 ROGUE ONE: A STAR WARS STORY

Felicity Jones reprised her *Rogue One* Jyn Erso role for the animated short series *Star Wars: Forces of Destiny* (2017–present). Her character also appears in the official tie-in prequel novel, *Catalyst: A Rogue One Novel*, written by *New York Times* bestselling author James Luceno.

5 ▷ A MONSTER CALLS

Of Felicity Jones' 36 acting credits, her 33rd was playing the mother in J. A. Bayona's adaptation of *A Monster Calls*. The novel, by Patrick Ness (based on an original idea by Siobhan Dowd) and illustrated by Jim Kay, deals with a boy who befriends a tree monster while trying to cope with his mother's cancer.

TOP 10 BIGGEST FELICITY JONES MOVIES

The British actress leads the heroics in *Rogue One* and was nominated for an Academy Award for her performance in *The Theory of Everything*...

	MOVIE	YEAR OF RELEASE	BOX OFFICE ($ WORLDWIDE)
1	ROGUE ONE: A STAR WARS STORY	2016	1,055,494,429
2	THE AMAZING SPIDER-MAN 2	2014	708,982,323
3	INFERNO	2016	219,304,189
4	THE THEORY OF EVERYTHING	2014	123,726,688
5	A MONSTER CALLS	2016	43,422,375
6	BRIDESHEAD REVISITED	2008	13,451,186
7	HYSTERIA	2012	9,504,139
8	CHÉRI	2009	9,366,227
9	COLLIDE	2017	4,811,525
10	TRUE STORY	2015	4,719,695

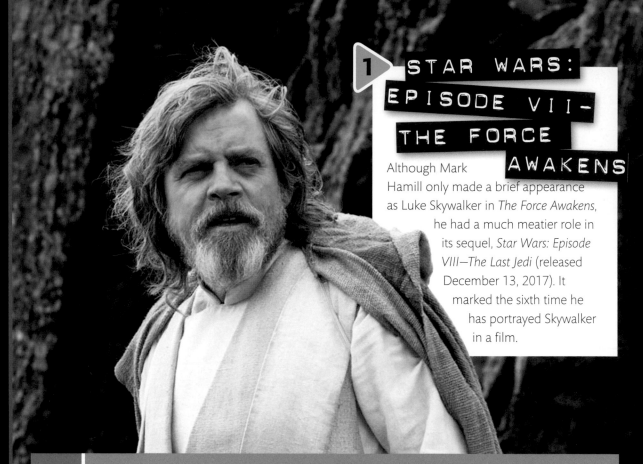

1 STAR WARS: EPISODE VII— THE FORCE AWAKENS

Although Mark Hamill only made a brief appearance as Luke Skywalker in *The Force Awakens*, he had a much meatier role in its sequel, *Star Wars: Episode VIII—The Last Jedi* (released December 13, 2017). It marked the sixth time he has portrayed Skywalker in a film.

TOP 10 BIGGEST **MARK HAMILL MOVIES**

As well as playing Luke Skywalker, Mark Hamill's eclectic career includes voicing the Joker in many episodes of animated *Batman* productions...

	MOVIE	YEAR OF RELEASE	BOX OFFICE ($ WORLDWIDE)
1	STAR WARS: EPISODE VII—THE FORCE AWAKENS	2015	2,068,223,624
2	STAR WARS: EPISODE IV—A NEW HOPE	1977	775,398,007
3	STAR WARS: EPISODE V—THE EMPIRE STRIKES BACK	1980	538,375,067
4	STAR WARS: EPISODE VI—RETURN OF THE JEDI	1983	475,106,177
5	KINGSMAN: THE SECRET SERVICE	2015	414,351,546
6	JAY AND SILENT BOB STRIKE BACK	2001	33,788,161
7	SLEEPWALKERS	1992	30,524,763
8	CORVETTE SUMMER	1978	15,514,367
9	THE NIGHT THE LIGHTS WENT OUT IN GEORGIA	1981	14,923,752
10	NAUSICAÄ OF THE VALLEY OF THE WIND*	1984	13,411,645

*ENGLISH DUB VERSION

BIGGEST **CARRIE FISHER MOVIES**

Beyond her beloved Leia Organa character, Carrie Fisher was a hugely talented screenwriter, author, singer, and stand-up comedian...

	MOVIE	YEAR OF RELEASE	BOX OFFICE ($ WORLDWIDE)
1	STAR WARS: EPISODE VII—THE FORCE AWAKENS	2015	2,068,223,624
2	STAR WARS: EPISODE IV—A NEW HOPE	1977	775,398,007
3	STAR WARS: EPISODE V—THE EMPIRE STRIKES BACK	1980	538,375,067
4	STAR WARS: EPISODE VI—RETURN OF THE JEDI	1983	475,106,177
5	CHARLIE'S ANGELS: FULL THROTTLE	2003	259,175,788
6	SCREAM 3	2000	161,834,276
7	THE BLUES BROTHERS	1980	115,229,890
8	WHEN HARRY MET SALLY...	1989	92,823,546
9	AUSTIN POWERS: INTERNATIONAL MAN OF MYSTERY	1997	67,683,989
10	HEARTBREAKERS	2001	57,756,408
11	THE WOMEN	2008	50,007,546
12	SHAMPOO	1975	49,407,734
13	THE 'BURBS	1989	49,101,993
14	HANNAH AND HER SISTERS	1986	40,084,041
15	SOAPDISH	1991	36,489,888

3 STAR WARS: EPISODE V— THE EMPIRE STRIKES BACK

Carrie Fisher's (October 21, 1956–December 27, 2016) third *Star Wars* film (following *A New Hope* and *The Star Wars Holiday Special*) saw her role greatly expanded. *The Empire Strikes Back* was her eighth acting credit. Fisher went on to act in a further 80 productions, including the 2017-released *Star Wars: Episode VIII —The Last Jedi* and the drama *Wonderwell*.

3 ▶ STAR WARS: EPISODE IV— A NEW HOPE

This, the first *Star Wars* movie, brought Harrison Ford's Han Solo to the big screen. Ford (born July 13, 1942) played the character a total of five times, the last being in 2015's *Star Wars: Episode VII—The Force Awakens*.

TOP 10 BIGGEST HARRISON FORD MOVIES

The American actor behind Han Solo, Indiana Jones, and the *Blade Runner* films' Rick Deckard has more than 70 acting credits...

	MOVIE	YEAR OF RELEASE	BOX OFFICE ($ WORLDWIDE)
1	STAR WARS: EPISODE VII—THE FORCE AWAKENS	2015	2,068,223,624
2	INDIANA JONES AND THE KINGDOM OF THE CRYSTAL SKULL	2008	786,636,033
3	STAR WARS: EPISODE IV—A NEW HOPE	1977	775,398,007
4	STAR WARS: EPISODE V—THE EMPIRE STRIKES BACK	1980	538,375,067
5	STAR WARS: EPISODE VI—RETURN OF THE JEDI	1983	475,106,177
6	INDIANA JONES AND THE LAST CRUSADE	1989	474,171,806
7	INDIANA JONES AND THE RAIDERS OF THE LOST ARK	1981	389,925,971
8	THE FUGITIVE	1993	368,875,760
9	INDIANA JONES AND THE TEMPLE OF DOOM	1984	333,107,271
10	AIR FORCE ONE	1997	315,156,409
11	WHAT LIES BENEATH	2000	291,420,351
12	PRESUMED INNOCENT	1990	221,303,188
13	CLEAR AND PRESENT DANGER	1994	215,887,717
14	THE EXPENDABLES 3	2014	206,172,544
15	PATRIOT GAMES	1992	178,051,587

TOP 10 BIGGEST **WARWICK DAVIS MOVIES**

British actor Warwick Davis also stars in *Star Wars: Episode VIII—The Last Jedi*. Prior to its release, these are his biggest films...

	MOVIE	YEAR OF RELEASE	BOX OFFICE ($ WORLDWIDE)
1	STAR WARS: EPISODE VII—THE FORCE AWAKENS	2015	2,068,223,624
2	HARRY POTTER AND THE DEATHLY HALLOWS: PART 2	2011	1,341,511,219
3	ROGUE ONE: A STAR WARS STORY	2016	1,055,494,429
4	STAR WARS: EPISODE I—THE PHANTOM MENACE	1999	1,027,044,677
5	HARRY POTTER AND THE PHILOSOPHER'S STONE	2001	974,755,371
6	HARRY POTTER AND THE DEATHLY HALLOWS: PART 1	2010	960,283,305
7	HARRY POTTER AND THE ORDER OF THE PHOENIX	2007	939,885,929
8	HARRY POTTER AND THE HALF-BLOOD PRINCE	2009	934,416,487
9	HARRY POTTER AND THE GOBLET OF FIRE	2005	896,911,078
10	HARRY POTTER AND THE CHAMBER OF SECRETS	2002	878,979,634

3 ROGUE ONE: A STAR WARS STORY

Aside from playing Weeteef Cyubee (pictured right) in *Rogue One: A Star Wars Story*, Warwick Davis has acted in a total of seven *Star Wars* productions. Davis's first was playing the Ewok called Wicket W. Warrick in *Return of the Jedi* (1983). He reprised the role in the TV movies *Caravan of Courage* (1984) and *The Battle for Endor* (1985).

1 STAR WARS: EPISODE VII— THE FORCE AWAKENS

Prior to first playing Kylo Ren in *The Force Awakens*, California-born actor Adam Driver was known for his acclaimed roles in dramas *Lincoln* (2012) and *This is Where I Leave You* (2014). He has also played a character investigating a child with special powers in *Midnight Special* (2016).

TOP 10 BIGGEST ADAM DRIVER MOVIES

The actor who plays the malevolent Kylo Ren returned in *Star Wars: Episode VIII—The Last Jedi*, released December 13, 2017...

	MOVIE	YEAR OF RELEASE	BOX OFFICE ($ WORLDWIDE)
1	STAR WARS: EPISODE VII—THE FORCE AWAKENS	2015	2,068,223,624
2	LINCOLN	2012	275,293,450
3	THIS IS WHERE I LEAVE YOU	2014	41,296,320
4	INSIDE LLEWYN DAVIS	2013	32,935,319
5	WHILE WE'RE YOUNG	2015	17,287,309
6	WHAT IF	2014	7,847,000
7	MIDNIGHT SPECIAL	2016	6,212,282
8	SILENCE	2017	5,322,414
9	TRACKS	2013	4,878,242
10	FRANCES HA	2013	4,069,826

BIGGEST **JAMES EARL JONES MOVIES**

The actor who provides the commanding voice for Darth Vader is also highly celebrated for his dramatic, comedic, and animation roles...

	MOVIE	YEAR OF RELEASE	BOX OFFICE ($ WORLDWIDE)
1	ROGUE ONE: A STAR WARS STORY	2016	1,055,494,429
2	THE LION KING	1994	968,483,777
3	STAR WARS: EPISODE III—REVENGE OF THE SITH	2005	848,754,768
4	STAR WARS: EPISODE IV—A NEW HOPE	1977	775,398,007
5	STAR WARS: EPISODE V—THE EMPIRE STRIKES BACK	1980	538,375,067
6	STAR WARS: EPISODE VI—RETURN OF THE JEDI	1983	475,106,177
7	ROBOTS	2005	260,718,330
8	SOMMERSBY	1993	140,081,992
9	JUDGE DREDD	1995	113,493,481
10	SNEAKERS	1992	105,232,691
11	THE NAKED GUN 33⅓: THE FINAL INSULT	1994	51,132,598
12	WELCOME HOME, ROSCOE JENKINS	2008	43,650,785
13	A FAMILY THING	1996	10,125,417
14	THE METEOR MAN	1993	8,016,708
15	CLEAN SLATE	1994	7,355,425

3 STAR WARS: EPISODE III— REVENGE OF THE SITH

This, the third film of the prequel trilogy, was written and directed by *Star Wars* creator George Lucas. Although Hayden Christensen played Anakin Skywalker / Darth Vader, the voice of Vader was, as in every *Star Wars* film, performed by James Earl Jones.

1 STAR WARS: EPISODE VII— THE FORCE AWAKENS

John Williams began his scoring work for this, his seventh *Star Wars* film, in late 2014. Recording sessions concluded in November 2015. The released soundtrack features 23 cues from the film, totaling more than 67 minutes of music.

TOP 10 BIGGEST JOHN WILLIAMS MOVIES

This American composer is the man behind the much-hummed themes to major blockbusters in several different genres...

	MOVIE	YEAR OF RELEASE	BOX OFFICE ($ WORLDWIDE)
1	STAR WARS: EPISODE VII—THE FORCE AWAKENS	2015	2,068,223,624
2	JURASSIC PARK	1993	1,029,153,882
3	STAR WARS: EPISODE I—THE PHANTOM MENACE	1999	1,027,044,677
4	HARRY POTTER AND THE PHILOSOPHER'S STONE	2001	974,755,371
5	HARRY POTTER AND THE CHAMBER OF SECRETS	2002	878,979,634
6	STAR WARS: EPISODE III—REVENGE OF THE SITH	2005	848,754,768
7	HARRY POTTER AND THE PRISONER OF AZKABAN	2004	796,688,549
8	E.T. THE EXTRA-TERRESTRIAL	1982	792,910,554
9	INDIANA JONES AND THE KINGDOM OF THE CRYSTAL SKULL	2008	786,636,033
10	STAR WARS: EPISODE IV—A NEW HOPE	1977	775,398,007
11	STAR WARS: EPISODE II—ATTACK OF THE CLONES	2002	649,398,328
12	THE LOST WORLD: JURASSIC PARK	1997	618,638,999
13	WAR OF THE WORLDS	2005	591,745,540
14	STAR WARS: EPISODE V—THE EMPIRE STRIKES BACK	1980	538,375,067
15	STAR WARS: EPISODE VI—RETURN OF THE JEDI	1983	475,106,177

LONGEST-RUNNING
STAR WARS TV SERIES / SPECIALS

There have been more TV specials, live-action series, and animated spin-offs in the *Star Wars* universe than you may think...

	NAME	YEARS ON AIR	TOTAL EPISODES
1	STAR WARS: THE CLONE WARS	2008–14	121
2	STAR WARS REBELS	2014–PRESENT	63
3	STAR WARS: EWOKS	1985–86	35
4	STAR WARS: CLONE WARS	2003–05	25
5	STAR WARS: DROIDS	1985–86	13
=	LEGO STAR WARS: THE FREEMAKER ADVENTURES	2016	13
7	LEGO STAR WARS: THE YODA CHRONICLES	2013–14	7
8	LEGO STAR WARS: DROID TALES	2015	5
9	LEGO STAR WARS: THE PADAWAN MENACE	2011	1
=	LEGO STAR WARS: THE EMPIRE STRIKES OUT	2012	1

1 STAR WARS: THE CLONE WARS

Star Wars: Clone Wars was the 2003–05 miniseries created, cowritten and directed by Genndy Tartakovsky, the creator of the animated series *Samurai Jack* (2001–04 and 2017). The theatrically released animated film *Star Wars: The Clone Wars* (2008) kick-started the TV series of the same name that ran for six years.

TOP 10 BIGGEST SUPERHERO MOVIES

Whether inspired by a Marvel, DC, or independent superhero comic book, these are the 10 adaptations that have dominated the box office...

	MOVIE	YEAR OF RELEASE	BOX OFFICE ($ WORLDWIDE)
1	THE AVENGERS	2012	1,519,557,910
2	AVENGERS: AGE OF ULTRON	2015	1,405,413,868
3	IRON MAN 3	2013	1,215,439,994
4	CAPTAIN AMERICA: CIVIL WAR	2016	1,153,304,495
5	THE DARK KNIGHT RISES	2012	1,084,439,099
6	THE DARK KNIGHT	2008	1,004,558,444
7	SPIDER-MAN 3	2007	890,871,626
8	BATMAN V SUPERMAN: DAWN OF JUSTICE	2016	873,260,194
9	SPIDER-MAN	2002	821,708,551
10	SPIDER-MAN 2	2004	783,766,341

4 CAPTAIN AMERICA: CIVIL WAR

Captain America: Civil War (2016) marks the fourth time that Anthony Mackie played Sam Wilson (aka Falcon). Mackie first appeared as Wilson in Captain America: The Winter Soldier (2016), then in Avengers: Age of Ultron (2015), and Ant-Man (2015). His fifth time as Falcon is in Avengers: Infinity War (2018).

7 HELLBOY II: THE GOLDEN ARMY

Hellboy II: The Golden Army followed the events in *Hellboy* (2004), the first big-screen adaptation of the comic book created by artist-writer Mike Mignola. Ron Perlman played the title role in each movie, and voiced the character in the 2006–07 animated series.

TOP 10 BIGGEST INDEPENDENT CREATOR-OWNED COMICS MOVIES

Even if you have seen several of the films in this top 10, how many did you know were adapted from comic books?

	MOVIE	PUBLISHER(S)	YEAR OF RELEASE	BOX OFFICE ($ WORLDWIDE)
1	TEENAGE MUTANT NINJA TURTLES	MIRAGE STUDIOS / IDW	2014	493,333,584
2	THE MASK	DARK HORSE	1994	351,583,407
3	WANTED	TOP COW	2008	341,433,252
4	TEENAGE MUTANT NINJA TURTLES: OUT OF THE SHADOWS	MIRAGE STUDIOS / IDW	2016	245,623,848
5	THE GREEN HORNET	DYNAMITE	2011	227,817,248
6	TEENAGE MUTANT NINJA TURTLES	MIRAGE STUDIOS / IDW	1990	201,965,915
7	HELLBOY II: THE GOLDEN ARMY	DARK HORSE	2008	160,388,063
8	JUDGE DREDD	FLEETWAY / REBELLION	1995	113,493,481
9	HELLBOY	DARK HORSE	2004	99,318,987
10	TMNT	MIRAGE STUDIOS / IDW	2007	95,608,995

TOP 10 BIGGEST MARVEL MOVIES

This chart includes films considered part of the Marvel Cinematic Universe as well as any movie that is an official adaptation of a Marvel comic...

	MOVIE	YEAR OF RELEASE	BOX OFFICE ($ WORLDWIDE)
1	THE AVENGERS	2012	1,519,557,910
2	AVENGERS: AGE OF ULTRON	2015	1,405,413,868
3	IRON MAN 3	2013	1,215,439,994
4	CAPTAIN AMERICA: CIVIL WAR	2016	1,153,304,495
5	SPIDER-MAN 3	2007	890,871,626
6	SPIDER-MAN	2002	821,708,551
7	SPIDER-MAN 2	2004	783,766,341
8	DEADPOOL	2016	783,112,979
9	GUARDIANS OF THE GALAXY	2014	773,312,399
10	THE AMAZING SPIDER-MAN	2012	757,930,663

9 GUARDIANS OF THE GALAXY

Rocket Raccoon (voiced by Bradley Cooper) and Groot (voiced by Vin Diesel) feature in both 2014 and 2017 *Guardians of the Galaxy* movies, as well as in 2018's *Avengers: Infinity War.*

4 ▶ SUICIDE SQUAD

In this action movie, Will Smith played Deadshot, and Margot Robbie brought Harley Quinn to life. Jared Leto became the 12th actor (on screen or as a vocal performance) to portray the Joker. Christopher Allen Nelson, Alessandro Bertolazzi, and Giorgio Gregorini won the 2017 Academy Award for Best Makeup and Hairstyling.

TOP 10 BIGGEST DC MOVIES

Up to the May 30, 2017, release of *Wonder Woman*, these are the 10 most successful films based on characters from DC Comics...

	MOVIE	YEAR OF RELEASE	BOX OFFICE ($ WORLDWIDE)
1	THE DARK KNIGHT RISES	2012	1,084,439,099
2	THE DARK KNIGHT	2008	1,004,558,444
3	BATMAN V SUPERMAN: DAWN OF JUSTICE	2016	873,260,194
4	SUICIDE SQUAD	2016	745,600,054
5	MAN OF STEEL	2013	668,045,518
6	BATMAN	1989	411,348,924
7	SUPERMAN RETURNS	2006	391,081,192
8	BATMAN BEGINS	2005	374,218,673
9	BATMAN FOREVER	1995	336,529,144
10	SUPERMAN	1978	300,218,018

9 BATMAN: THE ANIMATED SERIES

Based on the character created by Bill Finger and Bob Kane, this series' voice artists included Kevin Conroy as Batman / Bruce Wayne, Mark Hamill as the Joker, and Arleen Sorkin as Harley Quinn.

TOP 10 LONGEST-RUNNING
COMIC BOOK TV SHOWS (ANIMATED)

Thousands of cartoon series have been produced, but these are the most popular ones that are based on comic books...

	SHOW	YEARS ON AIR	TOTAL EPISODES
1	TEENAGE MUTANT NINJA TURTLES	1986–96	193
2	TEEN TITANS GO!	2013–PRESENT	167+
3	TMNT	2003–10	158
4	HERGÉ'S ADVENTURES OF TINTIN	1957–64; 1991–92	141
5	TEENAGE MUTANT NINJA TURTLES	2012–PRESENT	130+
6	DUCK TALES	1987–90; 2017–PRESENT	123
7	DENNIS THE MENACE & GNASHER	1996–98; 2009–10; 2013	120
8	CAPTAIN PUGWASH	1957–66; 1974–75	107
9	BATMAN: THE ANIMATED SERIES	1992–95	85
10	X-MEN	1992–97	76

LONGEST-RUNNING
COMIC BOOK TV SHOWS (LIVE ACTION)

From zombie-filled dramas to witchy comedies, comic book worlds have been turned into TV shows for decades...

	SHOW	YEARS ON AIR	TOTAL EPISODES
1	SMALLVILLE	2001–2011	218
2	SABRINA THE TEENAGE WITCH	1996–2003	163
3	BATMAN	1966–68	120
4	ARROW	2012–PRESENT	106
5	ADVENTURES OF SUPERMAN	1952–58	104
6	SUPERBOY	1988–92	100
7	THE WALKING DEAD	2010–PRESENT	99
8	TALES FROM THE CRYPT	1986–96	93
9	LOIS & CLARK: THE NEW ADVENTURES OF SUPERMAN	1993–97	88
10	THE INCREDIBLE HULK	1978–82	86 (INCL. 3 F.F)

8 TALES FROM THE CRYPT

This series was based on EC Comics' anthology horror comic book of the same name, published between 1950 and 1955. The HBO (Home Box Office)-produced TV series ran for seven seasons. Guest directors included titans of horror such as Tom Holland, the writer-director of the vampire classic *Fright Night* (1985), and Mary Lambert, director of the Stephen King adaptation *Pet Sematary* (1989).

TOP 10 BIGGEST ANIMATED MOVIES

After comparing all of the different types of animated feature films that have been made, these 10 are the box office winners...

	MOVIE	YEAR OF RELEASE	BOX OFFICE ($ WORLDWIDE)
1	FROZEN	2013	1,276,480,335
2	MINIONS	2015	1,159,398,397
3	TOY STORY 3	2010	1,066,969,703
4	FINDING DORY	2016	1,026,431,305
5	ZOOTOPIA	2016	1,023,761,003
6	DESPICABLE ME 2	2013	970,761,885
7	THE LION KING	1994	968,483,777
8	FINDING NEMO	2003	940,335,536
9	SHREK 2	2004	919,838,758
10	ICE AGE: DAWN OF THE DINOSAURS	2009	886,686,817

5 ZOOTOPIA

Zootopia is Disney's 55th animated feature. Voice actors included Ginnifer Goodwin (from the ABC TV series *Once Upon a Time*), who played bunny cop Judy Hopps, and Jason Bateman (director and star of 2013's *Bad Words*) as fox Nick Wilde.

TOP 10 LONGEST-RUNNING
US ANIMATED TV SERIES

Some of the entries on this animated chart first appeared on TV screens more than 25 years ago...

	SERIES	YEARS ON AIR	TOTAL EPISODES
1	THE SIMPSONS	1989–PRESENT	622+
2	FAMILY GUY	1999–2003; 2005–PRESENT	286+
3	SOUTH PARK	1997–PRESENT	277+
4	KING OF THE HILL	1997–2010	259
5	ADVENTURE TIME	2007; 2010–PRESENT	258+
6	AMERICAN DAD!	2005–PRESENT	256+
7	SPONGEBOB SQUAREPANTS	1999–PRESENT	242+
8	ARTHUR	1996–PRESENT	232+
9	BEAVIS AND BUTT-HEAD	1993–97; 2011	222
10	TEENAGE MUTANT NINJA TURTLES	1986–96	193

7 SPONGEBOB SQUAREPANTS

The worldwide success of this TV series led to the 2004 film *The SpongeBob SquarePants Movie*. It took in $140,161,792, leading to its 2015 sequel *The SpongeBob Movie: Sponge Out of Water*, an even bigger hit, making $325,186,032.

5 OJARUMARU

This long-running TV series and manga comic book was created by Rin Inumaru. The franchise also includes video games and a 47-minute feature film released in 2000 called *Ojarumaru the Movie: The Promised Summer—Ojaru and Semira.*

TOP 10 LONGEST-RUNNING ANIME TV SERIES

Japanese animation (known as "anime") has millions of fans all over the world, resulting in these thousands of episodes being produced...

	SERIES	YEARS ON AIR	TOTAL EPISODES
1	SAZAE-SAN	1969–PRESENT	7,466+
2	DORAEMON	1973; 1978; 1979–2005; 2005–PRESENT	2,593+
3	NINTAMA RANTARO	1993–PRESENT	1,953+
4	OYAKO CLUB	1994–2013	1,818
5	OJARUMARU	1998–PRESENT	1,590+
6	KIRIN NO MONOSHIRI YAKATA	1975–79	1,565
7	KIRIN ASHITA NO CALENDAR	1980–84	1,498
8	MANGA NIPPON MUKASHI BANASHI	1975–85	1,488
9	HOKA HOKA KAZOKU	1976–82	1,428
10	SOREIKE! ANPANMAN	1988–PRESENT	1,315+

2 ▶ SPIRITED AWAY

This is Studio Ghibli's most successful film. It won more than 30 international awards, including the 2003 Academy Award for Best Animated Feature. Its composer, Joe Hisaishi, has more than 100 credits, including the scores for *My Neighbor Totoro* (1998) and the video game *Ni no Kuni: Wrath of the White Witch* (2011).

TOP **10** BIGGEST **ANIME MOVIES**

With a production budget that is a fraction of those commanded by superhero movies, anime films can still score big box office numbers...

	MOVIE	YEAR OF RELEASE	BOX OFFICE ($ WORLDWIDE)
1	YOUR NAME	2016	288,803,434
2	SPIRITED AWAY	2002	274,925,095
3	STAND BY ME, DORAEMON	2014	266,542,714
4	HOWL'S MOVING CASTLE	2005	235,184,110
5	PONYO	2009	201,750,937
6	POKÉMON: THE FIRST MOVIE	1999	163,644,662
7	PRINCESS MONONOKE	1999	159,375,308
8	THE SECRET WORLD OF ARRIETTY	2012	145,570,827
9	POKÉMON: THE MOVIE 2000	2000	133,949,270
10	THE WIND RISES	2014	117,932,401

TOP 10

BIGGEST
MOVIES ABOUT VIDEO GAMING

These 10 films are not based on a specific video game franchise, but their stories are about video gaming in one way or another...

	MOVIE	YEAR OF RELEASE	BOX OFFICE ($ WORLDWIDE)
1	WRECK-IT RALPH	2012	471,222,889
2	TRON LEGACY	2010	400,062,763
3	PIXELS	2015	244,874,809
4	SPY KIDS 3D: GAME OVER	2003	197,011,982
5	WARGAMES	1983	79,567,667
6	SCOTT PILGRIM VS. THE WORLD	2010	47,664,559
7	TRON	1982	33,000,000
8	THE LAST STARFIGHTER	1984	28,733,290
9	STAY ALIVE	2006	27,105,095
10	AVALON	2001	15,740,796

6 SCOTT PILGRIM VS. THE WORLD

This fantasy comedy was based on Canadian comic book writer-artist Bryan Lee O'Malley's *Scott Pilgrim* series, published by Oni Press between 2004 and 2010. The movie's director, Edgar Wright, was also behind the TV series *Spaced* (1999–2001), the horror-comedy *Shaun of the Dead* (2004), as well as *Hot Fuzz* (2007), and *Baby Driver* (2017).

2 DIGIMON

The billion-dollar franchise of *Digimon* started its life in 1997 as Bandai's keychain Digital Monster virtual pet. As well as the multiple TV series, more than 40 video games have been released, as well as 21 feature films, and a card game series.

TOP **10** LONGEST-RUNNING
TV SHOWS BASED ON VIDEO GAMES

Beyond *Pokémon* and *Digimon*, how many TV shows adapted from famous video games can you think of?

	SHOW	BASED ON GAME FRANCHISE	YEARS ON AIR	TOTAL EPISODES
1	POKÉMON	POKÉMON	21 (1997–PRESENT)	944+
2	DIGIMON	DIGIMON	12 (1999–2011)	332
3	KIRBY: RIGHT BACK AT YA!	KIRBY	2 (2001–03)	100
4	SATURDAY SUPERCADE	VARIOUS	2 (1983–85)	97
5	SONIC X	SONIC THE HEDGEHOG	2 (2003–05)	78
6	MEGA MAN STAR FORCE	MEGA MAN	2 (2006–08)	76
7	MONSTER RANCHER	MONSTER RANCHER	2 (1999–2001)	73
8	ADVENTURES OF SONIC THE HEDGEHOG	SONIC THE HEDGEHOG	3 (1993–96)	67
9	THE SUPER MARIO BROS. SUPER SHOW!	SUPER MARIO BROS.	1 (1989)	65
10	BOMBERMAN JETTERS	BOMBERMAN	1 (2002–03)	52

TOP 10 BIGGEST STOP-MOTION ANIMATED MOVIES

You may have heard of computer-generated animation, but "stop-motion" is the painstakingly patient art of creating moving images from thousands of still photos...

	MOVIE	YEAR OF RELEASE	BOX OFFICE ($ WORLDWIDE)
1	CHICKEN RUN	2000	224,834,564
2	WALLACE & GROMIT: THE CURSE OF THE WERE-RABBIT	2005	192,610,372
3	CORALINE	2009	124,596,398
4	THE PIRATES! IN AN ADVENTURE WITH SCIENTISTS!	2012	123,054,041
5	THE CORPSE BRIDE	2005	117,195,061
6	THE BOXTROLLS	2014	109,285,033
7	PARANORMAN	2012	107,139,399
8	SHAUN THE SHEEP MOVIE	2015	106,031,284
9	FRANKENWEENIE	2012	81,491,068
10	THE NIGHTMARE BEFORE CHRISTMAS	1993	75,082,668

KUBO AND THE TWO STRINGS

Just missing out on a place in this top 10, *Kubo and the Two Strings* (2016) earned $69,929,545 at the box office. Written by Chris Butler and Marc Haimes (based on a story by Haimes and Shannon Tindle), the Travis Knight-directed stop-motion epic earned 2017 Oscar nominations for Best Animated Feature and Best Visual Effects.

TOP 10 BIGGEST CELL / TRADITIONAL ANIMATED MOVIES

In the world of traditionally crafted (non 3D / CGI) animation, these are the movies we love the most, including two bonus off-the-chart entries...

	MOVIE	YEAR OF RELEASE	BOX OFFICE ($ WORLDWIDE)
1	THE LION KING	1994	987,483,777
2	THE SIMPSONS MOVIE	2007	527,071,022
3	ALADDIN	1992	504,050,219
4	TARZAN	1999	448,191,819
5	BEAUTY AND THE BEAST	1991	424,967,620
6	POCAHONTAS	1995	346,079,773
7	WHO FRAMED ROGER RABBIT?	1988	329,803,958
8	THE HUNCHBACK OF NOTRE DAME	1996	325,338,851
9	MULAN	1998	304,320,254
10	SPIRITED AWAY	2002	274,925,095
11	LILO & STITCH	2002	273,144,151
12	THE PRINCESS & THE FROG	2009	267,045,765

2 THE SIMPSONS MOVIE

Based on the animated TV series, which debuted in 1989, the script for the 87-minute-long movie was tweaked more than 100 times. Continuing the tradition of the series, several special guests appeared, including rock band Green Day and actor Tom Hanks.

THE RED TURTLE

This 2016 coproduction between Studio Ghibli and Wild Bunch, which does not feature any dialogue, took more than $3 million at the box office worldwide. It won three international awards, including the 2017 Annie Award for Best Independent Animated Feature. It was directed by Dutch filmmaker Michaël Dudok de Wit.

TOP 10 BIGGEST STUDIO GHIBLI MOVIES

Visionary Japanese filmmaker Hayao Miyazaki cofounded Studio Ghibli in the 1980s and they have produced more than 20 feature films, including these hits...

	MOVIE	YEAR OF RELEASE	BOX OFFICE ($ WORLDWIDE)
1	SPIRITED AWAY	2002	274,925,095
2	HOWL'S MOVING CASTLE	2005	235,184,110
3	PONYO	2009	201,750,937
4	PRINCESS MONONOKE	1999	159,375,308
5	THE SECRET WORLD OF ARRIETTY	2012	145,570,827
6	THE WIND RISES	2014	117,932,401
7	TALES FROM EARTHSEA	2006	68,673,565
8	FROM UP ON POPPY HILL	2011	61,037,844
9	THE CAT RETURNS	2002	53,918,847
10	WHEN MARNIE WAS THERE	2014	34,949,567

BIGGEST **ANIMATED PREHISTORIC MOVIES**

Dinosaurs and all manner of ancient animals and tribes have been central to countless hit animated features...

	MOVIE	YEAR OF RELEASE	BOX OFFICE ($ WORLDWIDE)
1	ICE AGE: DAWN OF THE DINOSAURS	2009	886,686,817
2	ICE AGE: CONTINENTAL DRIFT	2012	877,244,782
3	ICE AGE: THE MELTDOWN	2006	660,940,780
4	THE CROODS	2013	587,204,668
5	ICE AGE: COLLISION COURSE	2016	407,727,743
6	ICE AGE	2002	383,257,136
7	DINOSAUR	2000	349,822,765
8	THE GOOD DINOSAUR	2016	332,207,671
9	BROTHER BEAR	2003	250,397,798
10	THE LAND BEFORE TIME	1988	84,460,846

10  THE LAND BEFORE TIME

Directed and produced by Don Bluth, this Saturn Award-nominated feature film spawned 13 home video sequels and a 2008 TV series. Bluth's other directing credits include *Anastasia* (1997) and the 1983 video games *Dragon's Lair* and *Space Ace*.

TOP 10 BIGGEST MOVIES BASED ON TOYS

Fantastic plastic creations don't just ring the money bell on the toy shelves when their movie selves are this popular...

	MOVIE	YEAR OF RELEASE	BOX OFFICE ($ WORLDWIDE)
1	TRANSFORMERS: DARK OF THE MOON	2011	1,123,794,079
2	TRANSFORMERS: AGE OF EXTINCTION	2014	1,104,054,072
3	TRANSFORMERS: REVENGE OF THE FALLEN	2009	836,303,693
4	TRANSFORMERS	2007	709,709,780
5	THE LEGO MOVIE	2014	469,160,692
6	G.I. JOE: RETALIATION	2013	375,740,705
7	TROLLS	2016	337,268,818
8	BATTLESHIP	2012	303,025,485
9	G.I. JOE: THE RISE OF COBRA	2009	302,469,017
10	THE LEGO BATMAN MOVIE	2017	297,237,542

5 THE LEGO MOVIE

The official premiere for *The LEGO Batman Movie* was held in Paris, France, on February 1, 2016. Will Arnett, who provides the voice for Batman / Bruce Wayne, has 98 acting credits. These include *BoJack Horseman* (2014–present), where he voices the titular character, and Gob Bluth in *Arrested Development* (2003–present).

5 **THE DARK CRYSTAL**

The fantasy epic was codirected by Jim Henson and Frank Oz. The duo also voiced Kermit the Frog and Fozzie Bear from The Muppets, also created by Henson. A 10-episode prequel series, *The Dark Crystal: Age of Resistance*, was produced by Netflix in 2018.

TOP 10 MOST SUCCESSFUL **PUPPET MOVIES**

The one and only Jim Henson and his company were the creatives responsible for nine of the 10 films in this chart...

	MOVIE	YEAR OF RELEASE	BOX OFFICE ($ WORLDWIDE)
1	THE MUPPETS	2011	165,184,237
2	MUPPETS MOST WANTED	2014	80,383,290
3	THE MUPPET MOVIE	1979	65,200,000
4	TEAM AMERICA: WORLD POLICE	2004	50,907,422
5	THE DARK CRYSTAL	1982	40,577,001
6	MUPPET TREASURE ISLAND	1996	34,327,391
7	THE GREAT MUPPET CAPER	1981	31,206,251
8	THE MUPPET CHRISTMAS CAROL	1992	27,281,507
9	THE MUPPETS TAKE MANHATTAN	1984	25,534,703
10	MUPPETS FROM SPACE	1999	22,323,612

5 BRIDESMAIDS

This comedy was cowritten by Kristen Wiig and Annie Mumolo, who both scored a 2012 Academy Award nomination for Best Original Screenplay. It was not the last time lead actress Kristen Wiig worked with *Bridesmaids'* director Paul Feig—the two reunited for 2016's *Ghostbusters*.

TOP 10 MOST SUCCESSFUL WEDDING MOVIES

If you respond, "I do," when asked if you love nothing better than a movie about marriage, then this top 10 is for you...

	MOVIE	YEAR OF RELEASE	BOX OFFICE ($ WORLDWIDE)
1	MAMMA MIA!	2008	609,841,637
2	MY BIG FAT GREEK WEDDING	2002	368,744,044
3	RUNAWAY BRIDE	1999	309,457,509
4	MY BEST FRIEND'S WEDDING	1997	299,288,605
5	BRIDESMAIDS	2011	288,383,523
6	WEDDING CRASHERS	2005	285,176,741
7	AMERICAN WEDDING	2003	231,449,203
8	SWEET HOME ALABAMA	2002	180,622,424
9	27 DRESSES	2008	160,259,319
10	LAST VEGAS	2013	134,402,450

TOP 10

BIGGEST **COOKING MOVIES**

Culinary skills being played out on the big screen are behind some of the most popular comedies, animated classics, and dramas...

MOVIE	YEAR OF RELEASE	BOX OFFICE ($ WORLDWIDE)
1 RATATOUILLE	2007	620,702,951
2 CHOCOLAT	2000	152,699,946
3 JULIE & JULIA	2009	129,540,499
4 NO RESERVATIONS	2007	92,601,050
5 THE HUNDRED-FOOT JOURNEY	2014	88,880,821
6 CHEF	2014	45,967,935
7 BURNT	2015	36,606,743
8 LIKE WATER FOR CHOCOLATE	1993	21,665,468
9 SOUL KITCHEN	2010	17,872,796
10 BIG NIGHT	1996	12,008,376

1  RATATOUILLE

Pixar's eighth production starred stand-up comedian and actor Patton Oswalt as Remy the rat. The film was written and directed by Brad Bird, who also helmed *The Iron Giant* (1999), *The Incredibles* (2004) and its 2018 sequel, as well as *Tomorrowland* (2015).

TOP 10 BIGGEST **WITCH MOVIES**

2016 saw the release of two very different witch-based movies, the terrifying sequel *Blair Witch* and 17th-century-based horror *The Witch*...

	MOVIE	YEAR OF RELEASE	BOX OFFICE ($ WORLDWIDE)
1	THE CHRONICLES OF NARNIA: THE LION, THE WITCH & THE WARDROBE	2005	745,013,115
2	THE CHRONICLES OF NARNIA: PRINCE CASPIAN	2008	419,665,568
3	THE CHRONICLES OF NARNIA: THE VOYAGE OF DAWN TREADER	2010	415,686,217
4	THE BLAIR WITCH PROJECT	1999	248,639,099
5	HANSEL & GRETEL: WITCH HUNTERS	2013	226,349,749
6	THE LAST WITCH HUNTER	2015	146,936,910
7	BEWITCHED	2005	131,426,169
8	SEASON OF THE WITCH	2009	91,627,228
9	THE WITCHES OF EASTWICK	1987	63,766,510
10	BEAUTIFUL CREATURES	2013	60,052,138

TOP 10 BIGGEST **ZOMBIE MOVIES**

If you thought that the undead only populated gore-filled shockers, check out the eclectic genres and movies that make up this list...

	MOVIE	YEAR OF RELEASE	BOX OFFICE ($ WORLDWIDE)
1	WORLD WAR Z	2013	540,007,876
2	RESIDENT EVIL: THE FINAL CHAPTER	2017	312,242,626
3	RESIDENT EVIL: AFTERLIFE	2010	296,221,663
4	RESIDENT EVIL: RETRIBUTION	2012	240,159,255
5	DEATH BECOMES HER	1992	149,022,650
6	RESIDENT EVIL: EXTINCTION	2007	147,717,833
7	RESIDENT EVIL: APOCALYPSE	2004	129,394,835
8	WARM BODIES	2013	116,980,662
9	PARANORMAN	2012	107,139,399
10	ZOMBIELAND	2009	102,391,540

1 ▸ THE CHRONICLES OF NARNIA: THE LION, THE WITCH & THE WARDROBE

British actress Tilda Swinton played the White Witch, the central villain of this movie. The film was based on C. S. Lewis's fantasy novel, first published in 1950. The screenplay's four writers included Christopher Markus and Stephen McFeely, most famous for their work on movies in the Marvel Cinematic Universe such as *Avengers: Infinity War*.

9 ▸ PARANORMAN

Animation studio Laika's second feature film (following 2009's *Coraline*) was nominated for an Academy Award, and is the winner of 14 international awards. Its composer, Jon Brion, also scored the 2010 Will Ferrell comedy *The Other Guys*.

PICTURE CREDITS

123RF Aliaksandr Mazurkevich 44-45; Elena Duvernay 20-21; Robert Wilson 129; Roman Slavik 130-131. **AC Comics** 84-85. **Alamy Stock Photo** AF Archive/Lucasfilm 271, 272; AF Archive/Saban Entertainment 288-289; AF Archive/Warner Bros. 262l; Agencja Fotograficzna Caro 153; Ahmad Faizal Yahya 155; A. Mirsberger/Tierfotoagentur 17; Amy Cicconi 135; Andrew Holt 144bl; Andrew Zarivny 86-87; Andrey Nekrasov 14-15; Atlaspix/Apaches Entertainment 269r, 269l; Atlaspix/Laika Entertainment 290-291; B.A.E. Inc. 182-183; Bertrand Gardel/Hemis 138-139; Buzz Pictures 68; Clarence Holmes Photography 128bl; Collection Philippe Clement/ Arterra Picture Library 80b; Courtesy Everett Collection/©NBC 266; Courtesy Everett Collection/©Netflix 266-267; Courtesy Everett Collection/©Walt Disney Co./Lucasfilm 274-275; Courtesy Everett Collection/©Walt Disney Co./Pixar Animation Studios 297; Courtesy Everett Collection/ Marvel Studios/© Walt Disney Studios Motion Pictures 280-281; CTK 264; Dan Selmeczi/Steve Bloom Images 32-33; Dinodia Photos 90; Disney Magic 144-145; Dmytro Pylypenko 65; Donna Ikenberry/Art Directors & TRIP 11; Entertainment Pictures/Walt Disney Co. 299; Everett Collection Inc. 78; Everett Collection Inc./Twentieth Century Fox 291; FLPA 13a; G. Lacz/Arco Images GmbH 18-19; Hipix 81cr; imageimage 144br; ITAR-TASS Photo Agency 111; ITPhoto 125; Ivan Batinic 52; Kateryna Kon/ Science Photo Library 79a; Kevin Elsby 44; Lee Dalton 156; Life on white 13b; Lucasfilm/Entertainment Pictures 273; Marc Rasmus/imageBROKER 140-141; Mark -9/Visual&Written SL 8; Michael Wells/fStop Images GmbH 69; Mike Theiss/National Geographic Creative 66; Mike Veitch 50-51; Moviestore collection Ltd./Universal Pictures 288; Moviestore collection Ltd/ Twentieth Century Fox 262-263; National Geographic Creative 141; Nobuo Matsumura 47; Oyvind Martinsen Wildlife Collection 12-13; pbpgalleries 154-155; philipus 126; Photo 12/Lucasfilm 277; Photo 12/Studio Ghibli/Prima Linea Productions 292-293; Photo 12/Universal Pictures 260, 293; Pictorial Press Ltd./Lionsgate 264-265; Picture Partners 128; pumkinpie/Nintendo 198-199; R. Richter/ Tierfotoagentur 19; Raga Jose Fuste/Prisma by Dukas Presseagentur GmbH 134-135; Randy Brandon/ Design Pics Inc 25; RGB Ventures/SuperStock 159; Robert Landau 92-93; Roman Tiraspolsky 124; SPUTNIK 61; Stefan Auth/imageBROKER 62-63; Stefan Huwiler/Rolf Nussbaumer Photography 16-17; Stephanie Jackson - Australian birds collection 43; Tobias Schwarz/Reuters 160-161; US Navy Photo 149; Vangelis Vassalakis/Nintendo 209ar; WaterFrame 29, 36-37; WENN UK/Focus Features/Laika Entertainment 298-299; Xinhua 119; ZUMA Press, Inc./© Lucasfilm/ Entertainment Pictures 268. **Bandai Namco** 221r,222. **Capcom** 229. **Dabashian** 160. **ESA**

Claus Vogl 176; DLR/FU Berlin, CC BY-SA 3.0 IGO 189; NASA 170-171; ROB 185. **Evan-Amos** Nintendo 201r, 204l, 208l, 209br; Sony Interactive Entertainment 200b. **Fregopie** 59. **Getty Images** Drew Angerer 262r; Michael Steele 108; © CORBIS/Corbis via Getty Images 80a; © Marco Bottigelli 55; Adam Pretty 112-113; AF-studio 208-209; Ahmad Zamroni/AFP 162-163; Alastair Macewen 38; Alberto Pezzali/Pacific Press/LightRocket via Getty Images 233; Alexander Safonov 30-31; Andy Lyons 98l; ansonmiao 122-123; Anton Petrus 56-57; Attila Kisbenedek/AFP 239; Ben Stansall/AFP 102; Bertrand Guay/AFP 240; Bettmann 85b; BeyondImages 166; Blackstation 136-137; Bloomberg 237; Brendan Moran/Sportsfile via Getty Images 103; Brian J. Skerry 36; Bruno Vincent 255; Burak Cingi/Redferns 234; Caiaimage/Martin Barraud 74-75; Caspar Benson 223bg; Chiaki Nozu/ Wirelmage 236; Chris Hendrickson 69b; christophe_ cerisier 70-71; Christopher Polk/TAS/Getty Images for TAS 253; Clive Rose 101; Daniel Reiter 94; Danita Delimont 40; Dave Fleetham/Design Pics 28-29; Dave Hogan 242-243; David Allio/Icon Sportswire/Corbis via Getty Images 99; David Kirkland 91; David Madison 167; Denise Truscello/Getty Images for Madame Tussauds Las Vegas 82; Dennis Oulds/ Central Press/Hulton Archive 151; Detlev van Ravenswaay 180-181; Diarmuid Greene/Sportsfile via Getty Images 114-115; Dimitri lundt/Corbis/VCG via Getty Images 107; Dong Wenjie 89; Eduardo Parra/FilmMagic 295; Elroy Serrao 66-67; Erika Goldring/FilmMagic 237; Ezra Shaw 150-151; Florentina Georgescu Photography 52-53; Franck Fife/ AFP 108-109; Francois Nel 106-107, 110; Frederick M. Brown 262c; Gareth Cattermole 256-257; Godong/ robertharding 60; Greg Wood/AFP 158-159; Gustavo Caballero 276; Henrik Sorensen 10-11; Ian McKinnell 258-259; in-future 230-231; Jack Taylor 83a; janetteasche 64-65; Jason Merritt 261; Jeff Dai/ Stocktrek Images 48-49; Jeff Kravitz/AMA2016/ FilmMagic 244; Jo Hale/Redferns 247; John Greim/ LightRocket via Getty Images 6-7; John Korduner/Icon Sportswire via Getty Images 120-121; John Lamparski 83br; John Russell/EyeEm 31; John Shearer/Wirelmage 246-247; Josh Brasted/FilmMagic 250; Juvenal Pereira 87; Karim Jaafar/AFP 100; Karwai Tang/Wirelmage 83al; Kevin Mazur/Getty Images for Live Nation 252; Kevin Mazur/Wirelmage 251; Kevork Djansezian 257; Kiyoshi Ota/Bloomberg via Getty Images 152-153; Kyodo News via Getty Images 104-105; Lisa Marcus/ Courtesy of the US Navy 164; Lorne Thomson/ Redferns 235; LUPOO/ullstein bild via Getty Images 139; mallardg500 42-43; Marevision 9; Masa Ushioda 34-35; Mauro Ujetto/NurPhoto via Getty Images 118-119; Michael H 88-89; Miemo Penttinen - miemo.net 127; Mina De La O 218-219; Mint Images 56; Nick Laham 112; Noel Celis/AFP 120; Ollie Millington/Redferns 242; Omar Sabik/Clasos.com/

LatinContent 248-249; peepo 96-97; Pete Oxford/ Minden Pictures 40-41; Peter Adams 58-59, 132; Pgiam 54-55; Phillip Massey/FilmMagic 232-233; Photo by JKboy Jatenipat 50; Rainer W. Schlegelmilch 162; Reinhard Dirscherl/ullstein bild via Getty Images 32; Richard Herrmann/Minden Pictures 34; Richard T. Nowitz 133; Rune Hellestad/Corbis via Getty Images 77; ryccio 196-197; Samir Hussein/Redferns via Getty Images 241; Scott Barbour/ALLSPORT 117; Scott Dudelson/Wirelmage 245; Scott Legato 238-239; Scott Mcquaide/EyeEm 146-147; Sergey Krasovskiy 23; Shaun Botterill 105; SSPL 81, 164-165; Steven Puetzer 202-203; The Asahi Shimbun via Getty Images 79b, 116-117; Theo Wargo/Getty Images for Tony Awards Productions 249; Tim Clayton/Corbis via Getty Images 114; Tom Brakefield 14; Topic Images Inc. 93; totororo 71; Valerie Macon/AFP 143; VCG/VCG via Getty Images 254, 254-255; VEGARD WIVESTAD GROTT/AFP 76; Walter Myers/Stocktrek Images 46-47, 184-185; Westend61 24-25; William Volcov/Brazil Photo Press/LatinConten 98r; Yamaguchi Haruyoshi/ Corbis via Getty Images 142; Yann Arthus-Bertrand 94-95. **istockphoto.com** DenisTangneyJr 72-73; estivillml 67; wrangel 26. **Konami** 218, 227. **LucasArts/Aspyr (OS X)/Eidos Interactive (GBA)** 226. **LucasArts/Electronic Arts** 224. **Nintendo** 198, 199l, 199r, 202a, 202b, 203, 203l, 203r, 204 ar, 204-205, 205r, 208r, 209l, 201, 212, 214, 216, 217, 219, 220, 223r. NOAA 63, 73 below; Satellite and Information Service 73a. **Microsoft Studios** 206-207. **Mojang Specifications** 211. **MovieStillsDB.com** Atlas Entertainment/DC Comics 281; DC Entertainment/ LEGO System A/S 294; Home Box Office (HBO) 283; Incorporated Television Company (ITC)/Jim Henson Productions 295; Lucasfilm 270-271; Marvel Studios 278; Studio Ghibli 286-287; United Plankton Pictures/ Nickelodeon Animation Studios 285; Universal Pictures 279, 296; Walt Disney Co. 284-285; Warner Bros. 282. **NASA** 170br, 170bl, 171, 172, 172-173, 174, 174-175, 177, 178bl, 178ar, 188, 195r, 195; ESA and Erich Karkoschka University of Arizona 183; ESA/Hubble 168-169; GCTC/Andrey Shelepin 173; Johns Hopkins University Applied Physics Laboratory/Southwest Research Institute 186; Johns Hopkins University Applied Physics Laboratory/Southwest Research Institute/Goddard Space 193; JPL 190, 191, 192-193; JPL-Caltech 187; JPL-Caltech/JSC 178-179; Robert Markowitz 180; SDO 194. **REX Shutterstock** Judy Leden 157. **Rin Inumaru** 286. **Rockstar Games** 214-215. **Roman Uchytel (www.prehistoric-fauna.com)** 21. **Shutterstock** Elenarts 22-23; Herschel Hoffmeyer 27; Lee Hua Ming 38-39. **Sony** 201, 204, 207. **Sierra Games** 225. **Square/Sony Computer Entertainment** 201l. **Takimata** Nintendo 204br. **US Navy Photo by General Dynamics Electric Boat** 148-149. **Warner Bros. Interactive Entertainment** 228-229. **Wikifrits** 131.

ACKNOWLEDGMENTS

Paul Terry would like to thank: all of the contributing sources, especially paleobiologists Luke Hauser and David Martill, Anna Loynes and BuzzAngle Music / Border City Media for the music intel, and the brilliant IMDb and VGChartz teams; my Editor extraordinaire Polly Poulter for knocking another T-10 book out of the park; my brilliant Editorial Director Trevor Davies for the ongoing support (and film recommendations); Team T-10's design team, picture researchers, sub-editors, proofreaders, and marketeers for all their hard work; all at Octopus Books and Readerlink; and as always, a massive thank you to my frequent collaborator Tara Bennett for all the support and encouragement.

DATA SOURCES:

Pages: 20, 21, 22, 23, 27, 46 – data sourced from Luke Hauser and David Martill, paleobiologists **Pages:** 198–229 – data sourced from VGChartz.com **Pages:** 124, 125, 126, 127, 130, 131, 134, 135, 136, 137, – data sourced from the Council on Tall Buildings and Urban Habitat **Pages:** 232–249 – data kindly provided by BuzzAngle Music (BuzzAngleMusic.com) and Border City Media Copyright (C) Border City Media. **Pages:** 182–191 – data sourced from NASA (https:// solarsystem.nasa.gov) **Pages:** 260–265, 268–281, 284, 287–299 – data sourced from IMDB.com. Box office information courtesy of The Internet Movie Database (http://www.imdb.com). Used with permission.